HONKY TONK
PARADE

OTHER TITLES BY JOHN LAHR

Biographies:

NOTES ON A COWARDLY LION: THE BIOGRAPHY OF BERT LAHR

PRICK UP YOUR EARS: THE BIOGRAPHY OF JOE ORTON

THE ORTON DIARIES (EDITOR)

COWARD: THE PLAYWRIGHT

DAME EDNA EVERAGE AND THE RISE OF WESTERN CIVILIZATION: BACKSTAGE
WITH BARRY HUMPHRIES

SINATRA: THE ARTIST AND THE MAN

SHOW AND TELL: NEW YORKER PROFILES

THE DIARIES OF KENNETH TYNAN (EDITOR)

PAUL DAVIS: SHOW PEOPLE

Criticism:

A CASEBOOK ON HAROLD PINTER'S *THE HOMECOMING*
(EDITED WITH ANTHEA LAHR)

UP AGAINST THE FOURTH WALL

ACTING OUT AMERICA

ASTONISH ME

LIFE-SHOW (WITH JONATHAN PRICE)

LIGHT FANTASTIC: ADVENTURES IN THEATRE

Novels:

THE AUTOGRAPH HOUND

HOT TO TROT

Plays:

ACCIDENTAL DEATH OF AN ANARCHIST (*ADAPTATION*)

DIARY OF A SOMEBODY (*ADAPTATION*)

THE BLUEBIRD OF UNHAPPINESS: A WOODY ALLEN REVUE (*ADAPTATION*)

THE MANCHURIAN CANDIDATE (*ADAPTATION*)

ELAINE STRITCH AT LIBERTY (WITH ELAINE STRITCH)

HONKY TONK PARADE

NEW YORKER PROFILES OF SHOW PEOPLE

JOHN LAHR

THE OVERLOOK PRESS
Woodstock & New York

The phrase "honky tonk parade" is taken from the song "It's Only a Paper Moon,"
written by E.Y. Harburg and Harold Arlen.

First published in the United States and the United Kingdom in 2005 by
Overlook Duckworth

LONDON
90-93 Cowcross Street
London EC1M 6BF
inquiries@duckworth-publishers.co.uk
www.ducknet.co.uk

NEW YORK
The Overlook Press
141 Wooster Street
New York, NY 10012

WOODSTOCK
The Overlook Press
One Overlook Drive
Woodstock, NY 12498
www.overlookpress.com
[for individual orders and bulk sales in the United States,
please contact our Woodstock office]

A CIP catalogue record for this book is available from the
British Library and the Library of Congress

ISBN (hc) 1-58567-703-5   ISBN (UK hc) 0 7156 3544 1
ISBN (pb) 1-58567-786-6   ISBN (UK pb) 0 7156 3552 2

Printed in the United States of America

1   3   5   7   9   10   8   6   4   2

To
Connie Booth
&
Deborah Treisman

"We must risk delight. We can do without pleasure,
but not delight. Not enjoyment. We must have
the stubbornness to accept our gladness in the ruthless
furnace of this world . . ."

—Jack Gilbert
"A Brief for the Defense"
Refusing Heaven

CONTENTS

HONKY TONK
PARADE

INTRODUCTION

When I was young, my father the comedian Bert Lahr used to let me and my sister Jane watch him from the wings. Over the years, wedged between the stage manager and the curtain, with a good view of the Broadway customers, we saw him become a woodsman, a baseball coach, a policeman, Queen Victoria, a tramp, even a Wagnerian valkyrie complete with horned Viking helmet. His outrageousness was wonderful, sometimes even visionary. No one else we knew had a father who made people laugh for a living. In one play, S. J. Perelman's "The Beauty Part," a fat man in the second row laughed so hard and so loud that he had to stuff a handkerchief in his mouth so the show could continue. Of course, these moments were vivid and thrilling; they were also mysterious and troubling. How did Dad become that funny guy? Where did it come from? Where did it go? The minute Dad hit the wings the person who was bellowing and madcap and powerful on stage deflated like a tire. Then the noise and the fun and the sureness vanished; he became a brooding, loveable lost soul who spent most of his time at home parked in his maple colonial desk chair, listening to the radio, the television, and working the crossword, sometimes all at once. At a very early age, therefore, the play world and the private world were two linked but dramatically different arenas which seemed to call out multiple personalities from the same apparent self. The play world was lively; the private world was deadly; yet, to me, they seemed to feed off one another the way that brilliance needs shadow to show itself. On stage, Dad was free and inventive and full of hijinx; his resources of energy were boundless. Why didn't he have energy to play with us? What did the stage offer that we didn't? The public seemed to get his best self, the family got the rest. When I was a teenager and old enough to put these questions to him, Dad was completely uninterested. When the lights were not on and the audience was not out front, he could not be coaxed to set even one foot on the stage. "Does a shopkeeper go back to the shop after he's locked up?" he told me. His answer, and the sharp note of irritation which accompanied it, remained an enduring and perplexing memory. Why was he so adamant? What was he protecting? The threshold between worlds became to me, even more confounding and fascinating, a liminal space in which some alchemy of the soul took place.

As I grew up and began to read about theatricals, the literature seemed to bear little relation to the murky contradictory behaviour of my father and his performing friends. These accounts were written from the outside, with none of the psychological complexity or the suggestive eloquence of the mutant breed. I hankered for something that didn't just honour their prowess but plumbed them, something that brought me closer to the process and to the special transition from civilian to artist. In my twenties, I decided to make my own inquiry. I spent five years writing a book about my father which addressed this narrative problem. Although "Notes on a Cowardly Lion" is still in print after thirty years, as its title suggests I reached no conclusive findings. In my forties, with another prodigious comic spirit, Barry Humphries, I tried again. I spent six weeks with Humphries backstage at the Drury Lane Theatre in London and then on the road. My book, "Dame Edna Everage and the Rise of Western Civilization"—a portion of which was my first-ever profile in the *New Yorker*—is included here. To the best of my knowledge, it's the only book ever written about a comedian from the wings. When Barry arrived each night at his dressing room, I was there to talk to him as he put on his makeup, to watch him as he revved himself up to metamorphose into Dame Edna and Sir Les Patterson, to track the movement from ordinary to extraordinary. The experience felt very familiar; the literary result, I think, got closer to the nub of the performing self, which is what I'd always had in mind. To bear witness to the joy and import of theatricals—the price paid for their ravishing connection to our imagination and to the thing accomplished—is what a great deal of my writing has been about. As the poet Mary Oliver says, "To pay attention— this is our endless and proper work."

In 1992, it was my luck to join the *New Yorker* as senior drama critic. The magazine gave me a fabulous field on which to play as well as the resources and the access to pursue my biographical curiosity. Since then, widening the remit to include writers, directors, lyricists, even critics— anyone, frankly, who gets the salmon in me going upstream—a large part of my *New Yorker* output has been pen portraits of theatricals. These mini-biographies take about four months to research and to write; the reading experience is meant to feel effortless, but the writing experience never is. The profile is a literary juggling act, and harder than it might seem. Besides my own point of view, I'm trying to interpret the subject's career, life, conversation, and a cast of subsidiary characters who come into the story— which always amounts to no less than a thousand pages of taped interviews. Sometimes when people talk to me about the profiles, they inadvertently refer to them as "interviews"; I can feel myself bristle. Certainly, the spine of each profile is a series of conversations, held over time, in a number of different venues; however, the purpose of the exercise and the prose are interpretive. A *New Yorker* profile is written, not transcribed. The aim is to fathom the subject by seeing him or her from as many angles as possible. For instance, for this volume, I have walked with August Wilson down the sour streets of the Hill District in Pittsburgh, the landscape his plays mythologize and the place where he came of age; travelled to Uganda, where the film director Mira Nair spends a good part of every year in order to understand the multicultural lens through which she views the world; ridden on the back of Laurence Fishburnes's Harley-Davidson as he negotiated the New York traffic and his own international fame; sat beside Tony Kushner at the opening of "Caroline, or Change," his first major work since "Angels in America," and incidentally the first opening night of his plays which he's ever attended. In these encounters, what I am listening for is not just what the subject is saying but what he or she is showing; I'm trying to pinpoint the thing in each artist which seeks expression. This takes time, luck, collaboration, and a certain amount of dogged scrutiny. (In the case of the late comedian Bill Hicks, who died of pancreatic cancer, in 1993, about four months after writing me a thirty-nine page account detailing his being banned from the *Late Show with David Letterman*, I have added a postscript to the original published profile to bring up to date the story of his last days and his legacy.) I enjoy the hunt. Sometimes, when the magazine's editor David Remnick sees me lugging my thick dossiers of interviews around the office, he rolls his eyes and I know what he's thinking: Why don't I just use a pad and take down the telling quote? But, if I did that, I'd spend more time writing than listening; I'd miss the tell-tale syntax and misspeakings and the subject's rhythms. A good profile, it seems to me, evolves out of the depth of connection between the writer and the subject, the sense of being heard and seen. Anyway, I'm finding the story as I'm hearing it. So, inevitably, I overdo the research and the writing; no matter how hard I try, most of these profiles are submitted at twice their published length. It's the only way I seem to be able to do the job. I seem to be looking for something that can never exactly be found, or maybe I'm refinding something that's been lost since 1967 when Dad died: the bittersweet mayhem of theatrical obsession, the gallantry of excellence. Maybe—this just struck me—it's my way of keeping Dad with me.

In our house, since neither of them got past junior high school, my parents had language but no vocabulary. When Dad started out in burlesque, and to a lesser degree throughout his career, his malaprops—"Pass me the salt if I'm not too inquisitive"—turned this linguistic impoverishment into fun. But it was no laughing matter. He kept a gigantic Funk & Wagnall's Dictionary on his desk and routinely poured over it with his magnifying glass. After my mother died, in 1995, I discovered elocution books hidden in the back of her closet. The acquisition of a word horde and the use of language became my project, something which my parents tacitly endorsed and which also set me apart from them. For me, words have always been full of wonder. I completely understand the feeling of the medieval calligraphers whose embossed letters are entwined with flowers and animals and magical beings. For me, words—whether on signs, in books, in conversation, or on the page—contained a mystery and a life of their own. They caught my imagination. They still do. Now, at sixty-four, I feel I'm just beginning to make words do what I want—to make them pop and twist and deliver those little surprises that even I can't anticipate. Much of this education has come from my years at the *New Yorker* and from keeping company with so many excellent writers and editors. In this never-ending study, my own editor Deborah Treisman has been the subtlest of teachers. She seems to have an uncanny ability to understand the special metabolism of her authors, myself included, and to help them find that unique voice which some-times gets lost in the thicket of tangled syntax. To her, to the fact-checkers, to the grammarians, and to the other editors—especially Dorothy Wick-enden and David Remnick, whose input on these profiles sometimes makes me boil but also makes them better—I owe a great debt. They have all played a part—greater than they know—in making my *New Yorker* years a joyous adventure. The joy comes from the impossible struggle to get it right. In "Endgame," Samuel Beckett says, "Try again. Fail again. Fail better." I like to think that in "Honky Tonk Parade" I've failed better than ever before.

John Lahr
May 23, 2005

AUGUST WILSON

BEEN HERE AND GONE

If anybody asks you who sang this song
Tell 'em
It was little Jimmy Rushing,
He's been here and gone.

THE PLAYWRIGHT AUGUST WILSON lives in a leafy, genteel part of Seattle intended by the city's founding fathers to be the site of the state capitol, and so named Capitol Hill. He moved here in 1994, with Constanza Romero, a Colombian-born costume designer who is now his third wife, and they share a rambling turn-of-the-century house with Azula, their three-year-old daughter. Azula has her father's ear and number, as well as total control of the living room, which, apart from a jukebox and a piano—props from Wilson's productions—hasn't a stick of adult furniture. Wilson, who doesn't drive, is more interested in the inner terrain than the external one; writing, he says, "is for me like walking down the landscape of the self. . . . You find false trails, roads closed for repairs, impregnable fortresses, scouts, armies of memory, and impossible cartography."

Wilson does most of his pathfinding below the living room, in a low-ceilinged basement, lit by neon bars, where he goes to sneak cigarettes, listen to records, and wait for his characters to arrive. He writes standing up, at a high, cluttered pine accounting desk, where he can prop his legal pad and transfer his jottings to a laptop computer. Pinned on a bulletin board, just beside where he stands to write, are two quotations, as bold as street signs: "TAKE IT TO THE MOON" (Frank Gehry) and "DON'T BE AFRAID. JUST PLAY THE MUSIC" (Charlie Parker). When Wilson looks up from his desk, at the dingy wall with its labyrinth of water pipes, he sees honorary degrees from the University of Pittsburgh, his home town, and from Yale, where his career as a playwright began, in 1982—just two of twenty-three he has accumulated so far, which is not bad for a fifty-five-year-old writer who quit school when he was fifteen.

For years, about two steps behind Wilson's writing table, an Everlast punching bag was suspended from the ceiling. When Wilson was in full flow and the dialogue was popping, he'd stop, pivot, throw a barrage of punches at the bag, then turn back to the work. Recently, however, during a particularly vigorous rewrite of his new play, "King Hedley II," which opens on Broadway this month, Wilson knocked the bag and its ceiling hook down, and it now rests mournfully in the corner. Wilson has a retired boxer's heft—thick neck, square shoulders, wide chest—and a stomach whose amplitude is emphasized by suspenders that bracket his belly like parentheses. Wilson is the product of a mixed marriage, but, he says, "the culture I learned in my mother's household was black." He has a handsome face that is dominated by a wide forehead and a concentrated gaze. He exudes a very specific sense of gravity. He gives away nothing at first, or even second, glance. But when his guard is down, and especially when he's telling a story, you feel what his wife calls "the sizzle."

Wilson, who was originally named Frederick August Kittel, after his German father, says that his model for manhood—"the first male image that I carry"—is not his father but an old family friend, "the brilliant Hall of Fame prize-fighter" Charley Burley. Archie Moore called Burley the best fighter he'd ever faced, and Sugar Ray Robinson refused to box him, but after his glory days as a pugilist were over Burley became a garbageman in Pittsburgh and lived across the street from the impressionable young Wilson. In Burley's Friday-night regalia—hundred-dollar Stetson, cashmere coat, yam-colored Florsheim shoes—Wilson saw something iconic. Burley was one of those black men, Wilson writes, who "elevated their presence into an art. They were bad. If only in an abstract of style."

Burley was known as "the uncrowned champion"; Wilson is known as "the heavyweight champion"—a nickname given to him by the director Marion McClinton, who is staging "King Hedley II." McClinton explains, "It's August's language—the rhythm of hurt, the rhythm of pain, the rhythm of ecstasy, the rhythm of family—which sets him apart and is why we call him the heavyweight champion." Between 1959, when Lorraine Hansberry had a hit with "A Raisin in the Sun," and 1984, when Wilson made his sensational breakthrough with "Ma Rainey's Black Bottom," a play about black musicians' struggle with their white bosses in the twenties, the number of African-American plays to succeed on Broadway was zero. (There were, of course, many other black playwrights during this time— Amiri Baraka, Ron Milner, Phillip Hayes Dean, Richard Wesley, and Ed Bullins, among them—who won critical praise and a coterie following.) "Ma Rainey" ran for ten months. Almost immediately, Hollywood came calling, mostly with offers for bio-pics of Louis Armstrong, Muhammad Ali, and the like; Wilson wasn't tempted. He asked the Hollywood nabobs why so many black playwrights had written only one play. "I go, 'Where is Lonne Elder? Where is Joseph Walker?' They go, 'They're in Hollywood.' And I go, 'Oh, I see,'" he says. "I wanted to have a career in the theatre."

Wilson's success also triggered what McClinton calls "one of the more major American theatrical revolutions." His audience appeal almost single-handedly broke down the wall for other black artists, many of whom would not otherwise be working in the mainstream. His plays were showcases for an array of first-rate performers, such as Charles S. Dutton, Samuel L. Jackson, Courtney Vance, Angela Bassett, Ruben Santiago-Hudson, and Laurence Fishburne. And the opportunities for African-American playwrights also increased. "What's happened since 1984 has been incredible," McClinton says. "A lot of black writers had doors opened to them basically because August knocked them open. So then you start seeing Kia Corthron, Suzan-Lori Parks, Keith Glover, Robert Alexander, Lynn Nottage, Sam Kelley, Carlisle Brown, Charles Smith, Michael Henry Brown—I could keep going. American theatre now looks toward African-Americans as viable members."

Wilson followed "Ma Rainey" with six critically acclaimed plays in a row—"Fences" (1987; Pulitzer Prize, Tony Award), "Joe Turner's Come and Gone" (1988), "The Piano Lesson" (1990; Pulitzer Prize), "Two Trains Running" (1992), "Seven Guitars" (1996), and "Jitney" (2000). He actually had drafts of "Fences" and "Joe Turner's Come and Gone" in his trunk before "Ma Rainey" made it to Broadway, and sometime after the success of that play, he has said, it dawned on him that each play he'd written so far was "trying to focus on what I felt were the most important issues confronting black Americans for that decade." Wilson gave himself a mission: to continue to chronicle, decade by decade, the "dazed and dazzling" rapport of African-Americans with the twentieth century. "King Hedley II" is set in the nineteen-eighties, which leaves only the first and last decades of the century to be written. The plays form a kind of fever chart of the trauma of slavery. Their historical trajectory takes African-Americans through their transition from property to personhood ("Joe Turner's Come and Gone"); their struggle for power in urban life ("Ma Rainey"); their dilemma over whether to embrace or deny their slave past ("The Piano Lesson"); the broken promise of first-class citizenship after the Second World War ("Seven Guitars"); their fraught adaptation to bourgeois values ("Fences"); stagnancy in the midst of Black Power militancy ("Two Trains Running"); and their historical and financial disenfranchisement during the economic boom ("Jitney" and "King Hedley II").

"The average struggling non-morbid Negro is the best-kept secret in America," Zora Neale Hurston wrote in 1950. Wilson has put that man—his songs, his idiom, his superstitions, his folly, and his courage—on the stage. His plays are not talking textbooks; they paint the big picture indirectly, from the little incidents of daily life. "People can be slave-ships in shoes," Hurston said. Wilson's characters are shackled together by something greater than poverty; their bondage is to the caprices of history. "We's the leftovers," Toledo, the piano player and only literate member of Ma Rainey's band, tells the other musicians. "The white man knows you just a leftover. 'Cause he the one who done the eating and he know what he done ate. But we don't know that we been took and made history out of."

Wilson's work is a conscious answer to James Baldwin's call for "a profound articulation of the Black Tradition." He says he wanted to demonstrate that black American culture "was capable of sustaining you, so that when you left your father's or your mother's house you didn't go into the world naked. You were fully clothed in manners and a way of life." In the past, playwrights such as Dubose Heyward, Paul Green, and Eugene O'Neill made blacks and black culture the subject of drama; Wilson has made them the object. "When you go to the dictionary and you look up 'black,' it gives you these definitions that say, 'Affected by an undesirable condition,'" Wilson says. "You start thinking something's wrong with black. When white people say, 'I don't see color,' what they're saying is 'You're affected by this undesirable condition, but I'll pretend I don't see that.' And I go, 'No, *see* my color. Look at me. I'm not ashamed of who I am and what I am."

Wilson's characters often scrabble desperately, sometimes foolishly, for an opportunity that rarely comes. But when opportunity knocked for Wilson he seized it with a vengeance. He has tried to live his writing life by the Buddhist motto "You're entitled to the work but not the reward"; nevertheless, he has become a very rich man—in 1990, he was the most produced American playwright—and he is only getting richer. After "Seven Guitars," he and his co-producer, Ben Mordecai, formed a joint venture called Sageworks, which allows Wilson to exercise unusual control over the destiny of his plays—and also to take both a writer's and a producer's share of their profits. A Wilson play has a gestation period like no other in the history of American theatre, and no other major playwright—not Arthur Miller, Tennessee Williams, Eugene O'Neill, or David Mamet—has negotiated the latitude to work so freely. Before a play arrives on Broadway, Wilson refines his story through a series of separate productions. In his rehearsal mufti— black turtleneck and cloth cap—he sits beside the director for almost every hour of every production, and, since "Seven Guitars," he's taken to "writing in the heat of the moment." By the time "King Hedley II" reaches New York, the play, which shows the fragmented life of a Pittsburgh ghetto during the Reagan years, will have been seen, digested, reconceived, and rewritten after productions in Seattle, Boston, Pittsburgh, Chicago, Los Angeles, and Washington. This long reworking, like a brass rubbing, brings the play's parameters and its filigree of detail into bold relief until the drama emerges, as Wilson puts it, "fat with substance."

"When I was writing 'Joe Turner,'" Wilson says, "I realized that someone was gonna stand up onstage and say the words, whatever the hell they were. That's when I realized I had a responsibility to the words. I couldn't have the character say any old thing. There couldn't be any mistakes." To achieve this sort of focus requires the kind of appetite for victory that is epitomized, for Wilson, by a breed of championship racehorses, which in order to win "bite their own necks to get more oxygen." He began his own extraordinary endeavor late, at about forty, and his time is valuable. He does not spend it on the telephone, or watching television, or going to movies (between 1980 and 1991, he saw only two, both directed by Martin Scorsese—"Raging Bull" and "Cape Fear"). His work requires a lot of "doing nothing" to generate "brain space." So Wilson, whom Azula calls "the slippery guy," is usually to be found puttering in the crepuscular gloom of his basement, where he communes with himself and, if he's lucky taps into what he calls "the blood's memory," that "deepest part of yourself where the ancestors are talking." To do so requires a kind of ritual preparation. "Before I write something, I wash my hands," he says. "I always want to say I approached it with clean hands—you know, a symbolic cleansing."

Wilson's plays, filled as they often are with visions and visionaries, have a kind of hoodoo of their own, which can seem strange to white viewers, who are often critical of his use of the supernatural. He is a collagist, making Afro-Christian parables, and his plays are best when the real and the spiritual are wedded ("Joe Turner," "Seven Guitars," "The Piano Lesson"), in order, as he says, "to come up with a third thing, which is neither realism nor allegory." Then, his intensity and his natural eloquence—what Henry Louis Gates, Jr., calls "an unruly luxuriance of language, an ability to ease between trash talk and near-choral transport"—most effectively highlight another comparatively unsung quality of his writing: the ability to unfetter the heart. Under his focussed gaze, characters take on uncanny, sometimes awesome, life, and, unlike most contemporary male playwrights, he can write memorable roles for women as well as men. Wilson's work is not much influenced by the canon of modern Western plays, almost none of which he has read or seen. "I consider it a blessing that when I started writing plays in earnest, in 1979, I had not read Chekhov. I hadn't read Ibsen. I hadn't read Tennessee Williams, Arthur Miller, or O'Neill," he says. By then, he had been writing poetry for fifteen years and had read all the major American poets. "It took me eight years to find my own voice as a poet. I didn't want to take eight years to find my voice as a playwright." To this day, as incredible as it seems, with the exception of his own productions and a few of his friends', Wilson has seen only about a dozen plays.

In the age of the sound bite, Wilson is that most endangered of rare birds—a storyteller. A Wilson tale takes about as long as a baseball game, which is to say a good deal longer than the average commercial play. Although audiences will happily watch sports contests into double overtime, the play of ideas and characters is another matter. In this arena, they are accustomed to what Shakespeare called the "two hours' traffic," and Wilson has taken a lot of flak for his capaciousness. According to "The Oxford Companion to American Theatre," his plays "lack a sense of tone and a legitimate, sustained dramatic thrust." This criticism is, to my mind, unjust, but it reflects a distinctive cultural and artistic difference. Virtually all the seminal white postwar plays—"The Glass Menagerie," "Long Day's Journey Into Night," "Death of a Salesman"—revolve around the drama of American individualism; they mark a retreat from exterior into interior life. Wilson, however, dramatizes community. "Community is the most valuable thing that you have in African-American culture," he explains. "The individual good is always subverted to the good of the community." Wilson's plays are distinctive—and longer—because society, not just a psyche, is being mediated. They demonstrate the individual's interaction with the community, not his separation from it.

In Wilson's plays, the white world is a major character that remains almost entirely offstage; nonetheless, its presence is palpable—its rules, its standards, its ownership are always pressing in on the black world and changing the flow of things. "I look around and say, 'Where the barbed wire?'" Hedley says, observing that as a slave he would have been worth twelve hundred dollars, and now he's worth three-fifty an hour. "They got everything else. They got me blocked in every other way. 'Where the barbed wire?'" To which his sidekick replies, "If you had barbed wire you could cut through. You can't cut through having no job." "Blacks know the spiritual truth of white America," Wilson says. "We are living examples of America's hypocrisy. We know white America better than white America knows us." Wilson's plays go some distance toward making up this deficiency. For white members of the audience, the experience of watching a Wilson work is often educational and humanizing. It's the eternal things in Wilson's dramas—the arguments between fathers and sons, the longing for redemption, the dreams of winning, and the fear of losing—that reach across the footlights and link the black world to the white one, from which it is so profoundly separated and by which it is so profoundly defined. To the black world, Wilson's plays are witness; to the white world, they are news. This creates a fascinating racial conundrum, one first raised by Baldwin: "If I am not what I've been told I am, then it means that *you're* not what you thought *you* were *either!*"

II

August Wilson was born in 1945 in Pittsburgh's Hill District. Although it was just four minutes by car from downtown, the Hill—known then as Little Harlem—was a lively, flourishing, self-contained universe, with its own baseball teams, night clubs, businesses, and newspaper, and its own people, some of them legends who had left its one square mile to sing their distinctive songs to the world: Lena Horne, Erroll Garner, Ahmad Jamal, Earl, (Fatha) Hines, Billy Eckstine, George Benson. When Wilson was a child, the Hill had a population of fifty-five thousand; since then, as a consequence of the 1968 riots, urban renewal, and competition from white neighborhoods, to which African-Americans now have putative access, the Hill's boundaries and its buoyancy have shrunk. Today, its rows of small, decrepit houses sit on the sloping land like a set of bad teeth—irregular, decaying, with large gaps between them. Beside one such desolate, littered vacant lot, at the rear of 1727 Bedford Avenue, Wilson grew up. You have to bush-whack your way through a tangle of branches that covers the ten steep steps to the boarded front door of the forty-dollar-a-month apartment where Wilson, the fourth of six children, lived with his mother, Daisy Wilson, and his siblings, Freda, Linda Jean, Donna, Richard, and Edwin.

Daisy ran a structured household that was centered on family activities. "Monday at seven, the Rosary came on the radio, so we said the Rosary," Wilson recalls. "Art Linkletter's 'People Are Funny' was Tuesday. We played board games. Then there was the Top Forty. Everyone got to pick a

song. If your song got to No. 1, you got a nickel." The back yard, where
Daisy planted flowers and played dodgeball and baseball with her children
and, on summer evenings, sat around a card table for games of Tonk, is
blocked off now and difficult to see, but in the set for "Seven Guitars" Wilson preserved the ramshackle solace of the place so exactly that when his
sister Linda Jean first saw the show she burst into tears. At the core of Wilson's personality is a kind of truculent resolve, which comes, he says, from
his mother's example. (Daisy, who planned her own funeral, down to the
gown she'd wear, died of lung cancer in 1983; for the past eighteen years,
Wilson has returned to Pittsburgh on her birthday to gather with his family
and visit her grave.) She was a tall, strong, handsome homebody, who had
left school after the seventh grade and lived by the gospel of clear-eyed
common sense and competitiveness. For Wilson, the best example of
Daisy's brand of bumptious integrity is an incident that took place around
1955. She was listening to a quiz program that was offering a new washing
machine to anyone who could answer a question correctly. Daisy knew the
answer, and knew that, with six children, a washing machine would be a
blessing. But when she won the contest and the promoters found out that
she was black, they offered her instead a certificate to the Salvation Army to
get a used washing machine. "Mother said she wanted the new machine or
she didn't want any," Wilson says. "I remember Julie Burley"—Charley Burley's wife—"saying to her, 'Oh, Daisy, you got all them kids, what difference does it make? Take the washing machine.' And my mother said,
'Something is not always better than nothing.'"

Wilson's sense of his own uniqueness came, at least in part, from his
mother's adoring gaze, what Baldwin called "the crucial, the definitive, the
all-but-everlasting judgment." Wilson was Daisy's much longed-for first
son. "My mother said she would have had eleven girls—she didn't care—
she would have kept trying till she had a son," says Wilson's sister Donna,
who remembers being told of her father's disappointment at her own birth.
"'Another split-ass,' he said." Freda says, "Mother seemed to have a need
for a male in the house to show leadership. She dearly felt that August was
the best and smartest of us, so he should be given the duty of going downtown at the age of ten or eleven to pay the bills. It wasn't just about paying
the bills. Her underlying reason was to prepare him for the world." "She

made me believe that I could do anything," Wilson says. He adds, "I wanted to be the best at whatever I did. I was the best dishwasher in Pittsburgh. I really was. I got a raise the first day I was there. When I sit down and write, I want to write the best play that's ever been written. Sometimes that's a fearsome place to stand, but that's when you call on your courage."

Wilson had a high I.Q.; he also had a gift for language. In kindergarten, he was already entertaining the class with his stories. By the sixth grade, he was turning out love poems for the girls he fancied: "I would I could mend my festering heart / Harpooned by Cupid's flaming dart / But too far the shaft did penetrate / Alas, it is too late." At his Catholic grade school, Wilson's intellectual overreaching drove the nuns crazy. "When they said no one could figure out the Holy Trinity, I was like, 'Why not?' I instantly wanted to prove it could be done," he says. As Wilson grew into adolescence, even his friends acknowledged a certain grandiosity in him; his nickname was Napoleon.

Wilson's hankering to be spectacular was fed not only by his mother's expectations but by his father's abdications. Fritz Kittel considered himself German, although when he had immigrated to America, with his three brothers, in 1915, he was an Austro-Hungarian citizen. The first time he met Daisy, at a neighborhood grocery store, she was shy. At the urging of her grandmother, the next time she saw him she was more flirtatious. They married, but by the time Wilson was born, Linda jean says, Fritz was staying at the house only on weekends and living in a hotel during the week. Wilson remembers him as "mostly not there," adding, "You stayed out of his way if he was there." Fritz was, Wilson says, "an extremely talented baker," who worked for a while at New York's Waldorf-Astoria. He was also a wine drinker—"Muscatel by the gallon"—and couldn't keep a job.

The only father-son experience Wilson remembers was being taken downtown by Fritz in a blizzard to get a pair of Gene Autry cowboy boots. "He gave me a bunch of change, about seventy-five cents, and told me, 'Jingle it.' To let them know I had money." Otherwise, his memories focus on his father's hectoring abuse. Wilson refers to ferocious arguments, which sometimes ended with Fritz outside heaving bricks at their windows. "We knew to hide," Freda says. "We ran together, we'd fall behind the bed together, then, obviously, someone would sneak up to the window and look down." If Wilson closes his eyes to conjure up his father, he sees a tall man singing a German song to himself as he comes home from work with three-foot-high brown bags full of baked goods. "When he got angry, the next thing you know, Dad was just throwing the bags on the floor and stomping and crushing all the doughnuts and things in the bag," Linda Jean recalls. "And we needed those morsels." One Thanksgiving, in a tantrum, Fritz pulled the door off the oven and Daisy had to prop it back up with a stick so the turkey could finish roasting. Fritz's tranquil moments could be as tyrannical as his outbursts. "He believed in reading the papers," Freda says. "We had to sit down. We were not allowed to talk. We were not allowed to play. It was complete silence." Freda saw him as a displaced person, "an off-the-boat-type person." She says, "I don't think he ever fit here in America. I don't think he ever accepted black people. Or the culture. I think for my whole family there's a deep sense of abandonment." By 1957, when Wilson was twelve, Daisy had divorced Kittel and taken up with David Bedford, a black man whom she later married. "I loved the man," Wilson says of Bedford, an avid reader who was a community leader, and who, Wilson learned, after his death in 1969, had spent twenty-three years in prison.

Wilson inherited his father's volatile temperament. "He was a kid with a temper," Freda says. "And a sorry loser, because, in his mind, if he played to win he should win because he should have figured out whatever strategy was needed to win. And not figuring out that strategy was just highly unacceptable to him." In this regard, Wilson hasn't changed much over the years. "My goodness, when he got emotional he was mad scary," says the professor and playwright Rob Penny, who was one of Wilson's closest friends on the Hill. "You'd think he was gonna snap out, attack you, or beat you up or something. He was very intense." When he was about twenty, Wilson cuffed his sister Donna and broke her jaw. I asked Constanza Romero what she had found most surprising about Wilson after she married him, and she said, "His temper—his temper scared me." She referred to an explosion over a misplaced telephone number. "He went crazy, absolutely bonkers," she said. "He starts speaking very strongly, cussing himself out. He really doesn't allow himself any mistakes, any leeway."

"I just always felt that the society was lined up against you," Wilson says. "That in order to do anything in the world you were going to have to

battle this thing that was out there. It wasn't gonna give you any quarter."
For Wilson, the battle began in earnest when he was a freshman at Central
Catholic High School, where he was the only black student in his grade and
was placed in the advanced class. "There was a note on my desk every single
day. It said, 'Go home nigger,'" Wilson says. The indignities—the shoving,
the name-calling, the tripping—were constant; so was Wilson's brawling.
The Christian Brothers frequently sent him home by taxi. "They would have
to walk me through a gantlet of, like, forty kids. I would always want to say
to them, 'But you're not saying anything to these forty guys. You're just
escorting me through them as though they have a right to stand here.'"
Then, one day when Wilson was in his early teens, a student standing in
front of him during the Pledge of Allegiance made mention of the "nigger"
behind him. "I said, 'O.K., buddy,'" and, at "liberty and justice for all," Wilson punched him. "We go down to Brother Martin's, and he's ready to send
me home. I said, 'Hey, why don't we just do this permanently? I do not
want to go to school here anymore.'" Wilson went next to a vocational
school, where the academic content was "I swear, like fifth-grade work."
When his shop teacher, angry that Wilson had knocked in a thumbtack with
a T-square, punched Wilson so hard that he knocked him off his chair, Wilson lunged at the teacher and "bounced him off the blackboard." "Give me a
pink slip," he said. "I'm leaving this school."

At fifteen, Wilson ended up at Gladstone High School, taking tenth-
grade classes but still officially in the ninth grade. He sulked in class, sat in
the back, and refused to participate. Then, in an effort to redeem himself in
the eyes of a black teacher, who ran an after-school college club Wilson
wanted to join, he decided to take one assignment seriously. It was an essay
on a historical figure, and Wilson chose Napoleon. "The fact that he was a
self-made man, that he was a lieutenant in the army and became the
emperor, I liked that," Wilson says. He researched it; he wrote it; he rented
a typewriter with money he'd earned mowing lawns and washing cars; he
paid his sister Linda Jean twenty-five cents a page to type it; and then he
handed it in.

"The next day, the teacher asked me to stay after class," Wilson says. On
the paper the teacher had written two marks—A-plus and E, a failing
grade. "I'm gonna give you one of these two grades," he told Wilson. Sus-

pecting that one of Wilson's older sisters had written the paper, he asked, "Can you prove to me that you wrote this?" Wilson remembers saying, "Hey, unless you call everybody in here and have all the people prove they wrote them, even the ones that went and copied out of the encyclopedia word for word, I don't feel I should have to prove anything." The teacher circled the E and handed the paper back. "I tore it up, threw it in the waste-basket, and walked out of school," Wilson says.

Every morning for the rest of the school year, rather than tell his mother he'd dropped out, Wilson walked three blocks to the local library. Over the next four years, by his own estimation, he read three hun-dred books, spending as many as five hours a day in the library. He read everything—sociology, anthropology, theology, fiction. "The world opened up," he says. "I could wander through the stacks. I didn't need anyone to teach me. All you had to do was have an interest and a willingness to extract the information from the book." It was about this time that Wilson began to see himself as a kind of warrior, surviving unapologetically on his own terms. The first person with whom he had to do battle was Daisy, whose dashed dreams for her son made her a furious opponent." She told him he was no good, that he would amount to nothing," Linda Jean says. "It was relentless. It was an agony for him. He suffered many indignities. He was often denied food. She would take the food out of the refrigerator, put it in her bedroom, lock the door, and then go out. He was made to live in the basement for a while. She said he was dirty. She didn't want him in the house upstairs."

By the time Wilson was banished to the basement, he had decided to become a writer. "I was like, 'O.K., I'm gonna sit here, I'm gonna write some stories. I'll show you,'" Wilson says. "I was gonna demonstrate my worth to her. I negotiated cooking privileges. I'd get fifteen cents and go buy me three pounds of potatoes. I was gonna demonstrate that I could feed and take care of myself." He lasted a week. "My mother was very disap-pointed," Wilson says. "She saw a lot of potential that I'd squandered, as far as she was concerned." To get out of the house, Wilson joined the Army. He took the Officer Candidate School test and came in second in his battalion, just two points behind the leader. Then, as often happens in Wilson's plays and in his life, he came up against the rules: to be an officer, you had to be nineteen; he was seventeen. And, if he couldn't be an officer, he wasn't interested.

Wilson headed across the country to California, where he worked in a pharmacy, until his father's terminal illness brought him back to Pittsburgh. Wilson and Linda Jean visited their father, who told them stories about being in the Army and the battle of the Argonne Forest. "Then he suddenly looked up and said, 'Who are you?'" Wilson says. "He basically chased us out of there, but for a couple of hours we had a great time." On his deathbed, Wilson's father called for his son "Fritz." Afterward, Wilson wrote a muted memorial, "Poem for the Old Man," which begins by evoking his father in his prime ("Old Fritz, when young / could lay a harem") and ends with Wilson himself ("his boxing boy / Is hitting all the new places / Too soon to make a mark").

Wilson took refuge in the African-American community, and it, in turn, nurtured him and contained him and his rage at his father's abandonment. "He's so faithful to the blackness. He's faithful like a father—that represents fidelity to him," says James Earl Jones, who starred in "Fences." Wilson found another father figure in Chawley Williams, a black drug dealer turned poet, who became his protector on the street. "August wasn't really black. He was half-and-half," Williams says. "He was too dark to be white, and he was too white to be dark. He was in no man's land. I knew he was lost. I was lost. Kindred brothers know one another. We were trying to become men. We didn't even know what it meant." In time, Wilson would write himself into the center of modern black American history. But when he hit the streets he had no money, no marketable skills, no proven talent. He was, he says, "searching for something you can claim as yours."

On April 1, 1964, Wilson walked into downtown Pittsburgh to McFerron's typewriter store and put twenty dollars on the counter for a heavy black Royal Standard in the window. He'd earned the money by writing a term paper—"Two Violent Poets: Robert Frost and Carl Sandburg"—for Freda, who was then at Fordham University. He lugged the typewriter up the Hill to the basement apartment he'd rented in a boarding house, placed the machine on the kitchen table, put a piece of loose-leaf paper in it, and typed his name. Actually, he typed every possible combination of his name—Fred A. Kittel, Frederick A. Kittel, Frederick A. Wilson, A. Wilson, August Wilson—and settled finally on the last because it looked best on paper. He then laboriously typed a batch of poems. He'd heard that *Harper's* paid a dollar a line, so he sent the poems there. "They came back three days later," Wilson says. "I said, 'Oh, I see. This is serious. I'm gonna have to learn how to write a poem.' I wasn't deterred by that. I was emboldened." But because he "didn't like the feeling of rejection," Wilson didn't send out another poem for five years. (His first published work was "Muhammad Ali," which appeared in *Black World* in 1969.) "It was sufficient for me to know that I wrote poetry and I was growing as an artist," he says.

Most sightings of Wilson on the Hill were in restaurants—the White Tower, Eddie's Restaurant, the B &W, Moose's—bent over, scribbling on his tablet or on napkins. Decades later, Wilson would walk through the neighborhood and people would stop him and ask, "You still drawin'?" "I found out later people thought I was a bum," Wilson says. "The thing that sustained me was that my idea of myself was different from the idea that society, my mother, and even some of my friends had of me. I saw myself as a grand person." He adds, "I saw the pictures of Richard Wright, Langston Hughes—all of them always had a suit on. I thought, Yeah, that's me. I want to be like that." At a local thrift shop, he bought white shirts for a dime, the broad ties he favored for a nickel, and sports coats for thirty-five cents. In the poetic sphere, he'd come under the influence of Dylan Thomas, and he went through the Black Power movement with a coat and tie and a pipe, intoning poetry in an English accent. "People thought he was crazy in the neighborhood," Chawley Williams says. He adds, "When I met August, I was in the drug world. Here come August. He's sensitive, he's articulate, he has talent, he's trying to write. And the hustlers of the streets is at him. They could get him to do things, 'cause he wanted to belong. He would allow them to come to wherever he stayed at to eat, to get high and shoot their dope, to lie up with different women. They were trying to get him to get high. I put a halt to that."

Fish love water, it is said, and are cooked in it. But although Wilson swam in this predatory world he never felt threatened. If you ask him now to imagine the street back then, a smile crosses his face; he holds out his big right hand and trembles it. "A shimmy," he says. "The avenue shimmered.

Hundreds of people on the sidewalks. Life going on." The vibrancy ravished him. Once, riding up Centre Avenue in a friend's convertible, Wilson heard gunshots. "I hopped out of the car and ran down to where the gunshots were," he says. "There's this woman chasing the man around the car, and—*boom!*—she shot him. He was bleeding, and he asked this guy, 'Man, drive me to the hospital.' The guy said, 'You ain't gon' get all that blood in my car!'" Wilson adds, "I remember one time I didn't go to bed for damn near three days because every time I'd go to bed I felt like I was missing something."

Although Little Richard, Frankie Lymon and the Teenagers, Chuck Berry, and other rock and rollers had spilled over the back-yard fences of Wilson's childhood, it wasn't until this time that he first heard the blues. For a nickel at a St. Vincent de Paul charity shop, he bought a bootleg 78-r.p.m. record on whose tattered yellow label he could make out the words "Bessie Smith: 'Nobody in Town Can Bake a Sweet Jelly Roll Like Mine.'" Smith's impudent, unabashed sound stunned him. "The universe stuttered and everything fell to a new place," he wrote later. Like James Baldwin, who wrote that hearing Bessie Smith for the first time "helped to reconcile me to being a 'nigger,'" Wilson saw the moment as an epiphany: "a birth, a baptism, and a redemption all rolled up into one." Wilson played the new record twenty-two times straight. "Then I started laughing, you know, 'cause it suddenly dawned on me that there was another record on the other side." He adds, "It made me look at the world differently. It gave the people in the rooming house where I lived, and also my mother, a history I didn't know they had. It was the beginning of my consciousness that I was the carrier of some very valuable antecedents."

Wilson considers the blues "the best literature we have." As a way of preparing the emotional landscape for each play of his cycle, he submerges himself in the blues of the period. For "Hedley," for instance, he's asking himself, "How'd we get from Percy Sledge's 'Warm and Tender Love' to 'You My Bitch'?" Even the structure of his sentences   the frequent reiteration of themes and words—owes much to the music's repetitions, its raucous pitch and improvised irony. From Two Trains Running":

A nigger with a gun is bad news. You can't even use the word
"nigger" and "gun" in the same sentence. You say the word "gun"
in the same sentence with the word "nigger" and you in trouble.
The white man panic. Unless you say, "The policeman shot the
nigger with his gun."

He particularly likes it when singers speak their names in song. "There's
something wonderful about that," he says. "They're making a stand. They're
saying, 'This is me. This is what I have to say.'" In the context of what Zora
Neale Hurston called "the muteness of slavery," the notion of singing solo
and making a personal statement is, for African-Americans, a comparatively
new and extraordinarily potent thing, which Wilson dramatizes in his plays.
In his theatrical vocabulary, "finding a song" is both the expression of spirit
and the accomplishment of identity. Some of his characters have a song that
they can't broadcast; others have given up singing; some have been brutal-
ized into near-muteness; and others have turned the absence of a destiny
into tall talk—the rhetoric of deferred dreams. But Wilson's most brilliant
demonstration of "carrying other people's songs and not having one of
my own"—as one character puts it—is in "Joe Turner's Come and Gone,"
where a conjure man called Bynum, who has a song, discourses with Loomis,
who has been separated from his. Bynum says:

> Now, I can look at you, Mr. Loomis, and see you a man who
> done forgot his song. Forgot how to sing it. A fellow forget that
> and he forget who he is. Forget how he's supposed to mark
> down life. . . . See, Mr. Loomis, when a man forgets his song
> he goes of in search of it . . . till he find out he's got it with him
> all the time.

Music, in Wilson's plays, is more than slick Broadway entertainment. A
juba dance banged out on a table, a work song beaten out with chairs and
glasses, a gut-bucket blues demonstrate the African-American genius for
making something out of nothing. They take an empty world, as Ma Rainey
says, and "fill it up with something."

* * *

Blues people, Ralph Ellison once wrote, are "those who accepted and lived close to their folk experience." On the Hill, the blues cemented in Wilson's mind the notion that he was somehow "the conduit of ancestors." West's Funeral Home—which figures in "Two Trains Running"—was just around the corner from Eddie's Restaurant, and Wilson, for some deep personal reason and not for art's sake, felt compelled routinely to pay his respects to whomever had died. "I didn't have to know them. I felt that this is a life that has gone before me," he explains. From Claude McKay's "Home to Harlem," he learned of a hangout in his own neighborhood called Pat's Place—a cigar store with a pool hall in the back—where a lot of the community elders congregated. Pat's Place became Wilson's Oxford, and its garrulous denizens—"walking history books," Wilson calls them—his tutors. They called him Youngblood. "I was just like, 'Hey, man, how did you get to be so old, 'cause it's hard out here.' I really wanted to know how they survived. How do you get to be seventy years old in America?" Wilson recalls meeting one old man at Pat's Place who said to him, "I been watchin' you. You carryin' around a ten-gallon bucket. You carry that ten-gallon bucket through life, and you gon' always be disappointed. Get you a little cup. And, that way, if somebody put a little bit in it, why, you got sumpin'." Wilson adds, "I managed to cut it down to a gallon bucket, but I never did get that little cup."

"What I discovered is that writing was the only thing society would allow me to do," he said in 1991. "I couldn't have a job or be a lawyer because I didn't do all the things necessary. What I was allowed to do was write. If they saw me over in the corner scribbling on a piece of paper they would say: 'That is just a nigger over in the corner scribbling on a piece of paper.' Nobody said, 'Hey, you can't do that.' So I felt free." On the street, as a defensive maneuver, Wilson says he "learned to keep my mouth shut," but, according to Chawley Williams, "when August stood onstage and read his poetry, there was a difference in him that didn't exist at no other time. He stood tall and proud. He stood with that definiteness." He was supported in this pursuit by his friends in the neighborhood—Williams, Rob Penny, and Nicholas Flournoy, who were all aspiring poets. The group founded the Centre Avenue Poets Theatre Workshop, out of which came the journal *Connection* (Wilson was its poetry editor), then the Halfway Art Gallery, and, from 1968 to 1972, the Black Horizons Theatre, which Wilson cofounded with Penny, who served as house playwright.

During this time, Wilson had a daughter, Sakina Ansari (to whom "Joe Turner's Come and Gone" is dedicated), in a marriage to Brenda Burton, which ended in 1973. "She moved out with the baby," Linda Jean says. "August came home to an empty house. The shock and pain were unbearable to him. In a nutshell, she thought his writing was a waste of time, he wouldn't amount to anything." Although Wilson himself always felt successful, he says, he still hadn't achieved what he calls, quoting the poet Robert Duncan, "surety—the line burned in the hand." He says, "I had been trying to get to that point. I didn't approach it lightly. I worked concertedly toward growth." Finally, in 1973, in a poem called "Morning Statement," Wilson found his poetic voice:

> It is the middle of winter
> November 21 to be exact
> I got up, buckled my shoes,
> I caught a bus and went riding into town.
> I just thought I'd tell you.

"The poem didn't pretend to be anything else," Wilson says. "It wasn't struggling to say eternal things. It was just claiming the ground as its own thing. For me, it was so liberating." But his liberation as a playwright didn't begin until March 5, 1978, when he moved away from the Hill, to St. Paul, Minnesota, where he married Judy Oliver, a white social worker. In doing so, he went from a neighborhood that had fifty-five thousand blacks to a state that had the same number. "There weren't many black folks around," he says. "In that silence, I could hear the language for the first time." Until then, Wilson says, he hadn't "valued or respected the way that black folks talked. I'd always thought that in order to create art out of it you had to change that." Now he missed the street talk and wanted to preserve it. "I got lonely and missed those guys and sort of created them," he says. "I could hear the music."

III

By the time Wilson reached St. Paul, he'd directed a handful of amateur
productions, and his friend the director Claude Purdy had staged a musical
satire based on a series of Wilson's poems. But despite a paying gig at the
Science Museum of Minnesota, where Wilson wrote children's plays on
science-related subjects, he was, by anyone's standard, a theatrical tyro. As
early as 1976, he'd begun work on a piece about Ma Rainey; but then, he
says, "it never occurred to me to make the musicians characters in the play.
I couldn't have written the characters." His dialogue had a kind of florid
artiness. In one of his early dramatic experiments, which involved a conversation between an old man and a woman on a park bench, the woman said,
"Terror hangs over the night like a hawk." Wilson had at least one play, "The
Coldest Day of the Year," produced in this stilted style. "It wasn't black
American language," he says. It wasn't theatre, either.

In the fall of 1977, Wilson came across the work of the painter Romare
Bearden. As he thumbed through Bearden's series of collages "The Preva-
lence of Ritual," he discovered his "artistic mentor." Bearden's paintings
made simple what Wilson's writing had so far only groped to formulate:
"Black life presented on its own terms, on a grand and epic scale, with all its
richness and fullness, in a language that was vibrant and which, made attendant to everyday life, ennobled it, affirmed its value, and exalted its presence." He adds, "My response was visceral. I was looking at myself in ways I
hadn't thought of before and have never ceased to think of since." In later
years, Wilson would stand outside Bearden's house on Canal Street, in New
York, "in silent homage, daring myself to knock." He didn't knock, but, he
has written, if Bearden "had answered . . . and if I were wearing a hat, I
would have taken it off in tribute." (In the end, Wilson's true homage was
his plays, two of which—"Mill Hand's Lunch Bucket," which became "Joe
Turner," and "The Piano Lesson"—took their titles from Bearden paintings.)

Years before, Wilson, who then "couldn't write dialogue," had asked
Rob Penny, "How do you make characters talk?" Penny answered, "You

don't. You listen to them." Now, in 1979, when Wilson sat down to write
"Jitney," a play set at the taxi stand that had been one of Wilson's hangouts
on the Hill, the penny, as it were, dropped. For the first time, he was able to
listen to his characters and let them speak. "I found that exhilarating," he
says. "It felt like this was what I'd been looking for, something that was
mine, that would enable me to say anything." For Wilson, the revelation was
that "language describes the idea of the one who speaks; so if I'm speaking
the oppressor's language I'm in essence speaking his ideas, too. This is why I
think blacks speak their own language, because they have to find another
way." While writing "Jitney," he proved to himself that he didn't have to
reconstitute black life; he just had to capture it.

Wilson sat at Arthur Treacher's Fish & Chips, a restaurant up the street
from his apartment in St. Paul, for ten days in a row until the play was finished. At Penny's suggestion, he submitted it to the O'Neill Playwrights
Conference, a sprawling estate in Waterford, Connecticut, where each
summer about a dozen playwrights are provided with a dramaturge, a
director, and a cast to let them explore their flawed but promising plays.
The O'Neill rejected "Jitney"; its incredulous author, assuming that no one
had read it, submitted the play again. The O'Neill rejected it again. Wilson
took serious stock of his newfound calling; his inner dialogue, he says, was
"'Maybe it's not as good as you think. You have to write a better play.' 'I've
already written the best play I can write.' 'Why don't you write above your
talent?' 'Oh, man, how can you do that?' 'Well, you can write beneath it,
can't you?' 'Oh, yeah.'" Wilson turned back to the play on Ma Rainey and
began to imagine it differently. "I opened up the door to the band room," he
says. "Slow Drag and Cutler was talking about how Slow Drag got his name.
Then this guy walked in—he had glasses, carrying the books—he became
Toledo. I had discovered them and got them talking."

On August 1,1982, the producer Ben Mordecai, who had recently become
the managing director of the Yale Repertory Theatre, drove up to Waterford to see his boss, Lloyd Richards. Richards, who is of Jamaican descent,
was the head of the Yale Drama School and, for more than thirty years,
worked during the summer as the artistic director of the O'Neill. He is a
man of few words, most of them carefully chosen. "Is there anyone here I

should meet?" Mordecai asked Richards. "Meet him," Richards said, nodding toward the porch of the main building, where Wilson was sitting. When "Ma Rainey's Black Bottom" was accepted at the O'Neill, Wilson stumbled onto the right person at the right place at the right time. Other African-Americans, such as Ed Bullins, whose "Twentieth-Century Cycle" did for South Philadelphia in the sixties and seventies what Wilson would do for Pittsburgh, were not as lucky. With access to theatres and to grant-giving agencies, Richards, who had directed "A Raisin in the Sun" on Broadway, was well positioned to usher Wilson's talent directly into the mainstream. Richards became, Wilson wrote, "my guide, my mentor, and my provocateur," and all of Wilson's subsequent plays until "Seven Guitars" would follow the same golden path—from the O'Neill to Yale to Broadway.

When "Ma Rainey" went to Yale, in 1984, Richards took over. "We go into the room with the actors, we read the play," Wilson says, describing the first day of rehearsal. "An actor had a question about a character. I started to speak, and Lloyd answered the question. There was another question, and Lloyd answered it again. I remember there was a moment when I thought, The old fox knows what's going on. This is gonna be O.K." "We had a pattern of work," Richards says of their partnership, which in time would become as influential as that of Tennessee Williams and Elia Kazan. "I would work on it, check it with him, so I included him, but I was the director." He adds, "August was very receptive in the early days. He had a lot to learn and knew it. He was a big sponge, absorbing everything." Richards sent him to the sound booth, to the paint shop, to the lighting designer. "As he learned structure—playwriting, really—he was also learning everything else," Richards says.

Richards is not a gregarious man, and his natural reticence complements his collaborative, indirect way of working: "I try to provoke the artist to find the answer *I* want him to find." When Wilson sent Richards a version of "The Piano Lesson," he says, "Lloyd calls me up and says, 'I think you have one too many scenes there.' 'O.K., Lloyd, I'll look at that.' End of conversation. I go to the play. I see this scene that looks like it's expendable. I pull it out. Talking to Lloyd about something else a couple of days later, I say, 'Oh,

Lloyd, by the way, I took the scene out.' Lloyd says, 'Good.' To this day, I don't know if we were talking about the same scene." Richards says, "He cut the scene that needed to be cut." He adds, "August writes wonderful scenes. He must think they're wonderful, 'cause they go on and on and on. To the point where they advance the play much further than it needs to be advanced at that moment." Wilson's "Fences," which was the second-most-produced play on American professional stages in 1989, was transformed by Richards, over several productions, from a four-and-a-half-hour first appearance at the O'Neill to its commercial length of less than three hours not just by cutting but by reorganizing. This began Wilson's practice of refining his plays in the regionals. "The Piano Lesson"—which involves a contest for ownership of a prized family piano between a sister, who wants to keep it as a symbol of her African-American heritage, and her brother, who wants to sell it to buy land on the plantation where their ancestors were slaves—had still not found a satisfactory ending after a year of touring. It finally got one when Richards suggested to Wilson that the battle between the brother and sister was missing a third party: the spirit of the white family who also had claims on the piano. "August wrote a wonderful speech describing how the piano came into the family and how they had stolen it from this white family," Richards says. "That brought the piece together."

When "The Piano Lesson" was made into a TV movie, in 1995, Wilson served as a producer, a shift in power that also augured a change in his relationship with Richards. At one meeting, a production designer, Patricia Van Ryker, who hadn't read the original play—which states that the piano's legs are "carved in the manner of African sculpture," to represent the characters' African heritage—laid out her plans to decorate the piano with images of plantation life that fit within the time frame of the play. Wilson exploded. "He was screaming," Van Ryker recalls. "'How dare you do this! You're insulting my relatives! My race!' It was like I'd thrown kerosene on him." Richards recalls the moment as "terrible," and says, "I don't function dictatorially. I don't give directives. I saw August in a position of power. I knew I couldn't work *for* him."

As Wilson grew in confidence, craft, and stature, it became increasingly difficult for him to play the protégé in the partnership. "The two of them artistically began drifting apart, which was, I think, a natural thing," Mordecai says. "The collaboration wasn't happening at the level it had in earlier years." As Wilson saw it, "Lloyd slowed down," but it's just as true to say that Wilson grew up. When a rewritten version of "Jitney" was up for production at the Pittsburgh Public Theatre, in 1996, Wilson chose as his director Marion McClinton, who had done inventive second productions of many of his earlier plays. Wilson may have lost a kind of father in the split with Richards, but in McClinton he gained a brother. Where Richards's productions were stately, McClinton's are fluid; where Richards's process was formal, McClinton's is relaxed. "The first conversation we had, August said to me, 'My style is I don't talk to the actors,'" McClinton recalls. "I said, 'I don't care if you talk to the actors. Whatever gets the information to them the clearest and cleanest, that's what I'm for.'"

"August is a soldier," McClinton says, and he's referring to more than Wilson's theatrical battles. Wilson, who cites the Black Power movement as "the kiln in which I was fired," describes himself as a "race man." And his very specific anthropological understanding of American history has led him to some hard, politically incorrect opinions. For instance, he believes that it was a mistake for African-Americans to leave the South. "The blood and bones of two hundred and fifty years of our ancestors are buried in the South, and we came North," he says. "I think if we'd stayed South and continued to empower ourselves, in terms of acquiring land—we already had acres of farmland that we owned—we'd have had ten black senators in the United States. We'd be represented. We'd be a more culturally secure and culturally self-sufficient people."

Wilson's insistence on preserving and sustaining an African-American identity led to a well-publicized argument with Robert Brustein, the artistic director of Boston's American Repertory Theatre, that culminated in a formal debate at New York's Town Hall, in 1997. Among many contrarian points, Wilson argued against the current fashion for "color-blind casting"— a bias shared by McClinton, who refers to the practice as "Cyclops casting." "It's color-blind in one eye," he says. "You're quite aware of the fact that we're black—that's why we're not asked to present that in our performance, where the white actors can bring whatever history and interior self-knowledge they have into a rehearsal process and into the making of character." In Wilson's view, to mount an all-black production of, say, "Death of a Salesman" is to deny us "the need to make our own investigations from the cultural ground on which we stand as black Americans." In his exchange with Brustein, Wilson pointed out the transparent inequity of having sixty-six regional theatres and only one that can be considered black. (He subsequently conceived and supported the African Grove Institute for the Arts, an organization that promotes African-American theatre.) In America, "the subscription audience holds the seats of our theatres hostage to the mediocrity of its tastes, and serves to impede the further development of an audience for the work that we do," he said. "Intentional or not, it serves to keep blacks out of the theatre, where they suffer no illusion of welcome anyway." This call for an African-American theatre was immediately seized upon by the press as separatist, despite the fact that Wilson himself disputed the label. "We are not separatists, as Mr. Brustein asserts," he said. "We are Americans trying to fulfill our talents. We are not the servants at the party. We are not apprentices in the kitchens. . . . We are Africans. We are Americans." The aftermath of the debate—something of a tempest in a teapot—still lingers (and is still misconstrued). "He took that hit for a lot of other people," McClinton says. "That's what a champion does—a champion fights." When Wilson gave me a book of his first three plays, he inscribed it, "The struggle continues."

My first sighting of McClinton and Wilson at work was last November, in the rehearsal room of Chicago's new Goodman Theatre, where "King Hedley II" was the inaugural production. They sat shoulder to shoulder at the rehearsal table. McClinton, a heavy man, wore a baggy white T-shirt and a black fedora; he chugged at an economy-sized Dr Pepper. Wilson, in his trademark cap, sat bent slightly forward and absolutely still. His eyes were trained on the figure of Hedley, a former killer trying to make a go of it on the Hill, as he knelt in front of a flower patch demarked in rehearsal by a few stones on the concrete floor. His mother, Ruby, stood nearby, watching him. "You need some good dirt," she told him. "Them seeds ain't gonna grow in that dirt." Hedley responded, "This the only dirt I got. This is me right here." The words—the opening of the play—linked Wilson's newest protagonist to all the other desperate heroes of his cycle, and to himself: men attempting, in one way or another, to claim their inheritance. Wilson leaned across to whisper something to McClinton, who, keeping his eyes on the actors, nodded, took another hit of soda, and stopped the rehearsal to adjust the blocking. "King don't listen well," the actor playing Hedley said. "He's a king," McClinton replied. "Kings don't listen."

At the break, Wilson headed off to the theatre's loading bay for a cigarette. There he brooded about Aunt Esther, the three-hundred-and-sixty-six-year-old character whose death the play announces. "See, Aunt Esther is the tradition," he said. "If you don't value that, then you lose it. So, in 1985, these kids are out there killing one another. Aunt Esther dies of grief. People quit going up to her house. The weeds are all grown over. You can't even find the door no more. So she dies." He added, "If you had a connection to your grandparents and understood their struggle to survive, you wouldn't be out there in the street killing someone over fifteen dollars' worth of narcotics. You have to know your history. Then you'll have a purposeful presence in the world."

As he readied "Hedley" for New York, Wilson had been trying to make a start on his nineteen-hundreds play, in which Aunt Esther is a central character. Like Romare Bearden, Wilson opens himself up to his subjects and communes with them until he finds a pattern: "I just invite some of the people I know to come into the room and give it an ambience." "Fences" began with the ending; Wilson says that he saw his hero, Troy Maxson, "standing out on this brilliant starry night with this baby in his arms, talking to this woman. I didn't know who the woman was." "Two Trains Running" began in a New Haven restaurant, where Wilson picked up a napkin and wrote, "When I left out of Jackson I said I was gonna buy me a big Ford. Was gonna drive by Mr. Henry Ford's house and honk the horn. If anybody come to the window, I was gonna wave. Then I was going out, and buy me a 30.06, come on back to Jackson and drive up to Mr. Stovall's house. Only this time I wasn't waving."

By contrast, Aunt Esther had been balky about making her presence known. "I said, 'O.K., Aunt Esther, talk to me.' And she says, 'There's a lot of things I don't talk about.' And that threw me, because I didn't have anything to write then," Wilson says. A month later, he tried again. This time, he asked Aunt Esther, "O.K., what *don't* you talk about?" "I don't talk about the trees. The trees didn't have spirits," she told Wilson. "What does that mean? What that means is that none of your world is present here. You're looking at this landscape that's totally foreign to you. So I started writing that," Wilson says. "Then she started talking about the water, and I find she's talking about the Atlantic Ocean. And she starts talking about a city, a half mile by a half mile, down in there. She has a map to the city," he adds. "I think the map is important, so I have to pick the right time to approach that idea about the map. If I do it this afternoon, I get something entirely different than if I do it next week. It's intuition. You have to keep your eyes and ears open for clues. There's no compass."

In "King Hedley II," Hedley's sacrifice keeps a dying black tradition alive; in life, Wilson has also made a sacrifice to renew a connection to the past. He seems to know that the price he's paid for his enormous accomplishment is other people; and he has recently begun to take stock of his life and resolve "to do something different." He is making noises about retiring. Not long ago, when he returned to Seattle, Wilson, who had been away, by his own admission, "for the past two years," was dismayed to discover that Azula didn't know he lived there. "You live in all the places," she told him. "Boston, New York, Pittsburgh." "No, I live here," he said. He took Azula upstairs and showed her his clothes in the closet.

Wilson, who is an insomniac, shares a bed with both Azula and Constanza. At lights-out, Azula will say, "Don't let the bedbugs bite." Wilson will reply, "If they do, take a few," which leaves his daughter the final word: "'Cause I got them from you." When they wake up, Wilson says, "Good morning, Sunshine." Azula replies, "Good morning, Big Old Dad." But these moment of connection are only one side of the story. Wilson, who has created a universe of fully imagined characters, whose histories he knows in minute detail, is not as curious about the history of those close to him. "I've been married before," Constanza says. "He's never asked me a single question about that. I mean a lot to him, but what is it I mean to him if I'm not a complete person with history, with wants, with needs?" Constanza met Wilson at Yale fourteen years ago, when she designed costumes for "The

Piano Lesson," and she has a kind of clear-eyed fatalism about her life with this ambitious storyteller. "It's been hard," she says. "I don't get the love from him that all of me would like. I don't have a partner through the little things in life. He just doesn't reach that intimate part of everyday life." She continues, "In his mind, he's a great father, a great man, a great husband. One time, I was saying to Azula, when she was going to sleep, 'I'm going to teach you how to choose a really good husband for yourself.' And then August said, 'Just like your daddy.' And I was thinking to myself, No!"

"Be where you are"—a maxim Lloyd Richards drilled into Wilson—is a habit that Wilson—is "still working at." When he is at home, Wilson is pretty much wrapped in his own solitude, "brewing," as his sister Freda calls it. "I call him the deepest pool have ever seen in my life," Constanza says. "You can throw a rock inside this man and you'll never see it hit bottom. He's a mystery to me in many ways. He's reachable only in concise sentences." Wilson's plays are brilliantly furnished with characters and incident, but he hasn't yet managed to furnish his own home. "It's gone beyond eccentricity," Constanza says. "It's an outward symbol of our marriage being so out of the ordinary. We can't even furnish our own house. I mean, that's sad." Wilson's critical eye and Constanza's conviction that he would disapprove if she took the decoration into her own hands keeps them at a stalemate. "He's extremely critical," Constanza says. "The closer you are to him, the more critical he is. That's a pattern that his mother passed on to him."

Ordinarily, according to his wife, Wilson "has a hard time laughing at himself." But in the presence of his daughter the sombre, self-absorbed Wilson drops away. "I've seen a different August with Azula," McClinton agrees. "She brings out such a playful side of him. He came to the first day of rehearsal in Seattle for 'King Hedley II' wearing a bunny mask with the ears sticking up." Wilson has taught Azula some of the nonsense songs that he learned at the age of five from an uncle: together, they sing, "Jo and Mo had a candy store / Tellin' fortunes behind the door / The police ran in / Joe ran out / Hollerin' 'Run, Mo! / Policeman holdin' my hand!'" Recently, he wrote a story just for her that involved what he calls "telescoping"—a fusion of the spiritual and the diurnal "that I'm trying to do in the plays." The tale starts off in Seattle with a little girl who won't go to bed. "My aunt in Africa will grant you a wish if you will go to bed at the proper time," her babysitter says. "O.K.," the little girl says. "My wish is that it be daylight all the time so I never have to go to bed." The story then moves from reality into a fantastical world of sun gods and kings of darkness and chess games where the pieces come alive. "I think it's close to what would be an African-American world view—tree spirits and all those kinds of things," Wilson says. "In this world, you can have a three-hundred-and-sixty-six-year-old woman and you also gotta pay your bills. They exist side by side. They infuse life with a something that lifts it up, almost into another realm. Closer to God." Even Azula understands that her father's undertaking is somehow special and heroic and big in the world. At the Goodman Theatre, catching sight of him as he walked toward her in the lobby, she threw open her arms and said, "August Wilson!" Around that time, she also asked him, "Daddy, why you a writer?" "To tell the story," Wilson said.

COLE PORTER

KING COLE

O<small>N</small> O<small>CTOBER</small> 24, 1937, C<small>OLE</small>
Porter went out for a horseback ride at the Piping Rock Club, in Locust
Valley, Long Island—one of those swank playgrounds whose names he liked
to rhyme in song and which signalled his fully paid-up membership in the
Elegentsia. In the woods, the skittish horse, which the forty-six-year-old
Porter had been warned against riding, shied and fell on him, crushing both
his legs. According to Porter—a story that William McBrien, the author of
"Cole Porter: A Biography" (1998), finds "difficult to believe"—he passed
the excruciating hours while he waited to be rescued composing the lyrics
to an elusive verse of his song "At Long Last Love."

The moment was pivotal in Porter's life; so, too, was his recounting of
it. The lyrics to "At Long Last Love" are, of course, exquisite—"Is it an
earthquake or simply a shock? / Is it the good turtle soup or merely the
mock? / Is it a cocktail, this feeling of joy? / Or is what I feel the real
McCoy?"—but Porter's talent for masquerade, for turning life's griefs and
glories into an impudent game, didn't end there. In gruelling pain for
decades after the accident, forced to walk with braces and canes, he
nonetheless had the humor to give his lame legs names: the left he christened Josephine, the right Geraldine, "a hellion, a bitch, a psychopath."
Even at the end of his life, his apartment at the Waldorf Towers, in New
York, was decorated with an embroidered pillow that advised, in French,
"Don't Explain—Don't Complain."

Porter's entire life was built around the act of decoying his depths.
From the moment in 1905 when the elfin fourteen-year-old from a powerful lumber and mining family in Peru, Indiana—the pampered and only
surviving one of three siblings—arrived at Worcester Academy, in Massachusetts, with his paintings and an upright piano for his dorm room, he cast

himself as a kind of dandy. The dandy's strategy is to combine daring with tact, flamboyance with distance. Instead of breaking the rules, Porter learned to play with them. "At boarding school I was always taught," he wrote in "I'm in Love," "not to reveal what I really thought, / Nor ever once let my eyes betray / The dreadful things I longed to say." At Yale, where he had a sensational undergraduate career, his salmon-colored ties, his slick, center-parted hair, and his manicured nails broadcast his privilege and his rebellion. "Porter did not fit easily into the social mold of a Yale man," his friend Gerald Murphy, who engineered Porter's entry into the most raucous of Yale fraternities, DKE, said. Still, music made a place for him on campus, allowing him both to tease the mainstream and to join it. He composed "Bull Dog" and "Bingo Eli Yale," football anthems that are still played today; he wrote his first musical, "Cora" (1911); he was a member of the Whiffenpoofs, Yale's most prestigious singing group, and the president of the Glee Club. Behind a piano, delivering his mischievous lyrics in a high-pitched, metallic voice—"I sing unpleasantly," he once said—Porter could confess and, at the same time, mask his feelings, keeping the world both engaged and at arm's length.

For the best part of his adulthood, Porter organized life so that his effervescent music and his emollient lyrics preceded him into a room. Manners defined the man and his songs, imposing on both a meticulous and elegant symmetry. Slim and courtly, the five-foot-seven Porter had black doe eyes and a burnished baby face, whose smoothness he enhanced by shaving twice a day. "You might describe me as a cross between Eddie Cantor and the Duke of Windsor," he said. His assault on American puritanism—what Gilbert Seldes called "the habits-of-rabbits school of songwriting"—rarely transgressed the bounds of propriety, deploying etiquette even as it mocked it. "If you're swimming at Newport with some old leech," he wrote, "And he wrestles you while you're wet, / Don't call him a son of a Bailey's Beach, / It ain't smart, / It ain't chic, / It ain't etiquette."

Propriety, however, bred boredom. Porter's songs are passionate, playful, and immediately accessible; he, by contrast, was slow to kindle. "People who meet Cole Porter for the first time often find his personality baffling," Margaret Case Harriman wrote in her 1940 Profile of him for this magazine. "He is by turns pensive, nervous, mercurial, and polite. When he is interested or amused, he talks with a rush of words which betrays him into a slight lisp. . . . At other times his air of boredom verges on the spectacular." "Poor Young Millionaire," written in the twenties, when Porter was living in gala style in Europe, spelled out his deep-seated ennui. (Because Porter had dropped out of Harvard Law School to dedicate himself to music, his tyrannical grandfather, J. O. Cole, disinherited him; his mother, however, gave him half of her own four-million-dollar bequest.) "I'm tired of betting, / Tired of sporting, / Tired of flirting, / Tired of courting, . . . / Tired of being / Tired, tired, tired." Songwriting was Porter's antidote to the entropy of self-indulgence. "He worked around the clock," Moss Hart, who collaborated with Porter on "Jubilee" (1935), said. "He used work as a weapon to shield himself from a boredom whose threshold was extremely low. He could withdraw and disappear before one's eyes with an almost sinister facility."

To see Porter clearly—the full audacity of his lightness and brightness—one must view him against the dowdy gravity of the America into which he emerged, in 1932, a country lumbered by the Depression, Prohibition, and social upheaval. Although Porter had had three variable outings on Broadway in the twenties ("Greenwich Village Follies," in 1924, "Paris," in 1928, and "Wake Up and Dream," in 1929), the thirties were the decade when he came into his own, with ten musicals for the stage and two for Hollywood. "You could follow a progression from Jerome Kern to Dick Rodgers to Gershwin," the lyricist Alan Jay Lerner said. "But Cole seemed to spring like Jupiter from Minerva's head—all made. What he did was so special and . . . unexplainable that he is really of them all, in a strange way, the most irreplaceable."

At a time when prosperity was imperilled, Porter—with his valets, his sixteen dressing gowns, his Art Deco Paris house, with zebra rugs on marble floors, his Venetian palace, where he composed in a ballroom hung with Tiepolos—personified the myth of American abundance. Unlike the other Broadway music-makers, he didn't aspire to be wealthy; he simply was, to use his term, "rich-rich." He was also an unrepentant hedonist; his songs conveyed an exhilarating wonder at the world's plenitude. In "You're the Top," for instance, he conjured up an eclectic picture of the American cornucopia: a Bendel bonnet, Mickey Mouse, Garbo's salary, cellophane, a turkey dinner, the Derby winner, a Waldorf salad, the feet of Fred Astaire, an O'Neill drama, Whistler's mama, and so on. This yoking together of high and low culture was part of Porter's sumptuous impertinence—and a pop landscape new to the musical.

Porter's Broadway cohorts were mostly striving middle-class Jewish New Yorkers who took their inspiration from jazz and from the city's momentum. Porter, in his attitudes and his influences, was essentially European. After the spectacular failure of his 1916 Broadway debut, "See America First," he lived abroad for nearly two decades. The memory of his travels in those years surfaces in the rhythms of his songs. "What Is This Thing Called Love?" and "Night and Day" grew out of strains of Moroccan music; he discovered the offbeat of "Begin the Beguine" while watching a native dance in the Dutch East Indies; the fast-paced wit of the popular songs performed in Paris *boîtes* worked its way into Porter's "list songs"—a style that he originated and which was, according to its creator, "the Tin-Pantithesis of a melody."

Porter's songs evoked an adult existence—a world of pleasure, travel, wealth, and promiscuity. They goosed and seduced society; part of their frisson was their composer's antic impulse to put it ever so gently to his high-society friends. In "I'm Dining with Elsa," the flamboyant, beefy hostess Elsa Maxwell, who was at the center of Porter's deluxe crowd, got this jolt: "I've got Bromo Seltzer / To take when dinner ends, / For I'm dining with Elsa / And her ninety-nine most intimate friends!" But the songs' driving force was something else. Each of the great masters of the Broadway lyric had his source of special inspiration: Lorenz Hart had loneliness; E. Y. Harburg had Marxism; Oscar Hammerstein II had optimism; Ira Gershwin had his brother; Porter had sex. His songs glorified "the sweetness of sin," and were dished up with what Kenneth Tynan called his "bedside wit." Of the great lyricists, only Porter could have written, "I'd love to make a tour of you / The eyes, the arms, the mouth of you, / The east, west, north, and the south of you." "Night and Day," "Begin the Beguine," "In the Still of the Night," "So in Love," and "I've Got You Under My Skin"—his most famous ballads—show off Porter's sultry emotional power. He didn't want just to invoke love; he wanted to taste it.

In the arena of relationships, Porter was bracingly laissez-faire. With songs such as "Let's Misbehave" and "Please Don't Make Me Be Good," he counselled pragmatism of the heart, not idealism. He was, as Alan Jay Lerner quipped, "a homosexual who had never seen the closet"—"Anything Goes" was his motto, as well as his hit. In "Experiment," he wrote, "Be curious, / Though interfering friends may frown. / Get furious / At each attempt to hold you down." Porter was not above winking indirectly at his own appetite for a bit of rough. "Find me a primitive man / Built to a primitive plan," he wrote in a song for the show "Fifty Million Frenchmen" (1929). "I don't mean the kind that belongs to a club, / But the kind that has a club that belongs to him." His lyrics are often full of distinctly phallic fun. In "Brush Up Your Shakespeare," he joked, "When your baby is pleading for pleasure / Let her sample your 'Measure for Measure.'" But like Casanova, whom he sang about in "Nymph Errant" (1933), Porter was also "a human stove"; when he was actually in love, the blasé postures of his wit abandoned him. In song, he was cool; in life, he burned. "The only thing I really want to do is climb to the top of the bell tower and announce to the piazza that I'm desperately in love," he wrote to the dancer Boris Kochno, in 1925. "I love you so much that I think only of you—I see only you and I dream only of the moment when we'll be reunited."

Porter's homosexuality is the news at the center of Irwin Winkler's latest film, "De-Lovely," which stars Kevin Kline as Porter and Ashley Judd as Linda, his wife of thirty-five years, and which manages somehow to tell Porter's story without any of the three stylistic ingredients that defined him: rhythm, elegance, and wit. Hollywood's first stab at the subject, "Night and Day" (1946), with Cary Grant, made no reference to Porter's sexuality. In "De-Lovely," Porter's preference is shown as a problematic and regrettable intrusion on his abiding romantic attachment to his wife. There is some truth to this approach, but not enough.

Tall, blond, with deep-blue eyes, Linda Lee Porter was a famous Southern beauty. At seventeen, she had married the newspaper mogul Edward K. Thomas, whose empire included the New York *Morning Telegraph*. Eleven unhappy years later, she divorced the sadistic Thomas—the first American ever to have killed anyone with an automobile—and the settlement made her a wealthy woman. When she married Porter, in 1919, he was twenty-eight and she was thirty-six. Linda gave her ambitious young companion access to all of Europe's grandees. She was smart and supportive; he was a live wire who needed connections. Together, they formed an adoring partnership, a companionate marriage. But to the aesthete Bernard Berenson, a confidant of Linda's, who saw the newlyweds on their honeymoon, Porter was "a little music man fifteen years younger." (It's a barometer of Porter's boyishness that Berenson overstated the age difference by seven years.) She "has nearly worn herself out going at his rattling pace," he added. "I saw their future in the blackest terms."

"De-Lovely" makes the opposite of Berenson's mistake: it portrays Linda as significantly younger than Porter, a miscasting that completely skews Porter's psychosexual reality. The film turns Linda into a romantic object when, in fact, she was a maternal one. Like Porter's devoted mother, Linda believed in his talent. At first, according to Gerald Murphy, she "rather hoped he would devote himself to serious music." She wrote to Arnold Bennett, Bernard Shaw, and John Galsworthy for librettos from which her husband might compose an opera, and she invited Igor Stravinsky to the Riviera to instruct her husband in harmony and composition. "She goaded me along," Porter said. He invested Linda with a sort of parental authority, even going so far as to seek her approval of his lovers. "You made a friend today—it was Linda," he wrote to Kochno. "I don't know how to tell you how grateful I am—you did it. And that makes everything much easier."

"Marriage excuses no one the freak's roll call," the playwright Joe Orton wrote; Porter certainly proved this point. Although "De-Lovely" tries to depict Porter as bisexual, he was an avid member of the brotherhood. (Linda evidently had a miscarriage early in their relationship, but if it had occurred when the film positions it she'd have been in her fifties.) On their world junkets, "les Coleporteurs" travelled with a largely male entourage. At the Waldorf Towers, they lived in separate apartments; at their estate in Williamstown, Linda occupied the main house and Porter a small house nearby, which he dubbed "No Trespassing." The marriage, as Brendan Gill delicately put it in "Cole," was "not without intermittent warfare and cobbled-up truces." The couple fought primarily over Porter's increasingly reckless sexual escapades and his disregard of the "good form" of their heterosexual masquerade, which humiliated Linda and, inevitably, created a distance between them. "Porter had needs he could not satisfy with Linda, not only sexual needs but social ones as well," William McBrien writes of Porter's mature years. "He could not, for instance, discuss the beauty of young males. Nor could he lament to her about living without an intimate companion—a man with whom he might have shared a home." Linda was the darlin' to whom Porter was, as he memorably wrote, always true in his fashion.

In "De-Lovely," the masterly Kevin Kline invests Porter with a whiff of emotional complexity that the script doesn't earn. Porter's songs, however, do earn it. Many of his melodies, written in haunting minor keys, express a palpable sadness that his public persona kept hidden. "The thrill when we meet / Is so bittersweet / That, darling, it's getting me down," he wrote in "Get Out of Town." In "Down in the Depths," he noted, "Why, even the janitor's wife / Has a perfectly good love life / And here am I / Facing tomorrow / Alone with my sorrow." Promiscuity and songwriting were Porter's antidepressants, at once an expression of and a relief from his neediness—the "oh, such a hungry, yearning burning inside of me" that he wrote about in "Night and Day."

Porter seems never to have found the love that he eloquently invoked in song after song. In 1951, battered by pain, he had shock treatment for depression. In 1954, Linda died of emphysema. In 1958, after some thirty operations, his right leg was finally amputated. It was "a cruel decision to have to make and involves much sex vanity and many fears of being repellent," Noel Coward wrote, after visiting Porter in the hospital. "Wouldn't It Be Fun," written for a 1958 TV production of "Aladdin," was Porter's last song, and it carries a bitter autobiographical aftertaste: "Wouldn't it be fun not to be famous, / Wouldn't it be fun not to be rich! / . . . Wouldn't it be fun to be nearly anyone / Except me, mighty me!"

Porter survived another six years, but, when his music—that lifelong attempt to forestall the immanence of emptiness—stopped, he stopped, too. "He was terribly uninterested," Diana Vreeland wrote. "He just couldn't get up the old interest to do anything . . . and then he stopped speaking." Music was how Porter had negotiated life and created it around him. "Old songs are more than tunes," the playwright Ben Hecht said. "They are little houses in which our hearts once lived." In that sense, Porter was one of the great architects of the twentieth century. We still happily inhabit the pleasure palaces he built for us. He manufactured joy, that rarest of commodities, with which he excused everything, even himself.

BILLY CONNOLLY

CHASING THE WITCH

The Scottish comedian Billy Connolly likes to date his enduring optimism to his days in the shipyards of Glasgow, where he worked as a welder from the ages of sixteen to twenty-four. One day, he says, he went to buy a pack of cigarettes from Tam, the chain-smoking old worker who ran the company store:

> He started to cough. It was like a storm building up—a thundering storm from miles away. He ended up with these noises that sounded like a platoon of cavalry galloping through a swamp in Wellingtons full of vomit. Then it came to an end; all calmed down. I says, "Jesus, Tam, that's some cough." He says, "Fuck off?" He says, "Did you pass the graveyard on the way in here?" I says, "Aye." He says, "Well, the graveyard's full of people that would fucking love my cough." And that's basically my philosophy: if you think you're having a bad time, the graveyard's full of people who would love to be doing what you're doing.

In a thirty-three-year career, which has included some two thousand stage appearances, eighteen videos, and fifteen CDs, Connolly has almost never written down a line of material. Instead, onstage, for two and a half hours, he holds a sort of séance with himself. (One of his daughters once referred to his profession as "comedium.") A comedian performing without a script is like a high-wire artist working without a net: it creates a particular kind of immediacy. Connolly's free-associating hodgepodge of personal revelation, fantasy, and bawdry often takes him, as well as the audience, by surprise. "All this shit comes out," he told me in his distinctive burr. "All this fear and angst and learning." He added, "If I'm talking about something during the day, it'll pop up in the night. I remember talking about sex to Pamela"—his wife, the former comedian Pamela Stephenson—"when we first met. My point was that it was an animal act, and the worst thing you could do to it was put on it the manners of the dining room." In his routine, that idea became "You mustn't take the animalism of the bedroom into the dining room—except for foreplay. . . . It's handy to remember, when it comes to the cutlery, that it's the same as foreplay: start at the outside and work your way in."

The cross-dressing British comedian Eddie Izzard, whose own humor was inspired by Connolly's early, pathfinding performances, explains, "He'd just sort of say whatever he wanted to say; it didn't seem to bear any relationship to any structure that had come before." Last January, at a tribute to Connolly organized by the BBC and the British Academy of Film and Television Arts, Izzard said, "He shall lead you from the world of 'my wife' jokes to the promised land of the comic philosopher." Eric Idle, part of the "Monty Python" menagerie and Connolly's neighbor, agrees. Connolly offers the thrill of "ruthless honesty," he says. "He's not censoring anything. You see the whole Billy." (As did more than twelve million British television viewers two years ago, when Connolly, in order to raise money for charity, streaked naked around the statue of Eros in Piccadilly Circus.)

Connolly is an instinctive disturber of the peace, an enemy of blandness—of "the beigists," as he calls the humorless bourgeoisie. But although he makes a few million dollars annually from his comedy—he spends up to half of every year on tour—the American public is still, for the most part, unaware of him and his role as the progenitor of alternative British comedy. A beloved Scots Everyman, Connolly has never quite managed to sell himself as an American Everyman. Pamela Stephenson's insightful book about Connolly's life, "Billy," was a No. 1 best-seller on both hardback and paperback lists in Britain for twenty-four weeks, selling two million copies and earning Stephenson the 2002 British Book Awards' Book of the Year prize. (Her second Connolly volume, "Bravemouth," was published in England last month and is already No. 2 on the *Sunday Times* best-seller list.) In the

United States, however, "Billy" was acquired by Overlook Press for a four-figure advance and only sixteen thousand copies were printed. Although Connolly has lent his charm to two American sitcoms—"Head of the Class" and "Billy"—and was featured in a 1990 HBO special, "Whoopi Goldberg Presents Billy Connolly," he is still perhaps best recognized in America as the swaggering manservant John Brown, whose plain speaking won the heart of Judi Dench's Queen Victoria in the 1997 film "Mrs. Brown" (a performance whose subtlety surprised fans of Connolly's brazen comedy).

Connolly's lack of renown in this country is, in fact, one of the reasons that he has chosen to live here—in California—since 1991. "To let go of some of that fame I have in Europe is a wonderful thing," he says. "At first, you think it's like a big spear, but actually it's a big shield." One of Connolly's maxims is "Don't work *out*, work *in*." He knows that the hardest battle a star wages is an internal one: the world wants the extraordinary, but the performer—who is, by definition, a salesman of himself—risks losing himself in the management of the ordinary. Still, Connolly, who occasionally catches himself trying to call room service from his home phone, has more or less come to terms with normality. He lives among the good and the great of Hollywood (his house in Laurel Canyon, which overlooks Universal Studios, is just a few doors down from David Hockney's), but in his daily life he experiences a more mundane version of Los Angeles. He picks his children up from school; he eats with his family; he lets other people speak at dinner parties. It's his detachment from the Hollywood scene that allows him to do the work of comedy, he says: "Life without that adoration is so nice. The volume goes down. You don't move so fast. You can go for walks. You can look in shopwindows. You can feed your brain." He adds, "You have to look at the world. Absorb it, read, look, stay awake. It isn't what you're hearing that's important; it's what comes out again."

One of Connolly's havens is a cigar store in the Valley called the Big Easy. Here, in a crepuscular boys'-club atmosphere of beer signs, red leather chairs, old baseball mitts, boxing gloves, and pinball machines, Connolly can carouse and enjoy the invigorating company of "honest guys," who remind him of the men he knew in Glasgow (which he calls "Liverpool without deodorant"). "They know about football and baseball and politics," he says. "They're very, very aware. They're men. They're not new men." Connolly refers to himself as an "end-of-the-pier comedian," who aspires to be "beer-down-your-nose funny," and his noisy bravado is essentially a Friday-night pub style—"ludicrous storytelling, lying, and bragging that gets up to such a pitch." For the half hour that it took him to smoke his Bahia Gold one afternoon at the Big Easy, Connolly, who will be sixty-one this month but has the lanky body and the attitude of a much younger man, paced beside the counter in his usual mufti of cowboy boots and jeans and bantered with his mates: Mikey, who makes solder; Stevie G., an actor; and Billy, a union man. They argued about George Bush, Rush Limbaugh, the Kennedy assassination, Tom Petty's voice, the moon landing, and formerly American-backed operatives—Osama bin Laden, Manuel Noriega, Saddam Hussein—who turned against the United States. ("There's one thing about young assholes," Connolly said. "They tend to become old assholes. There's no blinding flash on the road to fucking Damascus here!") The discussion ended on the topic of corporate crime, and, playing a vigorous air guitar, Connolly broke into song:

> So you lost your money
> And your pension's fucked,
> Enron-Ron-Ron-Ron
> Enron-Ron-Ron!

It struck me that the warmhearted palaver I was overhearing was a version of Connolly's standup performance—a chat to friends in a room, except that, in the latter case, the room holds more than a thousand people.

At one point, Billy the union guy brought up the book "Billy," and Connolly joked about his wife's literary success. "She's got rich," he said. "When it's *about* you, you don't get anything. Who's on the cover? Who gets the money? Wrong again, Bill. She got this weird gold thing"—the British Book Award. "I get the Center of the Doughnut Award. Zip." On the way to the cigar store, Connolly had spoken more seriously about the memoir. "All it did was lighten my load," he said. "I didn't want to be seen as a victim. I'm not a victim. I'm a survivor." Stephenson, who was born in New Zealand and who was a piquant comedian in her youth, is now a clinical psychologist (her dissertation analyzed the experience of fame), and in the annals of emotional impoverishment her telling of Connolly's story ranks alongside the biographies of Charlie Chaplin, who was embraced by his father for the first time at the age of eleven, and of Buster Keaton, whose father literally wiped the floor with him—he was billed as "the Human Mop" in a family vaudeville act that turned child abuse into an art form.

One evening in 1945, when Connolly was three and his sister Florence was four, their twenty-one-year-old mother, Mamie, walked out of their two-room flat on Dover Street in Glasgow. Her husband, William, had been with the Royal Air Force in Burma for three years and wouldn't return from the war for another year. It wasn't unusual for Mamie to go out in the evening—she enjoyed a good time—and she frequently left the children alone. On one occasion, according to Stephenson's book, Florence fell into the embers of the fireplace and subsequently lost the sight in one eye, an incidence of neglect that brought the family to the attention of the Royal Scottish Society for the Prevention of Cruelty to Children. This time, however, Mamie had no one to answer to for her absence; she was gone for good. Connolly and his sister were eventually found by neighbors, crying, unkempt, and hungry.

The children went to live with their father's sisters Margaret and Mona, Connolly recalled in "The Big Yin," a 1994 biography by Jonathan Margolis (Big Yin, "Big One" in Scottish slang, is Connolly's nickname). "They were both single and in their twenties. One was just out of the Wrens"—the women's corps of the Royal Navy—"in Portsmouth, and the other one was a career nurse. I think they deeply regretted it. Especially the older one, Mona, who took the real mother place in my life. It kind of cost her marriage and happiness and stuff, and she took it out on me." When Mamie relented and turned up to visit the children sometime later, Mona blocked the door. There was a fracas. Mamie floored Mona with a punch and stalked off. "She had lots of fire and character," Connolly says of his mother. "She was a fast runner. If she had been an upper-class person, she would probably have achieved some kind of notoriety." Mamie settled thirty miles away, in Dunoon, where she remarried, raised a second family of four, and worked in a hospital canteen. But Connolly had no contact with her. In his teen-age years, he says, "I would cycle down to her town. I didn't know what she fucking looked like, but I thought maybe she would know what I looked like. So I would saunter about and have cups of tea and hope she would say, 'Excuse me, are you Billy Connolly?'"

Connolly was twenty-five and achieving his first success—as half of a folk-singing duo called the Humblebums—when he finally heard his mother say those words. He had come offstage at the Glenmorag Hotel in Dunoon. "She said, 'I'm your mother,'" he recalls. "I remember just staring at her. I thought, Oh, my God, you are, too. There's a line in a Peter McDougall play: 'You never forget your mother's smell.' I gave her a wee cuddle. I kissed her neck, and—*ding!*—it just came roaring back to me. I said, 'Let's go in the lounge bar here.' She said, 'I hope you don't drink too much.' I thought, What? You're fucking worried about me? A birthday card would have been nice."

In 1990, Connolly was betrayed by Mamie a second time, in an envious attack printed in a Scottish tabloid. "I'm quite happy sitting here in my wee house the ragman would not give me a balloon for," she told the newspaper, adding, "I don't watch his TV shows and have never seen any of his films. If he was your son, would you? I just feel his material could be embarrassing." Connolly responded, two years later, from the stage. "The *Sunday Mail* did a story on her. On Mother's Day . . . (Nice fuckin' touch, lads!) She said I'd abandoned her. Fuckin' who abandoned who around here?! I remember the day she left! 'Fuck off out of here,' I said. 'Don't show your face around here. I'll be fine. I'm gonna be a welder.'" When Mamie was dying, in 1993, at the age of sixty-nine, Connolly drove to Dunoon to see her. "I got there, and I just couldn't do it," he says. "I drove back to Glasgow again. I wanted to love her, and I wanted to love my father. I wanted him to love me back. I wanted the thing that everybody else gets. As far as I can see, everybody gets it free."

Connolly's first memory of any kind of physical affection is of a kiss from a school friend, at the age of seven or eight. ("Gracie McClintock! I can remember it today like it was yesterday. I never got over it.") His birthday was never celebrated; the first time he saw a birthday cake was on a trip to the circus when he was eight. Laughter was rare at home; family meals were a source of friction, not connection. "It was no joy when we all sat down," Connolly says of dinner with his aunts. "It was a time to be picked on. As far as they were concerned, I was a failure, an embarrassment, a loser." His gruff, taciturn father, who, after the war, had moved in with his sisters and got a job in a machine-parts factory, was mostly an absent parent, with the disconcerting habit of misplacing his son on outings—he lost Connolly at the Glasgow zoo and on a hike over the Barrowlands. According to "Billy," William Connolly only once managed to acknowledge his son's accomplishments, and he offered no explanation for Mamie's behavior or for his own. "It was very frustrating," Connolly says. "Sometimes when he was drunk, I would try and get him talking. He would cry sometimes, but you'd never get anything decent going." In 1988, as his father was dying in a hospital, Connolly confessed to Stephenson that, from the age of ten until he was fifteen or so, he had shared a bed with his father, who molested him. "The most awful thing was that it was kind of pleasant, physically, you know," Connolly told Stephenson in "Billy." "That's why nobody tells. I remember it happening a lot, not every night, but every night you were in a state thinking it was going to happen, that you'd be awakened by it. I would pray for the holidays. I couldn't wait for us to go to the seaside, because then we had separate beds."

"They just kept making us live in their dark side," Connolly says of his parents now. "I had no example of light." Florence, to whom he was very close, was his only solace. He was "always in trouble—all scars, stitches, broken bits from falling off things and getting punched in the mouth." Mona, who was later institutionalized, beat him almost every day throughout his childhood, hitting him with her fists, her feet, wet towels, and high-heeled shoes, and rubbing his face in his dirty underwear. Years later, in his routines, Connolly parsed his family's violence, using laughter as a form of shadowboxing. He ridiculed his "fuckin' mad auntie's" approach to child rearing: "She found a shop in Glasgow: Clothes for the Child You Didn't Want in the Fuckin' First Place!, Clothes Guaranteed Never to Be in Fashion." Describing taking a sucker punch to the chest from his father, which sent him flying over the sofa, he joked, "I'd never seen a couch from that angle before." "Have you had enough?" he remembered being asked by his guardians. "What a stupid question! . . . I think you're supposed to say, 'Would a kick in the testicles be out of the question?' " From the gravity of his grief, he created an atmosphere of lightness:

> Men will tell you a couple of times not to do a thing, then they'll lose patience and go for you. It's like being hit by a building. It's like having a Volkswagen dropped on you. Your father would do that. He'd kick, punch, bite, elbow, and gouge your eye all at once. You knew it was coming when sentences and words would start to fragment. "Get down off that wall. I won't tell you again. What did I tell you? Get that—! For Chri—! For fuck sa—! Jesus! Ya fu—! Oh! Come here!" It was like being run over by a herd of cattle. Women—they hit you in the rhythm of the argument. "Don't-you-ever-let-me-see-you-do-that-again!" Usually there's two real hay-makers to start— "DON'T!—YOU—Ever-let-me-see-you-do-that-again!!!"

School, for Connolly, was as brutalizing as the bedlam of home. Like many children who have endured early abuse, he had difficulty absorbing information. His mind, he says, "was jumping all over the place," and things came out "higgledy-piggledy." "I was bright enough," he adds. "I liked French, mathematics, equations. But I couldn't remember it on examination day. I'm not very academically bright. I don't retain very much, and I never have. I've got that attention-deficit-disorder thing. I always thought I was kind of stupid. I was told that all the time at school." For many years, Connolly refused to do homework. "I used to get belted for it every day," he says. "I thought, Fuck you. Fuck homework. If your teachers are nightmares and it's a nightmare when you go home, everybody who represents authority seems to be a bit of an asshole. So fuck 'em all. It's the only way to survive." Connolly was an avid reader, but when he left school, at fifteen, his only qualification was a letter from the headmaster saying that he was "always punctual." Nowadays, "just to make an atmosphere" in the middle of a riff—where Connolly's habit of "thinking sideways" has become a glorious asset—he will sometimes scream out his teachers' humiliating rebukes:

CONNOLLY, YOU'RE HOLDING THE WHOLE CLASS BACK! AND YOU
BROKE YOUR MOTHER'S HEART, STUPID BOY! Now, Connolly, go
out and count the school railings. Go on. Waste of fuckin'
space. I don't know why we let him wear the school blazer at
all. Disgrace to the tie. You'll come to nothing, Connolly.
You're a jellyfish, a spineless jellyfish. You've held the whole
class back for three and a half years. And you're spineless and
You'll Come to Nothing.

Well . . . I'm fuckin' rich! Fuck all of you—I hope you're
happy in your semi-detached shite houses. I'm your fuckin'
worst nightmare.

For years, Connolly saw himself as small (though he is now six feet one,
until he turned eighteen he was only five feet six), unattractive, unsuccessful, uneducated, and unwanted. In Glasgow, he started his own gang, the
Connollys, and he spent a lot of time performing dangerous stunts and
fighting in the streets, an activity he "quite looked forward to—long division scared me more." He also became obsessed with funerals. When he
was fourteen or fifteen, he decided to cut school and go for a long walk,
perhaps to London, which was four hundred miles away. He'd walked about
ten miles when he met up with a funeral procession. "I followed it into like
a crematorium place and just hung around," he says. By the end of the service, he says, he was "filled with joy," and he turned around and headed
home. Death seemed a perfect fit with the climate of Connolly's childhood,
its aura of absence. "I was incomplete," he says. "It was like being a limb
short, like going through life perpetually thinking you'd forgotten something. There was something completely missing, like having nine fingers.
Until I started being funny."

At the age of seven, Connolly was pushed into a puddle in his school playground. Instead of crying or pushing back, "I went right into the middle of
it and sat down in my shorts as if it was very comfortable," he recalls. "The
boys exploded with laughter. I remember the moment as clear as if it was
yesterday afternoon. My other limb grew back." He adds, "The atmosphere

changed radically. They admired what I'd just done. You could feel it in the air. I thought, Oh, that's the key. This is my role. Instead of being somebody's football all my life, I can actually have a function here. They've given me the O.K." What Stephenson calls Connolly's "fiery, evangelical fuckyouness" started in that playground puddle. "Once you agree to that role, you have to do it every day," he says. In one stunt, Connolly, pretending to be Superman, had wedged himself into the school-bathroom towel dispenser, when a teacher barged in and walloped him. "I didn't give a fuck," he says. "Did you hear the laugh? It was the roar of approval."

Connolly has always believed that comedy is linked to vulnerability. "When your knickers are down, you're funny," he frequently says. "I love life with knickers down." For five decades, he has had a persistent nightmare about drowning, which sometimes makes him cry out in his sleep. "What normally happens," Stephenson writes, "is he discovers he can breathe underwater." In life, laughter is what allows Connolly to breathe; it elevates his spirit and eliminates the things that weigh him down. Connolly likes to say that "there is no such thing as bad weather, there's only the wrong clothes"; for him, jokes have always been a sort of raiment that repels emotional storms. As a child, he filled up his bewildered emptiness with comic articulacy, and this made him what he most needed to be: visible. People who, like Connolly, are afraid of the dark (until he was fifty, he often slept with the lights on) are afraid not of not seeing but of not being seen. The worst thing about his parents and his aunts, he says, was that they were oblivious of him: "Nobody was out to torture me. They just kind of forgot." But once he'd learned how to be funny, his daily rants at school always drew a crowd of listeners. After years of being ignored, Connolly, who calls himself a "patter merchant," had found a way to be remembered. "You might say I've talked myself out of a corner," he said.

One day when we were together, this point was brought home by a fax he received from an Australian woman whose son had recently committed suicide. A fan, she was writing to thank Connolly for a fondly remembered phrase from one of his routines—which she and her son had often quoted. In the riff to which the letter referred, Connolly, who likes to collect unintentionally funny signs, such as "Keep Dogs Off Grass" and "This Door Is

Alarmed," told of looking in the window of a Glasgow dressmaker's shop and seeing a jacket modishly displayed with a small tag pinned to it that read, "Lovely on." "We would say, 'Lovely on what?'" Connolly says. "'Lovely on the mantelpiece? Lovely on toast? Lovely on fire?' We'd look at people's clothes and say, 'Lovely on.'" When he read the fax, Connolly said, "I had a little party in my heart." He went on, "When you're doing it right, in your own society, you become the sort of fluff in people's belly buttons. You become something they wear, something they carry around. You would need a forensic scientist to tell you what it was. But it's yours." He explained his particular brand of humor this way: "It's not because you've said something terribly funny; it's because you've reminded them of something very bright in their lives, because you're so passionate about telling them this tiny thing. It's a girl you love, it's fly-tying, it's a banjo—all the things that make you dance."

Learning how to make people laugh and how to play the banjo—"the musical choice of the antisocial," according to Eric Idle—were Connolly's first steps toward self-transformation. By the time he worked up the courage to go into show business, he had already been performing in one way or another in shipyard canteens, on oil rigs, and with the Parachute Regiment of the Territorial Army, in which he enlisted in 1962—and where, in addition to leaping out of planes (he made seventeen jumps in his three-year stint), he was renowned for leaping onto tables to do the "Dance of the Flaming Arseholes," a barroom competition to see who could last the longest with a lighted newspaper in his butt. Amid paratroopers chanting, "Oh the girls in France / Take their knickers down and dance," Connolly was the undefeated champion.

Although he compares his singing voice to "a goose farting in the fog," he lent it, and his banjo skills, to a number of folk groups, including the Skillet Lickers, the Acme Brush Band, and the Humblebums, the last of which had several hits and even made a Royal Command Performance before disbanding, in 1970. He loved the tunes, he says, but not the exaggerated gravity of the singers or their lyrics. Connolly's partner in the Humblebums, the songwriter Gerry Rafferty, was, Connolly says, "a better musician than me, but I was better at stagecraft. I just had to get funny. You can't go on singing about dead sailors forever. You have to own up." Connolly would joke about his métier ("One of those lines you never hear: 'She's shaggin' the banjo player'") and about the songs he played. "I'm gonna save you a lot of time here," he'd say, by way of introduction. "I've written a song here and it'll do your folk requirements for the evening, and then I can just get on with my banjo-playing: 'The tailor sat cross-legged on the workbench / One eye on his needle, another on the wench. / Oh, little girl, will you marry me? / Oh, no, I love a sailor / And he's far away at sea.'" During his solos, Connolly, who uses the rhythmic Appalachian technique of drop-thumbing to play the banjo, would cheer himself on, saying, "Go, Big Yin!" "I ruthlessly used folk music as a platform," he says now.

The Garrian Hotel, in Motherwell, Scotland, marks the spot where, in 1970, Connolly first began to "chase the witch," as he calls his comic soul-searching. Although he still brought his banjo onstage and sang songs, comedy was now the core of his performance; so was self-revelation. In the middle of his set, he suddenly threw himself on the floor and began speaking as if to a psychiatrist. "I was screaming, 'I've got issues! I've got issues! I've been abandoned!'" Connolly recalls. "Blah, blah, blah, blah. And the stuff about my mother and father came screaming out. Everybody laughed, 'cause they didn't believe it. I was really, really out there," he adds. "Nobody talked about stuff like this. No one on earth. I was plowing a field. It was just a brilliant feeling." Elton John, who hired Connolly as the opening act for his 1976 tour of America, says of his early shows, "I'd never seen anything like it in my life. He talked about his life, about everyday things, about chocolates and going to the seaside and swimming in the sea and the swimming costumes he had to wear, those horrible woolly things. Humor at that time was all about jokes, and people assuming other identities. Billy was being himself."

Connolly's combination of outrage and vulnerability struck a nerve. His series of comedy albums in the midseventies—which in Scotland sold as well as the Beatles and the Who—broadcast his outlandishness and won him a large fan base. The Scottish football team called on him for motivation in its bid for the 1974 World Cup; and, that same year, soon-to-be

Prime Minister Harold Wilson sought Connolly's support in stumping for Labour voters. By 1975, at the age of thirty-three, Connolly had his own No. 1 U.K. hit single, a parody of Tammy Wynette's "D.I.V.O.R.C.E." After just five years of solo performing, he had become the most renowned Scottish entertainer since the genial music-hall star Harry Lauder. When he made his début at the London Palladium, on January 12, 1975—he booked the venue himself, "to prove to London I exist"—the curtain came up on Connolly singing Lauder's sentimental anthem, "Keep Right On Till the End of the Road," with his head sticking through a life-size cardboard cutout of Lauder in kilt and sporran. After the song, the lights dimmed; when they came back up, Connolly was standing before the audience in a purple polka-dot suit. "I've come to bury Lauder, not to praise him," he said, and, in essence, that's what he did. (The Palladium's fire curtain had to be brought down at the finale because the management feared that the excited spectators would storm the stage. For a long time, the audience refused to leave the theatre.)

With his rough and raucous routines, Connolly brought the sludge of the Glaswegian streets to the stage. Although he had never sworn at home as a kid, he took profanity to new levels onstage. "It's a rhythm thing," he explains. "It's commas, exclamation marks, question marks—nothing to do with language. It's the rhythm of the street as compared to the rhythm of the drawing room." Connolly's swearing earned him a variety of journalistic epithets: "the Caliph of Crudity," "Scot of the anarchic," "the laureate of the loo," and "Man of the Devil"—this last from Scottish Presbyterians who took issue with Connolly's version of the Last Supper, which he reimagined in Gallowgate, Glasgow, with Jesus rolling into a pub, blind drunk, and urinating on the Roman soldier who pierced him with a spear on the Cross. Connolly's slangy meditations, counterpointed by his shaggy mane, turned the notion of the picturesque Scotsman on its head, and sent up the Scottish nationalism that such caricatures habitually conveyed. To the tune of "Scotland the Brave," for instance, he sang, "Land of polluted river / Blood-shot eyes and sodden liver / Land of my heart forever / Scotland the brave."

What Michael Caine calls Connolly's "almost barbaric humor" bridged cultures and got non-Scottish audiences past the barrier of his thick low-country accent. To Steve Martin, Connolly is "a Scottish timing machine, almost like a rapper with comic lines, opinions, and attitudes. He's physical onstage. It's like watching an opera." "He is the first comedian to represent the rock generation," the British talk-show host Michael Parkinson said, introducing Connolly to the BBC audience in 1975—a debut that, despite Connolly's obvious nervousness, almost instantly made him a household name in Britain. Parkinson says, "I think of all the people we've had on the show—and there have been four or five hundred—we never had a bigger single reaction than we had to Billy the first time around."

From his early days in the folk clubs, Connolly was a kind of dandy. He wanted the sight of himself alone to trigger an air of expectation. "When I walk in the door, they're gonna say, 'Wait till this guy gets on,'" he says of his loud shirts and striped trousers, which were also meant to broadcast the message, he explains, that "I'm not even defeated by me." As his venues got bigger, so did his sartorial ambitions: "I thought, I want to look like Alice Cooper. I want to look like rock and roll. I don't want to look like comedy. I want to be sexy. I want to be remembered." Polka dots, satins, and flared trousers became his trademark. "Wearing ridiculous clothes meant you could say what you pleased," he says. "You didn't represent anything, so you couldn't be blamed for anything." Connolly took to wearing "Banana Boots"—a pair of yellow boots in the shape of bananas (now enshrined in Glasgow's People's Palace)—or Wellingtons during his performances. For "The Great Northern Welly Boot Show," a 1972 musical he co-wrote and performed in, he sported a series of fabulous Wellies: the Wishing Welly, the Cowboy Welly, the Jack Buchanan Evening Welly—named for the debonair song-and-dance man—which had silk lapels. In his routines, Wellington boots replaced the kilt as the ironic icon of Scottish life, and he mythologized them in song: "If it wasn't for your Wellies where would you be? / You'd be in the hospital or infirmary, / 'Cause you would have a dose of the flu or even pleurisy, / If you didn't have your feet in your Wellies."

Connolly looked outrageous, he sounded outrageous, and he also lived outrageous. He had married the interior designer Iris Pressagh in 1969, and was the father of two children, Cara and Jamie, but the centripetal force of

Connolly's career increasingly pulled him away from his family—and from himself. If his humor onstage proved Nietzsche's dictum that "shame is inventive," his legendary drinking bouts offstage proved that it was also murderous. "A well-balanced person has a drink in both hands," he liked to say then, but drinking truly unhinged him. "I was flying. I was out there," he says. He took to naming his tours according to his beverage of choice: "The Gin Tour," "The White Wine Tour," "The Brandy Tour." Connolly, who said he saw himself "as a James Dean rock 'n' roll tragedy" and claimed to have "A-levels in guilt," would later indict himself as "a lousy father" and "a drunk absentee." He was "out of love," and rarely at home. "I had all the success I had ever dreamed of," he says. "My offstage life was in such an unsolvable mess, I thought, I'll just walk away from it. I decided to seek oblivion. I'll just drink, and then I'll die. It was a nice prospect." He adds, "The people I knew were very unattractive to me. Strangers were attractive to me. Strangers will do me better. There will be no judgment around here."

Connolly remembers calling his manager late one night because he was in a phone booth in Primrose Hill and couldn't find his way out. His manager eventually found him asleep in the booth. "There was nothing wrong with the door," Connolly says now. "I just couldn't find which wall *was* the door. That was my dilemma." At the London night club Tramps, in a feat that is still a record for the club, Connolly, in one sitting, downed thirteen bottles of Chablis, a drink he preferred to imbibe in pint glasses.

Alcohol kept his mood and his level of aggression elevated. "I didn't mind a good punch-up at all," he says. "I used to take delight in being the world's only violent hippie." On one occasion, after overhearing a patron make racist remarks to the owner of an Indian restaurant, Connolly ran across six tables to dive at the man and pull him into the street. "I remember the Beatles talking about him, saying, 'You have to run away,'" Idle says of Connolly. "Ringo will tell you he was a terrifying drunk." During the filming of "Water" (1985), in which Connolly co-starred with Michael Caine, the cast was riding in a bus up a mountain road in Toulouse, and Connolly recalls "putting my hands over the driver's eyes, which was a great trick of mine at the time." "Michael Caine got me down from that," he says, counting the star's intervention as "another one of those pennies that dropped." He adds, "He had a very long talk to me the following day about boozing. He said, 'Don't blow it.'" Stephenson says, "We see photographs of him sometimes from that period, and Billy will go, 'Look, the Bogeyman.' I notice there's a certain admiration there that scares me.

Although Connolly did eventually stop drinking—in 1985—the night in 1980 when he fell for Stephenson he downed thirty brandies at a London restaurant; the miniature bottles were lined up in front of him like chess pieces. At that time, Stephenson was starring with Rowan Atkinson, Mel Smith, and Griff Rhys Jones in the astringent BBC 2 satire "Not the Nine O'Clock News." (She subsequently did a season on "Saturday Night Live.") Cocky, well-educated, and beautiful, Stephenson was a bright young thing of twenty-nine, who aspired to be a wild young thing. "My I.Q. worked against my ability to be funny," she says. Always a good student, she needed the protection of a good script and a lot of rehearsal. She was blind-sided by the spontaneous Connolly, who was not like any comedian she'd ever met. He was "an alpha male, a crazy, hilarious, charismatic savage." Over dinner, she watched as he ate Dover sole with his hands—his dining style at the time. "What an animal!" she writes. "I was thrilled."

"It's a mysterious connection between the two of them," Steve Martin says. "It's a bit unseen." Connolly was divorced from Iris in 1983, and he had three daughters with Stephenson—Daisy, Amy, and Scarlet—before they were married, in Fiji, in 1989, while bagpipes played "You Take the High Road" and the theme from "The Archers," and the girls looked on. "I just recognized something I wanted," Connolly says. Stephenson's professional admiration and attentiveness as well as her compassion had a particularly potent allure for Connolly. "I replicated his sister," Stephenson says. "She was mother, friend, sibling—she was his protector. He internalized that." She adds, "That's why he's not in prison." In fact, when Connolly describes Florence, now a retired teacher living in Scotland—"She was the only person I could talk to about anything. She found my rebelliousness really funny. She was academic, bright, and intellectual"—he could just as easily be talking about Stephenson. "Pamela has saved my life on many occasions," he said at the BAFTA ceremony in January. Of the many things that changed in Connolly's life after he met Stephenson—his diet, his regimen, his social milieu—the biggest change was to his belief that a comedian had to be "either blasting light at the audience or in Stygian darkness." "I bullied him into letting go of that notion," Stephenson says. "He was fortunate that he did see what many comedians don't—that it's possible to let go of the mythology that says that in order to be funny you have to have this dark, untouchable, dangerous side to you that will eventually kill you." "Whatever it is that's driven me along with this odd talent that I have," Connolly said in 1992, "to do it without happiness, without solace, is a complete waste of time and energy. It's an incomplete journey. . . . I want my art to make me happy. . . . I don't want to be that clown with a tear in his eye."

When Connolly is pressed to define the differences between him and his wife, he says, "I'm Francis of Assisi. She's Cromwell." Certainly, Stephenson's rigor is apparent in their Los Angeles house, with its work and holiday flowcharts and a framed slate sign in the front hall that reads "Be Nice or Leave!" Connolly says that he brings "unpredictability" and "lightness to the party." Stephenson brings intellectual discipline and containment. "She is captain of a ship that's kind of a rudderless firework," Martin says. In her memoir, Stephenson writes of being joined to Connolly "at the wound." But for her Connolly's self destructiveness was counterbalanced by his talent. "She used to get very jealous at first, because I didn't prepare anything," he says. "She would be standing in the wings, just going, 'Oh, my God, how did you do that?' I'd say, 'I don't know'" He continues, "When she was a comedian, I didn't like it. When there's two people in the same business in the house, the one with the huge problem is the one for whom the phone rings all the time. You're saying, 'Oh, God, make it be for her.'" After their children were born, Stephenson, as she puts it, "fell out of love with performing." She decided to go back to school and study psychology. "Comedy and psychology are very closely linked—just different approaches to the examination of human behavior," she says. Besides, she adds, "one comedian per family is probably enough."

From the outset, Connolly and Stephenson's romance was tabloid fodder. By the time the couple decided to relocate to America, in 1991, Connolly, who says, "I've been booed longer and louder than Hitler," had been more or less rumbled by the British press. The end of his first marriage, his romance with Stephenson, his sobriety, his wealth, his upward mobility all contributed to the nation's steady drizzle of gossip—"the roar of the uninformed," he calls it—in which he was variously portrayed as working-class hero-traitor, renegade-softie, and blasphemer-bore. Connolly and Stephenson, who are both bumptious and outspoken when provoked, didn't always help their own cause. He took an occasional swing at intrusive paparazzi; she, in her punk pink-hair moment, once poured water down the back of a notoriously pompous Radio 4 pundit. Increasingly, in Connolly's eyes, Britain was becoming the Land of No, whose "lust for failure" was a subject for comment from the stage. "I hate my country for the way it holds people back, tells them they're not good enough," he said. "I hate the tabloid press for what it does to people, never letting them be intelligent." When Connolly imagines his funeral, he hopes for a skywriting plane to fly above his burial plot, spelling out "Fuck the Begrudgers!" From his catbird seat in California, his comic observations have assumed a kind of droll disenchantment. "In America, if you become successful they put your name on the pavement and let people walk on it," he said. "In Britain, they don't wait for your name to be engraved, they just walk all over you anyway."

America has, according to Connolly, slowed the rhythm of his speech, but it has done nothing to slow the pace of his career. "My career is in a growth state," he says, "which is very odd, because I've just turned sixty. The tickets are hotter than they've ever been." Still, he adds, "The Americans are determined to cut down on my tours. They keep bombing gigs of mine. Abu Dhabi, Dubai—that's a hot area for me. I've never done Baghdad—I'd get four thousand people a night, easy-peasy." The public's burgeoning interest in Connolly is a result both of the memoir and of his developing film career. "Movies cost me money," he says. "My manager looks on them as an expensive hobby." Nonetheless, since the late seventies, when he appeared in a television play, "The Elephants' Graveyard," written by his friend Peter McDougall, Connolly has turned in a series of convincing character portraits—in "Mrs. Brown," as a gay tennis pro in Stanley Tucci's "The Impostors," and as an aging rocker in "Still Crazy," among others.

The first time Connolly walked in front of a camera, he says, "I just did what I thought would be right. I looked right into the heart of it, right through the pupil of its eye." Connolly has grown more handsome over the years. "I've become windswept and interesting," he says. John Madden, the director of "Mrs. Brown," explains his appeal: "The camera either sees and builds upon somebody's physical presence or, in some way, it robs them of a physical presence. Billy had a really kind of towering and glamorous screen presence that one wouldn't necessarily have anticipated. He had a kind of transparency." At first, before the shooting of "Mrs. Brown" began, Madden had some apprehensions about Connolly in the role. He says, "Winging it is exactly where his genius resides. My concern was that winging it was going to be something that would automatically mean a casual, uninvestigated performance." He arranged a meeting with Connolly. "I basically sat him down and said, 'Look, this isn't a joke,'" Madden says. "What I was confronted with at that point was an extraordinary kind of humility. I didn't expect that."

Earlier this year, Connolly went to New Zealand to shoot a film called "The Last Samurai," which stars Tom Cruise. ("We're pretending to be in Japan," he explained from the set. "There's no room to have a battle in Japan, you see, without a high-rise building in the background.") "The Last Samurai" and another film in which Connolly appears, "Timeline," will be released later this month. Although this year's comedy tour was put on hold for his movie work, Connolly will tour New Zealand in early 2004. He has always been clear-eyed about his future—or lack thereof—in film. "I'm not a film star," he has said onstage, "and I don't think I will be. I'm being absolutely, ruthlessly honest here. But if they make 'Braveheart,' and they ask every Scotsman who can speak and stand upright and they don't fuckin' ask you, *then* . . ."

Connolly is a trout fisherman; he even has a black-green-and-gold fly named after him. In the late nineties, when he was scouting for property in Scotland, Connolly had, according to Stephenson, only one criterion: "I want to be able to go from my bedroom to where I can fish, without changing my slippers." In 1998, the couple took possession of Candacraig ("Pamelot," to their friends), a turreted seventeen-room baronial mansion in Aberdeen-shire, where they spend most of their summers. In the entrance hall of the mansion, a portrait of Connolly as a Scottish laird hangs above flickering votive candles ("Our leader," the frame reads); a painting of Stephenson as the Queen of Australia, with the Sydney opera house in the background and corgis at her feet, has pride of place in the living room. But Connolly can usually be found by a loch on the River Don, at the edge of the twelve-acre property, working the riffles. "Do you know what happiness is?" he says. "It's casting beautifully into the sun and watching your line unfold. It's a small thing. I always thought happiness eluded me. I had an image of happiness which was like throwing beach balls and laughing and throwing your children in the air. Like a railway poster. When I found contentment and replaced the word 'happiness' with 'contentment,' I realized I was happy all along." In many ways, Connolly resembles the venerable trout, which has only two functions: to conserve energy and to hide. "The more you come into the daylight and tell the truth, the happier you become, the more your shadow goes away," Connolly says. Yet, both on the road and off, he has the habit of solitude. "He's a little like a hermit," Stephenson says. "He just likes being alone."

Still, at his sixtieth-birthday jamboree, the summer before last (he was born in November, but he prefers summer celebrations), with the mansion decked out in ten thousand dollars' worth of tartan, Connolly played host to his many friends—among them Izzard, Idle, Martin, Dame Judi Dench, Robin Williams, Michael Parkinson, Ewan McGregor, the Duke and Duchess of York, and Prince Charles and Camilla Parker Bowles. (Balmoral, the Queen's Scottish estate, is just eighteen miles away.) While the guests amused themselves with activities organized by Stephenson, Connolly smoked his pipe, listened to the radio, and played his banjo.

Often, as they did that weekend, the Connollys gather friends and locals—"anybody we can find who can play a musical instrument, which could range from the best guitarist in the world to Bella, who teaches fiddle in the village," Stephenson says—and stroll down from the house to a clearing in a clump of ancient trees. There, sitting around a bonfire, they sing and play. "It's the best," Connolly says of the tradition. "We request stuff from each other, the same stuff all the time. Steve Martin's amazing at 'Sally Goodin'—'Strawberry pie, strawberry puddin' / I'd give it all up just to see Sally Goodin'." As the fire crackles and the sparks fly up, Connolly, who calls himself "the welder who got away with it," strums his banjo and sings into the night.

MIRA NAIR

TOUGH SISTER

To GET TO THE DIRECTOR MIRA Nair's house in Kampala, Uganda, you follow a single-lane highway north from Entebbe, dogleg right at the roundabout as you enter town, pass a service station where a sign announces "TOILETS NOW HALF OPEN," and proceed south toward the once unfashionable section called Buziga Hill, where real-estate prices have tripled since 1990, when Nair and her husband, the scholar Mahmood Mamdani, bought their two-acre property for about seventy thousand dollars. As Nair barrels along in a secondhand green Toyota RAV4, the road is an embodiment of the extremes in which her films revel—a confusion of enterprise and collapse, of modernity and tradition. On either side, raggedy shops are jammed together like rows of bad teeth. We pass Harrod's Tailors, a shipping container that's now a haberdashery. "People here use everything," Nair says. "There are no fripperies." Boys ride bicycles with fringed back seats; women hurry to work in colorful *gomesi,* weaving past swarms of *boda-bodas*—passenger motorcycles—and reckless *matatus,* the Volkswagen vans that ferry Ugandans around town; red dust rises from dirt roads that meander off into subtropical vegetation. By a rusted sign for the Kiwumulo Country Club ("Cold Beers, Soda, Snacks— Soft Music in Background"), Nair hangs a sharp right. The car jounces up a rutted road that winds a mile and a half, past shanties and the orange-roofed cinder-block vulgarities that have sprung up like gigantic barbed-wire mushrooms, to her house. Nair, who divides her time among Kampala, New York, and New Delhi, found her modest bungalow, which has a magnificent view of Lake Victoria, while scouting locations for her second feature, "Mississippi Masala." "I was looking for something unforgettable," she says. "Like Marilyn Monroe is shorthand for sex, I wanted something you could be nostalgic for. The sun was falling. It was a complete ruin. I fell in love with it instantly."

"Enjoy every part of the frame and make it pulsate with life," Nair tells her students at Columbia University's film school, where she is an adjunct professor. Her own frames are crammed with the contrasting textures of sight, sound, and sociology, and she often invokes Andre Gide's dictum that tyranny is the absence of complexity. "I have an eye and ear for paradox," she has said. "That is life—the gray area where no one person is less or more virtuous than the other." Nair ("It's Nair like 'fire'") exudes a cheeky dynamism that, in an earlier age, would have earned her the label of "bright spark." In 2000, she took on the seemingly lunatic task of making a film in thirty days in New Delhi, with a cast of sixty-eight and a budget of $1.2 million. Two years later, "Monsoon Wedding," a joyful and lyrical dissection of a Punjabi family and an upper-middle-class arranged marriage, has become the eighth-highest-grossing foreign film of all time in the United States. The movie took the top prize at last year's Venice International Film Festival, and its popularity accounted for why Nair's Chelsea production company, Mirabai Films, had been approached with three new proposals: a Ted Hughes–Sylvia Plath bio-pic, and film adaptations of Nick Hornby's "Fever Pitch" and Thackeray's "Vanity Fair." It was why Carsey-Werner-Mandabach Productions, which brought the world "Roseanne" and "The Cosby Show," had invited Nair to write a sitcom about an Indian-American family; and why Harvard University, which she attended in the late seventies, was planning to award her the 2003 Harvard Arts Medal.

"To be a filmmaker, you have to be diseased," Nair once said. She is, she explains, "permanently afflicted." Among the many accomplishments of "Monsoon Wedding," the most startling is that it conveys onscreen something that is palpable in Nair herself, what the Punjabis call *masti*—an intoxication with life. In film, which she chose as her métier at the age of twenty, Nair has found a form "where I can embrace life completely." She is now forty-five, and her relish for the world around her is fuelled, in part, by the knowledge that three horoscopes have predicted that she'll die at sixty-one. "I don't really believe it, but I don't forget it, either," she says. Nair, who is the youngest of three children reared in an upper-middle-class home in Bhubaneswar, a backwater—"remote even in Indian terms"— some two hundred and forty miles southwest of Calcutta, is a person of

color, and she celebrates color. Whether she is showing us Bombay strip-
pers in her documentary "India Cabaret" (1985), the racial divide between
blacks and browns in the South in "Mississippi Masala" (1991), or even a
white-trash Bayonne, New Jersey, no-hoper, who can't get a date (played,
improbably, by Uma Thurman) in the HBO movie "Hysterical Blindness"
(2002), Nair's films negotiate disparate ethnic geographies with the same
kind of sly civility she practices in life. Her approach is sometimes oblique:
she doesn't make political films, but she does make her films politically.
Her gift, to which "Monsoon Wedding" attests, is to make diversity irresistible.

Nair is, above all, a populist—a mass communicator who actually
maintains contact with the masses. When she was showing her 1996 erotic
movie "Kama Sutra: A Tale of Love" in India, where cinemagoing is a vocal,
largely male-dominated experience, she insisted that there be special
screenings for women. After making "Salaam Bombay!" (1988), her auda-
cious first feature, about street children in India, she started the Salaam
Baalak Trust, a program that now assists some four thousand homeless kids
a year in India. "I have always been drawn to the stories of people who live
on the margins of society—on the edge, or outside, always dealing with the
question of what and where is home," she says. Nair herself, who set off for
America at eighteen, exists in that weird, liminal expatriate zone, and the
complex negotiation of identity across cultural boundaries has become an
inevitable theme in her work. "To have a world view—to look at the world
through a point outside America—is crucial," she says. Even in India, she
notes, "the process of day-to-day living stops people from seeing the things
that I see when I come from the outside." One day in 1983, when she was in
Bombay, as her taxi idled in traffic, she recalls that a boy "with just a torso
and head, on a wooden platform with wheels," grabbed onto her cab. As we
approached the junction, he let go of the cab, pirouetted with the extra
velocity, and then made a big gesture, like he'd just finished his most important circus routine. It was just fantastic to have this flamboyant lack of self-
pity." She adds, "If I lived there, I might not have noticed the
extraordinariness of that." The moment was her inspiration for "Salaam
Bombay!"

*   *   *

When Nair was eight, her mischievousness and her fascination with the life stories of the village elders she befriended earned her the nickname Pagli—Hindi for "mad." Once, she even brought the milkman home. Nair grew up a tomboy—"I never had a doll"—with two older, athletic brothers, Vikram and Gautam. She has memories of playing hide-and-seek in the tall grass around the forgotten temples of Bhubaneswar, of collecting red velvet-backed beetles in her father's old cigar box, and of walking barefoot on asphalt roads as steam rose off them after the monsoon rains. But the beauty of the natural world stood in contrast to the sometimes bewildering life within the walls of her family's colonial-style bungalow, with its spacious veranda and terra-cotta-tiled floors.

Her father, Amrit, who is seventy-five and has been separated from her mother, Praveen, for the past twelve years, was then a high-ranking civil servant in charge of several ministries in the state of Orissa. By all accounts, he was a remote figure, who respected status and success and expected the household to revolve around him. "He was a regimented fellow—still is," Nair says. "Not much fun. When he would leave, it would be more relaxed." Amrit didn't have the ease or the grace with people that his beautiful, popular wife had. "Any demonstration of affection is not in me, but I feel that they know I love them," he says of his relationship with his children now. His abiding passion was Persian poetry. He immersed himself in Urdu and wrote poetry himself. He also played recordings of the great Persian singers and translated the lyrics for his children. "That's the time I would love him," Nair says. "He would transport us." But most of the time Amrit preached the gospel of attainment, and he insisted that his children employ their time usefully. During the summer holidays, for instance, he made them memorize and recite passages from Shakespeare and the story of Hannibal crossing the Alps. Nowadays, he's most proud of Mira for her ability to "utilize her time for something worthwhile." "Even I could learn from her, and I was a manager," he admits. But, over the years, his frustrated academic ambitions for Vikram and Gautam, who are now clothing manufacturers, led to acrimonious family battles. "Viki was often humiliated in front of people," Gautam recalls. "Mother was blamed for not having spent more time with him. It was a really messy situation."

"We used to beg them to separate," Nair says of her parents. She remembers "fighting and tension and drama in the house—terrible stuff. My mother would get hysterical, and my father would just relentlessly go at her." When she was eleven, the family moved for two years to Delhi, where they lived in a mansion. Nair has a vivid memory of crouching at the top of a marble staircase with wrought-iron railings while down below, in a vast living room, her parents were quarrelling. They were sitting at opposite ends of an L-shaped couch, by a table that held glasses and a Gilbey's gin bottle filled with water. "My mother took this gin bottle, picked it up, and smashed it over her own head," Nair says. "That's that Indian self-sacrifice."

Much of Nair's startling independence and her social awareness come from her mother's example. "I was very fearless," Praveen says. During Mira's childhood, Praveen did volunteer work, organizing, at one point, a home for the healthy children of lepers. (She is now the chairwoman of the Salaam Baalak Trust.) Because her own trajectory had been determined by marriage, children, and rural life, Praveen, who introduces herself these days as "the producer of the director," encouraged her daughter's intellectual ambitions. She says that she wanted only for Mira "to enjoy what she was doing" and "not settle." "Even though the boys were older, she was the leader," Amrit says. He recalls how Mira, at twelve, pulled a silver-painted wooden switchblade on two boys "who tried to get fresh with her"; how she insisted that a teen-ager who was driving without a license and knocked her into a ditch receive no punishment; and how, at eight, she gave the most senior civil servant in Orissa two rupees, "because you are so old."

If Nair got her confidence from her mother, her desire for harmony and her aversion to authority can be traced, in one way or another, to her confrontations with her father, who, not incidentally, had not wanted her to be born in the first place. "We always regarded me as a contraceptual blunder," Nair says. By 1956, the Indian population explosion had become a serious problem, and Amrit Nair was charged with the task of promoting birth control in the district. The government slogan was "Two or Three, That's Enough." Nair remembers her father saying, "Don't give two or three. You give them an inch, they'll take a mile. Make it 'Just Two, That's Enough.'" Praveen's announcement that she was pregnant with a third child was a political embarrassment to him. "He insisted she get rid of me," Nair says.

"One time, she thought she'd had the procedure, but it didn't work. He sent her back, apparently. My mother's sister took her to the clinic, but she couldn't do it." To Praveen, who had always wanted a daughter, Mira was a sort of miracle child. Nowadays, when people ask her where Mira got her drive, she answers, "She was determined to be born."

Nair never directly rebelled against her father, but in her early documentaries she attacked the bulwark of his attitudes. "Children of Desired Sex" (1987) challenges the Indian custom of aborting female fetuses; "India Cabaret" examines the hypocrisy of male notions of "virtue." When Nair announced to her family that she was going to spend four months living with the dancers at a cabaret on the outskirts of Bombay, her father sat her down for a talk. "'Scum,' he said, 'you are going to live with scum? Why are you doing this?'" Nair wrote in an essay about the film. The exchange continued:

> "I know about all these cabaret girls. They do anything for a quick buck, even sell their flesh." "How do you know about them?" I asked. "Never mind about that. I have experience about the world. A very fine friend of mine offered a whole lot of them to me once. Of course, I didn't take up the offer—but I do know what kind of girls they are. Scum." "But then," I asked, "how do you regard your friend? Is he also scum for offering these girls to you?" My father looked surprised. "Of course not! He is a very sophisticated man of the world. He simply offered what was available."

Nair concluded, "Many of my doubts and fears and anxieties about the idea fell away at that time. I knew that there was a film to make."

Nair grew up remarkably free in a household where her parents' attention and fears, she says, "were for my brothers, not me." Amrit was an intermittent presence; Praveen had enough confidence in her daughter's abilities not to worry too much about her. "That allowed me to have whatever interests I wanted, because nobody really cared," Nair says. "I was not listened to, ever. The one great thing about that is that you end up actually listening more." Left to fend for herself, Nair became her own project. In her teens, she taught herself to type and play the sitar; she tried painting, wrote poetry, got into amateur theatricals, and, inevitably, became an outstanding student. "She would sort of jump for joy when examinations were coming," Praveen remembers. Even in the case of her education, Nair manufactured her own destiny. After returning to Bhubaneswar from Delhi, where she had been at the top of her class, Nair was reënrolled at the mediocre local school, while her brothers were sent to distinguished boarding schools. When she complained, her father said, "Tell me everything that's wrong with your school, and I'll fix it." Instead of arguing, Nair set about orchestrating her escape. She started rigging her school essays—for which she consistently got A's—writing coherent first and last paragraphs but inserting gibberish in between, to prove that her teachers weren't even reading them. At the same time, she enlisted the help of her former headmistress in gaining midterm admission to an exclusive convent school called Tara Hall. Nair then presented her father with the problem and the solution. He capitulated. A few years later, bored during her first year at Delhi University, Nair applied for scholarships to a number of prestigious universities. She decided against Cambridge ("I had a chip on my shoulder about the Brits"); Yale lost her application; Wellesley wouldn't cover full tuition. So, in 1976, she went to Harvard, "by default." "I had seen it in 'Love Story,'" Nair says. "The only thing my father said—which made me throw up at the time—was 'Oh, yes, the Kennedys went there.'"

At Harvard, Nair quickly made an impression. "She was strikingly beautiful," says Sooni Taraporevala, a classmate who became her friend and later her screen-writing partner. "She wore this tweed cape. She was like a gale-force wind." In her first semester, Nair performed Jocasta's speech from Ted Hughes's translation of Seneca's "Oedipus" and won the Boylston Prize. She was coached in her performance by the classicist Robert Fitzgerald, who told her, she recalls, "You know, Mira, you have too many climaxes. You should really work toward one climax." "I sort of sweetly challenged him," she says. "I said, 'I think that could be a male view.'" The mobility and liberality of America emboldened Nair to pursue acting. "I was intuitively comfortable onstage," she says. "I also had a huge love of the written word. And theatre was the word in many ways." She had already done political street theatre in Calcutta, with the Bengali playwright Badal

Sircar; at Delhi University she had starred in boulevard drama ("Equus,"
"Habeas Corpus") and in Shakespeare (she played Cleopatra); and at Harvard she was Arkadina in "The Seagull" and Eva Perón in a Latino version of
"Antigone." The summer after her first year there, Nair headed to New
York to explore the theatrical avant-garde. She hung out at La Mama, in the
East Village, worked with the director Joe Chaikin, and met Judith Malina
and Julian Beck, the founders of the Living Theatre. But the pretensions of
the theatre world and her lack of control over her life as an actress damp-
ened Nair's enthusiasm for the stage. When she returned to Harvard, she
submitted some landscape photographs to the Department of Visual and
Environmental Studies, where the professors found them impressive
enough to admit her as one of an annual quota of ten students. But it wasn't
long before she dropped photography for film. The form, as well as allowing her to deploy her extraordinary social skills, assuaged her chronic rest-
lessness; it was a medium that answered her need both to embrace life and
to be listened to.

Nair hadn't taken to still photography but she had taken to her teacher
Mitch Epstein, a wiry, taciturn, meticulous twenty-five-year-old, who
taught the introductory-photography course she took in the summer of
1977. "She wasn't great in the class," Epstein remembers, but he nonetheless found her "magical, full in body and in spirit." Epstein, who had been
taught by the photographer Garry Winogrand, set Nair an example of
uncompromising artistic commitment to "the way in which image holds a
kind of symbolic possibility." "He taught me the importance of the frame,
how sacred it is," Nair says. "How, in framing the environment, you would
artfully talk to the audience about how to see that picture, how to see the
world."

Nair worked as Epstein's assistant on freelance assignments, helping to
create "atmosphere" for his shots and to edit his contact sheets. "We were
three-hundred-dollars-a-month sort of people," she says. They were
together for twelve years, eight of them as husband and wife, and their relationship was, according to Epstein, a symbiotic one. In 1978, on a trip to
India to meet Nair's somewhat scandalized family, Epstein worried about
how to connect with the people there so that he could photograph them.

He asked Nair for a few Hindi words to disarm the locals. "She said that whenever you meet anybody you should say *'Mujhe su-su karna hai,'*" Nair's brother Vikram recalls. "Which means 'I want to take a leak.'" Although Epstein was a Jewish boy from Holyoke, Massachusetts, the couple was married in India, in 1981, in the flamboyant Punjabi fashion that Nair recreated in "Monsoon Wedding": Epstein, wearing a turban, made his entrance on a white horse and sat by a bonfire with his bride as he said his *om shantis*. "For a long period of time, it was a blessed life," Epstein says. "She was a catalyst that made me shift. Her curiosity was infectious. She held out a hand that I attached myself to."

In the course of a seven-year career in cinéma-vérité documentary—a genre that was almost unknown in India at the time—Nair learned the art of narrative and of creating a kind of drama through editing. "It's all about intuitive rhythm," she says. The lessons were hard won. In the eighteen-minute film that Nair submitted as her thesis at Harvard, "Jama Masjid Street Journal"—named for a Muslim community near the great mosque in old Delhi—she walked the streets with her Rolex, using the camera as a kind of veil. "The film was about how people reacted to me on the street, as a woman who spoke the language, who was from there and yet not from there," she has said. It was meant to be silent, but at the urging of friends Nair added narration, a concession she later regretted, although it taught her what she considers her first lesson in cinema: "Never surrender your own idea of the film . . . for the momentary pleasure of pleasing those around you." While Nair says she is embarrassed by the film now, D. A. Pennebaker, the panjandrum of cinéma vérité, was charmed by its adventurousness and theatricality. Nair met Pennebaker in New York after she graduated (she claims to have "stalked" him). "I saw her as potentially a natural filmmaker," he says. "I could just feel the want." Pennebaker helped Nair get a grant to make her next film, "So Far from India."

The nonprofit-documentary life was not, according to Nair, exactly "comfy." "It was a mountain of rejection," she says—a constant battle to find money, followed by a constant battle to find an audience. "I was getting killed on both sides." Every year from 1980 to 1984, Nair spent weeks on a Greyhound bus, taking her work to unions, women's hostels, and colleges.

"I would make, like, three hundred dollars a pop, live in the dorms with the students, or in some assistant professor's house," she says. The questions from the audience weren't particularly encouraging. "It was depressing to be in bloody Minneapolis and have an old lady say, 'I noticed a tap in your documentary. Do you have running water in India?'" Nair says. "You'd think, Fuck, who am I doing this for? I'm not here to educate you about India." And, as she found out with "India Cabaret," which was bought by PBS, then rejected by Channel 13, PBS's New York affiliate, the Indian community could be just as misguided. "'What is this image of India you are presenting? When will you show us doctors and the Porsches I have in my garage?'" Nair says, imitating a Bollywood accent. "I said, 'When a doctor in a Porsche becomes an interesting character, I'll be there.'" Television, she says, "felt like a void. I didn't know whom I was reaching." She began to hanker for a wider audience and for more control over the gesture, the light, the story—"to be able to pick out the color of the actor's underwear." In other words, instead of waiting for the truth in hit-and-run documentary fashion, Nair wanted to organize it in a fictional way.

In 1985, "India Cabaret" opened the first Indian International Film Festival, in Hyderabad, where, as Nair wrote to Epstein, who had served as the documentary's cinematographer, it was "a pretty major sensation." In Nair's assessment, "People were really responding to the language, how people really talk in Bombay." Sooni Taraporevala attended the screening on her way to Orissa, where she and Nair had planned to do research for a film about Nair's childhood. "The audience was totally into it—you know, laughing and clapping," she says. "It wasn't just the language, to my mind. It was the sense of something's being relevant." Buoyed by the reaction to the film, Taraporevala reminded Nair of a subject they'd discussed before. "Why not develop your earlier idea on the Bombay kids instead?" she asked. Nair's response, as she wrote in her journals, was "It's too huge, too ambitious. . . . Sooni retorted in her fearless, nonchalant style: 'NO GUTS NO GLORY.'" Nair and Taraporevala changed their tickets and set off for Bombay.

The challenge was herculean. Nair had never been on a movie set, never made a feature film, never developed a budget, and had no access to real funding, though, by even a modest estimate, she would need almost a million dollars. "The cost of my film is the cost of a leg of one camel in . . .

'Ishtar,'" Nair told studio executives. Nonetheless, in June of 1987, Nair began the project without the money to finish it. She felt, she says, "like a warrior." The slogan on the production T-shirts bore witness to her bravado: " NO GUTS NO GLORY—52 LOCATIONS 52 DAYS—WHAT PROBLEM? NO PROBLEM."

The enterprise brought together the intellectual strands of Nair's life: theatre, politics, the documentary tradition. Acting workshops were organized for the street children Nair recruited—a hundred and thirty narrowed down to twenty-four, who were then issued official-looking I.D. cards to protect them from being carted off by the police and remanded to the almost Dickensian homes dramatized in the film. In a series of drafts, Nair and Taraporevala developed a plot from the stories of street children they had interviewed. The film, they decided, would follow an abandoned ten-year-old as he made his way through the choked Bombay slums, where he lived rough among beggars and drug addicts, progressing from bumpkin to street-savvy survivor. "Salaam Bombay!" would capture the pathos and bravery amid India's chaos, the realities of its lowlife and its low talk.

But the uncertainty of so many factors, according to Epstein, who was the co-producer and production designer, made the situation "hellish." "It was a David-and-Goliath situation," he says. "We were up against all the odds—how to get through it, how not to get sick, how to keep everybody together. It was larger than us." Dinaz Stafford, Nair's collaborator and trouble-shooter, remembers one moment of despair: "We'd been working on the film. We'd set up the workshop. This huge juggernaut had been moved into action, getting people to work for hardly any money. And Mira and I went up on the top of this building—it was sunset—and she told me she didn't have the money for the project. It was like, O.K., we may have to close this now." After a lot of filmflammery and economy with the truth, Nair managed to cajole completion cash out of a French company. At the end of the shoot, she wrote in her journal, "I am so worn out, worn out of feeling, insisting, demanding, hoping, making it happen. A section of my hair has turned almost completely gray, à la Indira." She was thirty years old.

Six months later, on May 19, 1988, only three days after she'd finished cutting the movie, "Salaam Bombay!" made its world premiere at the closing gala at Cannes. After the screening, a crowd of two thousand stood and applauded for more than fifteen minutes. "Salaam Bombay!" was the first

Indian film to win the Camera d'Or at Cannes; it also earned an Oscar nomination.

Nair's life changed again on March 29, 1989, when she and Taraporevala were in Nairobi researching "Mississippi Masala," this time with studio backing. The movie aimed to tell the story of some Indian-Africans, exiled from Uganda by Idi Amin, making a new life in the United States. It was Nair and Taraporevala's first visit to Africa. For her research, Nair had read Mahmood Mamdani's book "From Citizen to Refugee," which dealt with the Ugandan expatriation, and she had arranged to interview him in Kampala, where he lived. But Mamdani turned up early, in Nairobi, and called from the lobby of Nair's hotel to ask if she was free. "We thought he would be a fudsy-dudsy professor," Nair says. She told Taraporevala, "He's some sort of a lefty. Let's just hide the materialism." They were shoving the bags and sarongs they'd purchased earlier that day under their beds when the bell rang. Nair opened the door to Mamdani, a handsome Ugandan-Asian in his early forties, with playful eyes and a gentle authority. He looked over Nair's shoulder. "I'm looking for Mira Nair," he said. "I'd expected a middle-aged, sort of sagelike person," Mamdani explains. "I had no idea who Mira was. I lived in a city that didn't have a functioning movie theatre."

They met up again a few days later in Kampala. In that ghostly setting—the war had just ended, and the city was devastated—their relationship began. The trajectories of their lives had an eerie similarity: both came from small towns and now moved in multiple worlds; both had won scholarships to Harvard; and both blended the personal and the political in their work. By the time Nair left, she had become, she says, "humbled by love." In typically head-strong fashion, she returned to New York and, as she put it, "willed myself" out of a marriage that, on the surface, "had nothing wrong with it." "I thought, I can't control it. I can't stop," Nair says. "Mitch said I took a piece of his heart. It was true. And it was terrible. I turned my back on the home we had made. I felt like a foreigner again, totally outside." Epstein stayed on as the co-producer and production designer of "Mississippi Masala," but, he says, "the way we worked together had little of the grace and the quality of communication we had achieved over the years."

Nair soon moved to Kampala's Makerere University, where Mamdani was teaching political science, and where, in campus housing, they had running water for only an hour a day. "I went from Jacuzzi to jerrican," Nair says. "Love is like that."

Last May, in a screening room at Columbia, Nair watched a short film by a Turkish student and offered her critique. "Remember, I told you about my hesitancy with your doing something seemingly generic," she told the woman, who had produced a vignette about an American girl and her narcissistic mother. "The mother and daughter have got nothing to do with where you came from. It's showing to me in the film. In that sense, I have to say I am disappointed. The thing is you don't know these women. You don't actually love them or know them." She concluded, "See you in Istanbul." In a way, Nair was teaching the bitter lesson she herself had learned in the nineties.

"Mira's passed through a period of a certain amount of humbling," Epstein says. "I wouldn't say she got a little big-headed. I'd say she got very bigheaded." Certainly, for a time, something seemed to come between her and what she put on the screen. "The Perez Family" (1995), which was Nair's first experience of Hollywood, and the first story she hadn't developed herself, has none of her defining authenticity. All her obsessions are present—exile, family, home—but they are in the dialogue, not the subtext. The film is almost unwatchable as it tries to factor out its histrionic dramatic equations: a released Cuban political prisoner, mistaken by immigration officials for the husband of a high-spirited prostitute, tries in vain to reconnect with his real wife, while the prostitute works to build a family from whatever misfits cross her path. "There was too much plot, and that was part of the problem," Michael Nozik, one of the film's producers, says. "It was too overt. It was too obvious." As one critic wrote, "It looks like a musical after all the songs have been cut out." Although Nair claims that the film had a more magic-realist quality before the studio recut it for comedy, "The Perez Family" strains for life instead of exuding it. It feels as if Nair had never fully taken hold of her material, which in a way is true. "They really ran roughshod over us," the producer Lydia Dean Pitcher says. "We don't like to say that they took the movie away. She had a choice to walk away or to stick by it. . . . The whole experience made what she did next incredibly important. It had to be a comeback."

It wasn't. "Kama Sutra," which Nair now calls "an aberration," was a sumptuous, peacock-colored spectacle, sensual in its use of costumes and tableaux, but uncertain in its narrative. The movie recreates sixteenth-century India through the story of two virgins, who are competitive friends in childhood and sexual rivals in adulthood—one marries a king and the other seduces him, only to fall in love with a sculptor. ("Because I love you, my work has a power that even I cannot explain," he says.) But the period detail gets in the way of the characterization, which more or less peters out. "It sort of bombed," Mamdani says of the film. "It was a moment of learning for her, painful as it was. It is the issue that she wrestles with: narrative versus design."

The year that "Kama Sutra" was released, Nair moved to South Africa with Mamdani, who had been appointed the head of the African-studies program at the University of Cape Town. The next three years were hard ones. "She had very little to do," Mamdani says. "Her film career was going through a difficult time. She stagnated." The South Africans, he adds, "simply weren't interested in her. She was not invited to talk at the universities where film and cinema were being taught. She had a bout with a sort of racism." Her Indian clothes indicated to the South African community, Mamdani says, "that she was pre-modern, pre-rational, must be spoken to slowly in special English, with clear diction." Nair cared for their son, Zohran, who was born in 1991. She and Taraporevala worked on scripts and adapted Abraham Verghese's book "My Own Country: A Doctor's Story" for Showtime; and Nair spent six weeks helping children from the nearby townships make films of their lives. But, Nair's brother Gautam says, "She was very worried that she'd lost her touch, that in her life as a suburban housewife the edge had gone from her. She perhaps wouldn't see things and wouldn't be able to express things through her films as she could before."

When the photographer Adam Bartos suggested that they collaborate on "The Laughing Club of India"—a remarkable documentary account of a Bombay doctor who set up laughing clubs to improve people's well-being—Nair agreed. "She was very self-deprecating about her career at that point," Bartos says. "I thought it would be therapeutic." After the film was finished, Nair began to dream up her next project. "I had done the epic," she says. "I had done the millions of dollars. I had done the special effects. I had done the erotic. I wanted to get back to basics, to prove to myself that I needed the essence of drama and had something to say." The result was "Monsoon Wedding." "At least people won't meet me and say, 'Hi, Mira, love your early work,'" she says.

On a clear day in mid-May, as Orthodox Jews in long black *reklakh* and Muslims in flowing djellabahs scuttled past with their groceries and their kids in tow, Nair found herself in the Kensington section of Brooklyn, at the corner of Avenue C and McDonald. She was sitting in her *churidar-kurta*— the earth-colored Indian cotton pants and tunic she favors—on the stoop of one of the unprepossessing bungalows whose aluminum awnings give the neighborhood the sleepy feel of a Jersey Shore town. She was there to shoot her contribution to a French project that would include the responses of eleven directors to the events of September 11th. The movie's collective title, "11'09"01"—or eleven minutes, nine seconds, and a frame—was the challenge that its producers had extended to Nair, as well as to such far-dung independent filmmakers as Ken Loach, Claude Lelouch, Danis Tanovic, Youssef Chahine, Samira Makhmalbaf, and Sean Penn.

Nair had chosen a true story as her narrative: that of Mohammad Salman Hamdani, a twenty-three-year-old research assistant from Bayside, Queens, who took the subway to work that Tuesday and never returned. For a time, his parents thought that Salman was among the thousand or so Muslims detained for security reasons after the attack. Then, to the family's humiliation, the *Post* splashed his picture on its pages, along with insinuations of collaboration and treason. The Hamdanis protested to their congressman, and even to President Bush. Six months later, Salman's remains were found at the World Trade Center, where, it turned out, he had rushed to save lives, and he was given a hero's burial. The story would allow Nair, she said, to bear witness to the pervasiveness of what she calls "Islamophobia." "After September 11th, none of the media spoke of *why* this had happened," she says. "What *was* talked about was that Muslims equal

terrorists." ("11'09"01" has been distributed successfully in twenty coun-
tries but not in the United States, where a few of its segments are perceived, in some quarters, as anti-American. Loach's film, for instance,
reminded audiences that on September 11, 1973, America helped bring
about the downfall of Chile's democratically elected Socialist leader, Salvador Allende, and installed General Augusto Pinochet.)

On the set, Nair cast a droll eye over her skeleton crew and noted that
there was no director's chair, no trailer, no catering tent, in fact, "no nothing." "It's back to the low-budget slut thing," she joked. She walked me to
the end of the block, to a spot where she'd filmed the day before. Eight
months after the eleventh, American flags still hung from almost every
house on the street, which had a mosque, Baitul Jannah Masjid, at one end;
even the brick subway bridge across from the mosque had been spray-
painted with stars and stripes. "What I love about shooting in India is to
choreograph the chaos," Nair said. "Here it's all so dreadfully competent
and systematized—you have to create the electricity." Still, the previous
day, in the twilight, amid the rumble of the subway and the whine of cop
cars, with kids on skateboards maneuvering around a sign that read, in
English and Arabic, "Road Closed for Prayer," she had wrangled thirty-five
wary local Bangladeshi Muslim men onto a traffic island and filmed them
praying. "The great thing about yesterday was that we captured India in
Brooklyn," Nair said. "They were praying in the direction of Mecca, but in
front of them was graffiti. What I want is a tapestry of the banality of the
Muslim presence in New York. It's just absolutely normal."

The focus of Nair's film was Salman Hamdani's parents: Talat, a middle-
school English teacher, and Saleem, a convenience-store owner, who had
been living in America for more than two decades before the September 11th attack. In a kitchen laid out to resemble the Hamdanis', Nair sat
on an apple crate, hunched behind a video monitor. On the screen was the
rectangle—about five by three inches—where Nair does a significant part
of her work: composing the image. This morning, she was watching the
actress Tanvi Azmi playing Talat, making a curry at the stove as she day-
dreamed about her lost son. From her cramped command post, Nair called
for small angle adjustments from her director of photography, Declan
Quinn, and checked a line of dialogue with her script supervisor. Then she

pushed back the apple crate and walked into the shot to talk to Azmi. Nair never directs her actors from behind the video monitor; she needs to see them in real space and time and communicate face to face. As she huddled with Azmi, suggesting that she try humming as she cooked, the actress stood motionless, blinking, like someone caught in the headlights—which, in a way, is what Nair's dark, kohl-lined eyes are. Her scrutiny is at once penetrating and containing, it can feel like an embrace. "Her eyes are as strong as a camera," says the actress Sarita Choudhury, who starred in "Mississippi Masala" and "Kama Sutra." "It's almost like 'Oh, my God, this is my moment.' I know it's never a casual thing. Something's being registered. I get very excited."

Nair works with a handheld Aaton Super16. "A handheld camera means you have to be alive to the moment," she says. "It also means you have to have a lot of stamina." To build that stamina, Nair and many of her crew, including the resourceful women she keeps around her on location, whom she teasingly calls her International Bhenji Brigade ("not-so-hip sisters," in her translation), take a ninety-minute yoga class before each day's shoot. "Mira allows you to jump into her story, and you fall into her world," says Dinaz Stafford, who was about to start a second postgraduate degree, at Cambridge, when Nair enlisted her, in the late eighties, to help organize the Bombay street kids. I felt the centrifugal force myself when Nair persuaded me to join her early-morning yoga ritual. "I really think it promotes a kind of egolessness in the work," she said. When Nair and six of her Bhenjis arrived at the appointed place—a tenth-floor office in the West Village—they found it locked. Nair considered the problem for a moment, then threw down her lavender yoga mat in the neon-lit corridor opposite the elevators, stripped to her shorts, and, much to the amusement of some Russian workmen who ogled from a nearby office, began a series of headstands, handstands, and downward-facing-dog and warrior postures. Yoga's discipline of physical flexibility is, for Nair, also a lesson in intellectual flexibility. "The way the body is asked to be in those positions really teaches you the art of resistance and surrender," she said. "You stretch and then you pull. If the solutions aren't coming from one place, you have to look at another."

That morning, for instance, rain interfered with the movie's planned opening shot, which was to have been filmed in Flushing, Queens, in an area where planes swoop in close to the buildings before veering off to land at Kennedy Airport. The camera was to pan with a plane, then find Tanvi Azmi in a sea of non-white faces. Nair now had to conjure up a new opening, in the turquoise-tiled vastness of the Fatih Camii Mosque, in Brooklyn. As she improvised the logistics of the shot, kneeling barefoot by the screen that separates praying women from praying men, she looked up at her director of photography. "I want you to focus on her hands, not just her face," she said. "As soon as the hands hit her face, they should be in focus." Once the shot was established, Nair's attention went to a bank of lights on the side wall, which suddenly switched on, turning the gray day sunny. "Totally looking good. Totally looking good. God's here," she said.

At work, Nair is swift, clear, and good-humored. Even at the end of the day, after five failed attempts to coordinate her driver and the passengers in her car, Nair, with hands on hips, joked, "There is a limit to democracy!" "She has a kind of charmed humor," Epstein says, "a way of making somebody feel good." Sometimes she does it just by sidling up to a crew member and jostling him with her shoulder. Sometimes she does it with nicknames. Nair's talkative doe-eyed son, Zohran, who exudes the charm of the well-loved, is known by dozens of coinages, including Z, Zoru, Fadoose, and Nonstop Mamdani. Even her unsatisfactory assistant director—"He doesn't pay attention to what is involved in each shot," she complains—has an alternate name; she calls him Phuttone. In a kind of ersatz Hindi, "it means 'a broken drum,'" she says. "He has no idea." Most of the time, however, her naming is a strategy for intimacy, which allows her to play with people and to let others play with her. During the filming of "Salaam Bombay!," the child actors referred to her variously as Tough Sister, Danger Director, Atom Bomb, and Whirlwind.

Nair turned the final day of shooting at the mosque into a sort of extended family outing. In addition to orchestrating the cast, crew, and a platoon of extras, she was happily entertaining Zohran, Lydia Dean Pitcher and her seven-year-old son, and Taraporevala, who was visiting from Bombay with her two young children. Far from distracting Nair, the swarming confusion of realms seems to intensify her concentration. "Her orientation to relationships is very familial," Mamdani says. "She treasures loyalty, and therefore doesn't really work in terms of a purely one-to-one basis. She creates groups." Like the set for "Monsoon Wedding," which was almost a home movie filled with the props and the people of her Delhi circle, the "11'09"01" set was for Nair a sort of emotional safety net, a simulacrum of family love. As Santa Choudbury says, "She really wants to live in a village and go to the well with her friends."

By the time I visited Nair in Kampala, she was already beginning work on her next project. She had turned down "Fever Pitch" and the Plath-Hughes project but accepted "Vanity Fair"; and she had enlisted Reese Witherspoon to play Becky Sharp. Although Witherspoon usually plays "the cute pesky sort," Nair said, she sees her as a potentially "sensual and full-blown woman." "It's not there yet, but we're going to put it there," she added. Nair was also occupied with a fragrance garden that she was planting next to her house to attract butterflies and birds. A playing field had been levelled for Zohran, and she walked me down a steep embankment to a jacaranda tree, near which she planned to build an editing studio. The deliriums of the First World, with its "casualness of acquisition," as Nair calls it, felt very far away. What was renewing about Africa, she said, "is a real connection with the earth—one that I had in my childhood, but not since then." Inside Nair's house, the emphasis is on the homespun and the elemental: "It makes my imagination soar a bit," she says. In the garden, what excites her is the drama of color and shape. As she patrolled the flower beds, sizing up and reblocking the plants like so many actors in a scene, she pointed to a purple blossom that the gardener had tried to slip into her selection. "Peter?" she said, putting her hand on his shoulder. "Did you choose the chrysanthemums? I don't like them—a namby-pamby flower!" Her head swivelled toward the house. "Look!" she said. "The butterflies are already coming!"

Out shopping the previous day, Nair had seen a sign she wanted to buy: "LIFE IS SWEET BUT SHORT." The phrase spoke to her professional drive, but also to her sense of gratitude. "It's a privilege" were her words to me as we stepped for the first time into the spectacular luxuriance of her leafy hill. "Mira likes happiness around her," Taraporevala had told me, and the making of happiness, it seemed to me, was both Nair's ambition and her profession. It was also what had drawn her to "Vanity Fair" and to what she called the "yogic question" raised in the last sentences of the novel: "Which of us is happy in this world? Which of us has his desire? or, having it, is satisfied?"

Sitting on her veranda, paging through Thackeray, Nair recalled the former studio executive Scott Greenstein, who had first approached her with the "Vanity Fair" project, not long after "Monsoon Wedding" had come out. "It was kind of condescending," she says. "He said, 'You know, Mira, you gotta do a big English-language picture.' I said, 'Hello, Scott? "Monsoon Wedding" is sixty per cent English.'" She went on, "I was just teasing him—teasing doesn't exist there. So I bait them: 'So now that I can do brown people I can do white people, too! Thank you, Scott.'" She riffled through the pages of the novel, then pushed herself forward from the orange cushions of her wicker sofa to read me an underlined sentence: "So these two were each exemplifying the Vanity of this life, and each longing for what he or she could not get." She peered over her sunglasses. "If I can get that, it'll be so amazing," she said. Thackeray's comic philosophical detachment, in a way, is not unlike the detachment that Nair has engineered for herself by shifting cultures. "What is meaningful in one place is absolutely meaningless in another," she said. "You can't take yourself too seriously. It's a very good way of keeping the absurdity of fame in context. People who are venerated and think they're the answer are not students anymore. You have to be a student at all times."

As we talked, I noticed, beyond the patio's pink hibiscus and crimson bougainvillea, a brindled goat grazing in the field. I asked its name.

"Toofani," Nair said. "We gave it my old name—Whirlwind."

"A remnant of your old self?" I asked.

"I hope not too old," she said. "You must always have a little *toofani* in you."

LAURENCE FISHBURNE

THE SWINGER

IN THE HISTORY OF DRAMA, MANY
plays have been published with an author's note, but Laurence Fishburne's
"Riff Raff" is the only one, to my knowledge, that comes with a warning.
"Practitioners of the craft, be forewarned," he writes in the 1997 acting edi-
tion. "DON'T FUCK AROUND! COME CORRECT, COME TO GET DOWN. A 'RIFF' IS A
'RIFF.' SO SWING!"

"Swing" is Fishburne's favorite word to describe the nuanced and
dynamic force that he brings to his performances. "I mean it in the exact
sense that jazz musicians mean it," he explains. "'Don't mean a thing if it
ain't got no swing.' It's got to have a feel, a rhythm, a sense of melody and
tempo." In nearly fifty films, Fishburne, with his broad-shouldered swagger,
his heavy-lidded almond eyes, and his smoky, wet voice, has made his own
eloquent music, swooping between registers of sorrow and joy. "There is
hardly an actor of his age around who exhibits more flash, energy, and intelligence," David Thomson writes in "The New Biographical Dictionary of
Film." Acting, to Fishburne, means "being fearless—it's throwing yourself
off the bridge." He goes on, "Sometimes it's not appropriate; sometimes it
may be wrong. But it's gonna be O.K. You're gonna arrive at something
that's true. You're gonna fly. You're gonna catch the right fucking updraft,
man, and you're gonna go, 'Oh, oh, yes!—this is what I was trying to do.'"

The unjudgmental surrender with which Fishburne applies himself to
his roles has produced a collection of riveting character studies—from the cal-
low cannon fodder Clean in "Apocalypse Now" (1979) to the blood-curdling
hip-hop killer Jimmy Jump in "King of New York" (1990), the embattled
father Furious Styles in "Boyz N the Hood" (1991), the obsessive, abusive
Ike Turner in "What's Love Got to Do with It" (1993), and the perp turned
man of principle Socrates Fortlow in "Always Outnumbered" (1998). All of

these portraits find the epic in the ordinary; they exhibit Fishburne's signature dash and danger. In other words, they swing.

Fishburne's friend Arthur Mendoza, an acting coach who runs the Actors Circle Theatre, in Los Angeles, complains that "swing" is not a strategy for all actors. It's unhelpful, he argues, to tell "broken, emotionally unavailable actors to just let go and fly by the seat of their pants." It works for Fishburne, he explains, because of the "electric current of talent passing through him." He goes on, "He's a chameleon of body, voice, and movement. He'll walk one way with me in West Hollywood at eleven-thirty at night. He'll walk a different way down Madison Avenue in New York. He is so absorbed in his circumstances and his environment. His ear is attuned. His body is attuned. He can mimic and change."

Fishburne's improvisational skills were demonstrated at our first meeting, in New York, last October. At Brasserie 8½, a cavernous midtown restaurant on West Fifty-seventh Street, he bounded down the circular stairway in a green-and-yellow baseball cap and a sweatsuit, carrying what looked like a gym bag. But the most noticeable thing he brought into the buzzing room was his own specific gravity. Although Fishburne's bearing is statuesque, he is not conventionally handsome. His skin is pitted; the gap between his teeth reads like an exclamation point to every smile or scowl. His forehead is broad, and his cheekbones are high, drawing attention to his eyes, which are alternately brooding and twinkling. The defining quality in Fishburne's demeanor—and his performances—is stillness, a trick he says he learned from watching Clark Gable. His ability to meet the world without noise sharpens both his focus and the power of his presence. This aura of command makes it natural for Fishburne to play both kings and killers. (He was the first African-American to play Othello onscreen.) "He comes to the floor with a character and a dignity—quite the opposite of self importance," says Sidney Poitier, another model of reserve, who is one of Fishburne's mentors.

At the restaurant, when I mentioned that the happy hour was perhaps a little too happy for us to be able to tape our conversation, Fishburne immediately motioned to me to follow him. I did—up the stairs, through a scrum of pedestrians, and across Fifty-seventh Street, where he stopped at the curb. "How do you feel about motorcycles?" he asked me, eying a gray

BMW K1100 GT beside us. "A little scared," I said. He straddled the bike. "Just swing your leg over," he said. I did as I was told, and that was how I found myself, without a helmet, clinging to Fishburne's love handles as we pushed out into the mayhem of Manhattan rush-hour traffic. "Don't worry," he said, as a bus menaced us. "I've had Frank Gehry on the back."

Fishburne learned to ride in 1995, for the action comedy "Fled," and he starred last year in the best-forgotten Western-on-wheels "Biker Boyz." He now owns five motorcycles. Last summer, he took a three-day trip from Miami to Key West and back, and went on a five-day journey from Munich to Milan with the Guggenheim Motorcycle Club—a group of high rollers who enjoy playing low riders, among them Jeremy Irons, Dennis Hopper, and Thomas Krens, the director of the Guggenheim. It's not the speed of a motorcycle that Fishburne finds seductive but the freedom it offers. "It has to do with being able to move around under one's own steam," he said. "There are no minders, no assistants, no friends, no girlfriends. I don't have to talk to anybody; I have to make sure I survive!" He added, "This is how I gather stuff for myself."

Fishburne, who has been a professional actor for thirty-two of his forty-two years, is, thanks to his role as Morpheus in "The Matrix" trilogy, one of the most widely recognized actors in America. But with the visor of his helmet pulled down he becomes miraculously anonymous and free to observe. "I can stop on the bike and sit and watch people on the corner having coffee, having a conversation, having an argument," he said. He calls this a form of hunting and gathering—"the best sort of teaching." Riding also fulfills another of his needs. "I get to be a child when I'm on my motorcycle," he said. "Having a career as a child and having a childhood are in direct opposition. You don't get to be a child when you're working."

Fishburne likes to say that the stage chose him when he was ten. But his performing self was dreamed up long before, by his mother, Hattie, whom he describes as "a sassy brown woman with a brilliant mind and a razorlike tongue." Hattie Fishburne, who holds an M.A. in science education from Columbia Teachers College, was raised in Augusta, Georgia, the precocious third of her mother's eight daughters, all college-educated, and the only one to venture North. Her father, Jesse Crawford, who died when she was two, was a go-getter who managed a couple of businesses and whose "chutzpah" Hattie claims to have inherited. She felt short-changed, however, by her mother, Classie Anderson, who died in 1997, at the age of ninety-two. "For whatever reason, Mama could not embrace me," she says. "I always heard a different drummer. I heard a different whole band." Classie, who got by on Social Security and her own tenacity, was a strict disciplinarian. Her house was run on a rigid routine—dinner at four, lights out by ten or so. Hattie was a college student before she ever visited a friend's house. She played the piano, sang in a choir, read voraciously, and loved to dance, but she found no support at home for her artistic passions. "We were in the Deep South, in the Bible Belt," she says. "We didn't know that you could make a living writing or acting or singing. You had to have a real nine-to-five job and make a paycheck every week. I have always wanted to be a writer. I would have liked to be a singer. But there was no opportunity for me to do that."

In 1959, Hattie went to New York to visit Laurence Fishburne, Jr., a man she'd met a few years earlier at a U.S.O. function. They decided to marry, and, in the summer of 1960, she embarked for New York to enroll in graduate school at Columbia and begin her life with a sometime taxi-driver and gas-station attendant who later became a corrections officer. "She wasn't city-wise," Laurence Fishburne, Jr., who answers to the name Papa Fish, says of Hattie. "She was under the impression that in New York City the street was paved with gold. She wanted to have a mink coat and a maid." In the winter of 1960, Hattie became pregnant, and she returned to Augusta. "I knew that the marriage was over," she says. "He had no ambition." All her drive, resourcefulness, and longing came to rest, instead, on her son. "When Laurence was born," she says, "I looked at him and I said, 'We're gonna make it together.'"

By the time Fishburne was three or four, he and Hattie had moved back to New York, to a third-floor apartment in Park Slope, Brooklyn. "Me and Hattie had a great amount of fun," Fishburne says of his childhood. But if Hattie was Fishburne's caretaker—occasionally taking him to judo, theatre, and music lessons—he was increasingly vested with the unwanted responsibility of being hers. There were "men moving through the house all the time," Fishburne says, but he was the one who remained stalwart, listening to his mother's litany of grievances, bringing her coffee in the morning, zipping up her dresses for dates, and fetching the pills that she said were for her thyroid but which he now suspects were uppers and downers to control her frequent mood swings.

Fishburne learned to perform literally at his mother's knee, where, according to the photographer James Graham, who has been Fishburne's best friend since childhood, he embodied a whole repertory of supporting characters—"the houseboy, the servant, the trophy son, and the bad boy" among them. "I was seen only when I was being who she wanted me to be," Fishburne explains. His uncanny sensitivity—"He's like an open nerve that absorbs," Mendoza says—is due in part to his vigilance over Hattie's stormy emotional landscape. "When I walked into that home, I didn't know who I was gonna get," he says. "I didn't know if I was gonna get the woman who was really elated or really rageful." (Hattie once knocked out the female principal of the junior high school where she taught science.) One reliable antidepressant was to sing to her; she could always be resuscitated by her son's rendition of "Candy Man." But, until Fishburne discovered acting, his home life was fractious. "They used to fight," Fishburne's godfather, Maurice A. Watson, who is a professor of oral communication at Brooklyn College, says. "I mean, tug of war. I would say, 'Why y'all carry on like this? He's a child and you're a grown woman and why are y'all screaming at each other and calling names?'"

When Fishburne was about seven, Hattie, to supplement her income, set up a charm school in their apartment. One living-room wall was fitted with a ballet bar, the other with a full-length mirror. When Fishburne dressed for school, she says, "he had to look at himself in the mirror from head to foot, stand before the mirror to be sure all of his clothes were fitting right." The mirror served Fishburne the way it served Hattie's pupils: it made him forcibly aware of what he was presenting to the world. In front of it, Fishburne practiced his Pledge of Allegiance. For up to two minutes at a time, at his mother's insistence, he also looked himself straight in the eye. "She would say to me, 'I just want to make sure that when you are grown you will never encounter a white man and look down,'" Fishburne says.

"In the first grade, he had already established himself as the alpha male of the class," Graham recalls. "He could do incredible imitations of everybody. His vocal abilities were stunning." By the time he progressed from P.S. 321 to I.S. 88, Fishburne had won local celebrity as a regular on "One Life to Live," the first integrated network soap opera. He attributes his early success largely to Watson, who was involved with a semi-professional theatre group called the Afro-American Theatre Workshop. In third grade, Fishburne won the lead in a class production of "Peter Pan," and Hattie asked Watson to accompany her to the show. "She was ambitious for him," Watson remembers, and she wanted to know if he was talented. During the performance, Watson whispered to Hattie, "He's really quite good." Until then, Hattie had wanted her son to be a doctor; now she began to envision an acting career. In New York in the late sixties, there was a renaissance in black theatre—the Negro Ensemble Company, the New Lafayette Theatre, and the Public Theatre needed African-American child actors. Fishburne remembers refusing his mother's request that he audition for the musical "The Me Nobody Knows." "She came back to me a few weeks later and said, 'If you'd gotten the job, you'd make three hundred dollars a week,'" he recalls. "I looked at her and said, 'Well, why didn't you tell me that then?'"

Sometime later, Fishburne got his chance. Watson had been asked to appear in the New Federal Theatre production of Charles Fuller's play "In My Many Names and Days," which was about Jackie Robinson; he suggested that Fishburne audition for the part of young Jackie. "I brought him, he read, he was a natural," Watson says. "Controversy developed. He wasn't black enough." Hattie, who for years oversaw her son's finances and career, proposed that they solve the problem by putting shoe polish on her son. "I did my first performance in blackface," Fishburne recalls. On opening night, Watson says, "he was outstanding." Afterward, Fishburne found Watson. "It felt good, man," he said. Although he couldn't put it into words until years later, what excited Fishburne about his debut experience was not the sense of triumph it gave him but the sense of safety. The stage was a boundary that Hattie could not cross. "She couldn't get in there," Fishburne says. "It was my safe place, where I was in control of who I was and what I was gonna be." With his mother, Fishburne was emotionally under wraps.

Onstage, he discovered, he could express what was inside him. "I felt it was a homecoming," he says.

On Halloween of last year, Fishburne and I drove to his former stomping ground in Brooklyn, in the black Mercedes 600S that he gave his father in 2002. "My father needed to feel acknowledged in some small way by me," Fishburne said. "I know when my old man drives around in this car and people see him in it they go, 'Wow, man, nice car.' I know my old man's, like, 'Yeah, my son bought that for me.'" He added, "I always wanted to go, 'Hey, Dad, can I borrow the car?' So today I borrowed the car for the first time."

Papa Fish lives in the Bronx. When his son was growing up, he claims, he visited him every weekend. Fishburne puts those visits at once a month. Their main activity together—a barometer of the uneasy distance between them—was moviegoing, often, they'd see two or three movies in a day. "I don't really know my father that well," Fishburne says. "He has a really explosive personality. Very gregarious, very powerful. He's a funny cat. But I didn't need him to be funny. I needed him to be tender and gentle with me. He didn't know how to do that." As kids, Fishburne and Graham nicknamed him Idi Amin. "He was a man of few words," Graham says. "He was there just to put Fish in check. . . . There was no argument, no negotiation."

"Here it is!" Fishburne said, as the pavilion at the edge of Prospect Park came into view. "This is where my life starts—Grand Army Plaza, baby." Fishburne grew up on Fiske Place, between Seventh and Eighth Avenues, in the mid-sixties, when the neighborhood streets were filled with the polyglot din of first-generation Americans. "That's my base," he said, "the place I've always operated from as a human being. . . . It gave me an appreciation of different peoples and different cultures, man." When Fishburne was a boy, the notorious Puerto Rican gang the Brooklyn Homicides infiltrated the neighborhood. "On the other side of Thirteenth, there were gangs; on the other side of Seventh, there were gangs; on the other side of Fifth, there were gangs," he said. "White boys did not go across Seventh Avenue when I was a child because the whole block was Puerto Rican. I could cross the street because I was brown."

In Park Slope, Fishburne learned what he calls his "cool thing"—the posture of the street tough. Even as a boy, he was standing on corners with candy cigarettes dangling from his mouth, pretending to be "bad." On the basketball courts of P.S. 321, he became expert at standing up to older bullies by imitating their menace. "I would shut them down and put them off," he says. "I didn't find out until I was grown that they thought I was, like, some gang leader." As we drove, the neighborhood evoked stories from the old days. The bottom-feeders whose botched drug hustle is the premise of his play "Riff Raff"—Freddy Nine Lives, Tony the Tiger, Torch—were all based on Brooklyn figures "who didn't make it out." Fishburne's haphazard roll call—Tommy Costello, Mike Vigilante, Betty and Amos Saunders, Dave Rangelli—conjured up the gallimaufry of Americans whose lives and behavior he still draws on in his work. When Graham saw last year's "Mystic River," in which Fishburne plays a detective called Whitey Powers, he recognized in the characterization "a guy on our block—Whitey Higgins, a big bushy Irishman with a shock of white hair." He said, "I was seeing Whitey Higgins's voice come out of Laurence's head, and all his mannerisms. The guy channelled Whitey Higgins."

The landscape of Fishburne's Brooklyn youth has been refurbished over the years. Snooky's Pub is now Snooky's Fine Food and Spirits; Danny's Candy Store, where Fishburne stole comic books, is now a sushi bar; Greasy Jack's, the soda fountain, is a Starbucks. At a stoplight, Fishburne leaned his broad frame over the steering wheel and sighed. "You can't go home again," he said. A construction worker crossed in front of the Mercedes. "It's good to have money, huh?" he said in Fishburne's direction. "It ain't bad," Fishburne called back. "It don't hurt." (Though numbers conveniently elude him, by his own admission he'll be "making a whole lot of money" from "The Matrix" alone.) "But you know what they say—'Mo' money, mo' problems.'" The light changed, and Fishburne accelerated. "I wasn't aware of any world but this one," he said, "until I was snatched up and taken to the Philippines to do 'Apocalypse Now.'"

"My film is not about Vietnam," Francis Ford Coppola said of his masterpiece, at Cannes in 1979. "It *is* Vietnam. It's what it was really like. It was crazy. And the way we made it was very much like the way the Americans were in Vietnam. We were in the jungle. There were too many of us. We had access to too much money, too much equipment. And little by little we went insane." Fishburne came of age in this mayhem. Fresh from his first feature film, "Cornbread, Earl and Me," he was fourteen when he lied about his age to get the part of Clean. (Coppola had been looking for a sixteen- or seventeen-year-old.) "I wasn't on the swimming team, the track team or the basketball team," Fishburne told *Essence* in 1994. "I didn't go to the prom. I didn't have dates." Instead, he signed up for the war.

During the year and a half that he was on location—most of 1976 and half of 1977—Fishburne adopted Coppola as a father figure and mentor. "He was gentle with me," Fishburne says. "If I came to him and said, 'So what are you doing?,' he'd take a minute and go, 'Oh, I'm doing this. . . .' He wouldn't dismiss me like I was accustomed to being dismissed by adults like my mother and father." Fishburne never attended college or drama school; instead, he studied with some of the finest actors in the land—Robert Duvall, Albert Hall, Frederic Forrest, Sam Bottoms, Martin Sheen, Dennis Hopper, and Marlon Brando among them. "I learned how to swing from Dennis Hopper," he says. "I learned how to improvise from him and from Coppola, because Coppola didn't give me any words." (Coppola often generated dialogue by handing his actors index cards with activities written on them and letting them find the words.)

One moonlit night when he was sixteen, Fishburne was sitting in a boat on the water while Coppola and his cinematographer, Vittorio Storaro, talked about Orson Welles's failed attempt to make a film of Joseph Conrad's "Heart of Darkness," on which "Apocalypse Now" was also based. "Basically, they were patting each other on the back," Fishburne recalls. "They were talking about their intention to create a cinematic work of art that would last for generations. I went, 'You two motherfuckers are artists. You're making shit that's gonna influence people and touch people for generations. That means I must be one, too, 'cause I wouldn't be here if I wasn't.' I understood that the thing I was doing wasn't a lark." It was then, Fishburne said, that he began to think of himself "as an artist and to see film in artistic terms."

On camera, Fishburne's behavior was controlled; off camera, it was another matter. He had fallen under the spell of Dennis Hopper. "He was reckless," Fishburne told *Playboy* in 1994. "He was wild. I'd never seen a human being behave the way Dennis behaved and get away with it. And I wanted to know how he did it. I followed him around for about five months. His energy, power, sheer audacity and pure guts were things I wanted." Graham says of Fishburne's experience, "Take your fourteen-year-old kid. Tell him, 'Dennis Hopper is your babysitter.' They gave him a friggin' assault rifle with live ammunition, all the drugs and prostitutes he could do. And in this completely uncontrolled environment—the most corrupt degraded society since the fall of the Roman Empire—built and paid for by the U.S. government, who's in charge? This coked-to-the-tits megalomaniac filmmaker. And there you go!"

Hattie, who had recently remarried and had moved with her new husband to the Philippines for the duration of the shoot, sent an S.O.S. to Fishburne's father. "Crazy ain't the word for it," says Papa Fish, who spent the next year on location as his son's personal corrections officer. "I had to be the Gestapo. I had to go to extremes with him. I even made him write out a ten-point plan that he was supposed to follow while we were there." On a visit to the local authorities, Papa Fish was told, "Your son and his compatriots are walking down the street smoking Thai sticks. We can't have that." "I went home and waxed his ass," he says. "After I did that, Francis Coppola comes to me and says, 'Why did you have to react so violently?' I said, 'Let me tell you something. I don't give a fuck about your company, your picture, or his so-called bullshit career. The next time I catch any one of your cast giving my son any type of drugs, I'm locking their fucking ass up!'"

Fishburne matriculated from "Apocalypse Now" with an artistic pedigree and an attitude. "He did not integrate into society very well," Graham recalls. "He was smoking more pot than any of us, which is saying a lot. He was into all this wild new stuff. His head was filled with visions of the apocalypse—not a healthy place for a seventeen-year-old's brain to be." In order to capitalize on the momentum she anticipated for her son after the release of the movie, Hattie moved with him to L.A., where he enrolled at Hollywood High School. He spent most of his time there dancing to Rolling Stones records in the quad outside the school, dressed like Jimi Hendrix, whom he was beginning to resemble. After six weeks, he'd had enough; he returned to New York to finish high school with his friends, living for the first time with his father.

In August of 1979, "Apocalypse Now" broke big; Fishburne didn't. He and Graham spent most of that summer drinking near the Prospect Park band shell. "He was getting angrier and angrier, yelling at people," Graham says. Once, the two boys and their friend Gloria Rivera spent an afternoon drinking beer in Central Park. "We needed to find some bushes to pee in," Graham says. "We're walking past the wall on Central Park West, and he sees Tavern on the Green, which has these big bay windows all around it that look onto Central Park. And if you go there at 1 P.M. on a Wednesday, who's going to be sitting on the other side of that glass but two well-heeled Wasp ladies with blue hair having their Waldorf salads. I'm over in the bushes doing my thing. And I hear Gloria let out this wail. I turn, and, I swear to God, Fishburne has whipped out his schlong and is peeing on the window, right at eye level. We ran like banshees."

Finally, Fishburne called Coppola, who was about to start shooting "One from the Heart." He offered Fishburne and Graham work on the crew. "There were not a lot of roles for him out there," says Coppola, who later wrote Fishburne into "Rumble Fish" (1983) and "The Cotton Club" (1984), and cast him in "Gardens of Stone" (1987). I felt like he was one of my kids," he adds. Fishburne and Graham, with eighty dollars between them and a Fiat with a leaky gas tank, left Brooklyn for California. "We drove drunk," Graham says. "Neither of us had a license. I still have night-mares about that." But while they were on the road a writers' strike was called, and film production shut down for the best part of a year. Fishburne got no acting jobs for fifteen months. Instead, he worked as a doorman and a bouncer; he even cleaned offices with Graham, who briefly worked as a janitor in Culver City. "We were both alcoholics—full friggin' fledged," Graham says.

"Once I came home from 'Apocalypse Now,' I was no longer young and cute," Fishburne says. "I became tall, and a bit intimidating to people, par-tially because of the skin that I happen to come in." When people looked at him, they didn't see an eighteen-year-old boy; they saw, he says, "a twenty-six-year-old black male. Threatening." The only roles he was offered were as thugs and lowlifes. And Fishburne, who didn't deal well with rejection, could be scary. "There was no fucking way I didn't have some kind of skill," he says. "There was no way I didn't have something to offer. If I had been a white boy, them motherfuckers would have been dealing with me a whole lot differently. I didn't hide that. I walked in the room like I know where the fuck I've been, I know who I've been with, and I know what I know. And I know I'm a bad motherfucker, and I'm not coming in here trying to kowtow to you motherfuckers to give me a fucking job."

After a couple of years of being cast as a villain, Fishburne decided to turn a negative into a positive—to become, as he puts it, "the baddest motherfucker you have ever seen." His audition technique had a take-no-prisoners recklessness. To win the role of the mugger in Michael Winner's 1982 movie "Death Wish II" (Fishburne is the guy in the pink shades with his pants down during the gang bang of Charles Bronson's maid), he says, he "raped the chair, man." The day he went up for Paul Mazursky's "Willie & Phil" (1980), he ran into Graham and his girlfriend having a bad trip on psychedelic mushrooms. He took them along as props. "The film happened to be about a guy who teaches in an urban high school, and he's got all these freaky students," Graham says. "He challenges the one making all this trouble, and the kid delivers Hamlet's soliloquy." At the audition, while Graham sorted through the debris of a wastebasket he'd tipped over in the waiting room and his girlfriend shook the water cooler to watch the bubbles, Fishburne launched into the soliloquy. Afterward, according to Graham, "the casting director goes, 'O.K., do you think we could do that, but without, you know—' and he just looked at her and went, 'Nah, that's all I got for you today.' And picked us up and walked out of the room. They chased him down the hall and gave him the part."

When Fishburne, then twenty-two, was called to audition for "The Cotton Club," his agent told him to prepare a song and a dance step; instead, Fishburne put on shoes he'd spray-painted red, a pink shirt, and white pants, and walked into the audition, he says, "looking like some kind of crazy Mexican-American hoodlum." Gregory Hines asked him what he was going to sing. Fishburne said, "I'm not gonna sing anything for you today. If I'm gonna be in this movie, I'm gonna play a gangster, O.K.?" In the end, Fishburne was given the part of the Harlem numbers kingpin Bumpy Johnson. "I knew when he did Bumpy Johnson that he could be the star of a movie," Coppola says. "He had a presence. He has never lost his warmth and sweetness—and depth. A villain is always better when some-how you sense those bottom basements in him."

In 1986, Fishburne donned a purple Jheri-Curl wig and palomino chaps to play Cowboy Curtis on "Pee-wee's Playhouse." The part became a cult favorite and, finally, broke Fishburne out of the industry's profile of him. Two years later, he starred as the campus radical—and the only credible figure—in "School Daze," Spike Lee's musical satire about the tensions between middle-class black students. Then he won the role of Jimmy Jump in "King of New York," despite the fact that the director, Abel Ferrara, had originally conceived the part for a white actor. "I had to campaign for that," Fishburne says. "I went to Abel and I said, 'Listen, I have an idea about how this character can be played. And if you give me twenty-four hours to get the character together, I'll come in, present the character to you, and then, if you don't like it, cool. I'll do the part that you want me to do.'" (He had been pencilled in for the role of the policeman who was eventually played by Wesley Snipes.) Three days later, in the presence of Ferrara and the film's star, Christopher Walken, Fishburne arrived in all of Jimmy jump's iconic hip-hop flash—bowler, chain, gold tooth. For three hours, he told stories in character. In his version of the role, jump's menace was born of glee, not grudge. "Jump loved his life," Fishburne has said. "He loved the fact that he was fast, he was loose, he could kill people." He got the part. After almost twenty films, he admitted to the London *Guardian,* this was the first time that anyone had given him "something to run with."

But it was John Singleton's landmark "Boyz N the Hood," a shocking account of ghetto violence and anomie, that made him a star. Fishburne first met Singleton when the aspiring young director had just finished his fresh-man year at the University of Southern California film school and Fish-burne was working on "Pee-wee's Playhouse." "I was in awe of him," Singleton says. "I knew he had just done a film with Spike Lee. I asked him questions about it. After a while, I got him on the discussion of what I was doing with myself. I just said, 'Hey, maybe one day I'm gonna write some-thing for you.' He's, like, 'How old are you?' 'I'm nineteen, man.' He's like, 'Go on, brother, go ahead and do it!'" Fishburne was the first person to see the script for "Boyz." He became "the father of the film, the veteran actor that everyone went to," Singleton says. Singleton, who became the youngest director ever nominated for an Oscar, also consulted with Fishburne about how to deal with his cast. " 'Never give line readings,' " Singleton recalls him saying. " 'Try to give actors the space to explore.' "

When Fishburne played Ike Turner in "What's Love Got to Do with It," two years later, part of the energy that fuelled his performance was an ongoing disagreement between him and the director, Brian Gibson, who was white and British. "He was at a crucial moment of his career," Gibson, who died in January, told me. "He wanted to get away from playing heavies, and the real question in the community about Laurence Fishburne was: Can this man be a lead?" Gibson went on, "It was very, very difficult ever to give him a note. He often knew better, genuinely knew better. But sometimes notes were valuable. I remember one particular moment, which actually was one of the more important moments in the film, where Ike has a fight with Tina in the back of a limo. He takes off his shoe and whacks her, and she fights him back for the first time in their relationship. At that moment, we did a closeup. And I remember it was absolute ham—an unusual thing from Laurence because he is one of those people who judge their own performances incredibly well. I remember having to insist quite strongly to do it again, and thank God I did. Had we used that in the film, it probably wouldn't have got an Oscar nomination."

Still, much of the vivid force of the film is due to Fishburne, who rewrote, he says, "ninety per cent of the dialogue" in order to make the character of Ike Turner more than a caricature of a wife-beater, cokehead, and jailbird. "I was trying to humanize it," Fishburne said. "I was trying to give him some dignity. I was trying to make him a person." As Ike, Fishburne—with a pompadour, a pencil-thin mustache, and a brazen leer—could exhibit his own potent sexuality. "He's scary sexy," says Alfre Woodard, who co-starred with Fishburne in the 1997 HBO movie "Miss Evers' Boys." "He's the kind of sexy where your mother would say, 'O.K., this is the point when you get up and leave the room.' It's like, 'I better get out of here. I might follow this fool.' " Fishburne parsed Turner's psyche in such a complicated array of colors—at once ruthless, funny, tragic, terrifying, and lost—that even his ugliness was captivating. "Anybody who can make you like Ike Turner—he's gotta be a great actor," the playwright August Wilson says. "It was a brilliant performance."

Fishburne was thirty-one when "What's Love Got to Do with It" came out, and his career took on new amperage. In an eighteen-month period between 1992 and 1994, he earned an Oscar nomination, an Emmy Award (for a guest appearance on Robert DeNiro's show "Tribeca"), and a Tony (for "Two Trains Running"). "If Fish knew how to sing, he would be able to go up for a Grammy," Singleton says. After delivering a particularly eloquent acceptance speech at the Tony Awards, Fishburne ran into Wilson, who was in the lobby smoking a cigarette. "You've been holding out on me, man," Wilson said. "You're a writer." He pulled a pen from his pocket and handed it to Fishburne. "You should write something," he said. Shortly afterward, Wilson received "Riff Raff" in the mail.

Since his masterly "Othello," in 1995, Fishburne's most challenging roles have been on television (in "Miss Evers' Boys" and Michael Apted's "Always Outnumbered") and on Broadway (as Henry II in the 1999 revival of "The Lion in Winter"). The "Matrix" trilogy took three years of his time, but in those hyperactive futuristic thrillers, where the production design does most of the performing, Fishburne was required to pose more than to act.

For the past year, Fishburne has not acted at all. Instead, he is enjoying a new marriage, a new métier, and a new house. He lives in a two-story yellow villa in the Hollywood Hills, with his wife of a year and a half, the thirty-four-year-old actress Gina Torres—"This is my first home," he says. The house has high, vaulted ceilings; large, uncluttered rooms; tall, arched, glass-panelled doors that look out over Runyon Canyon Park; and a long, open kitchen that seems the size of a bowling alley. His office, where he writes, is the smallest room in the house. On the walls are photos of Bill Cosby, Gandhi, and Bumpy Johnson, and a framed letter from the King of Jordan inviting him to use the country as a location for a film version of Paulo Coelho's 1988 international best-seller "The Alchemist," a spiritual odyssey set in the time of the Inquisition. The film, in which he will star, will be his second directorial outing, and his first script written exclusively for the screen.

On his desk is a well-thumbed volume called "Structuring the Play," and tucked away in a corner is "Playwriting in Process: Thinking and Working Theatrically."

Fishburne, who has no trouble expressing feelings, is rather more challenged by the idea of constructing those feelings on the page. "What the fuck is 'theme'?" he says. "What the fuck is 'structure'? What the fuck is 'tempo'? I know that internally; I don't know it intellectually." In "Riff Raff," which was produced Off Broadway in 1995, with one claustrophobic set and three fine actors, emotion and energy carried the day. However, after writing and directing a messy film adaptation, "Once in the Life" (2000), Fishburne learned the pitfalls of feeling without form. Since then, he has written a second play, a sprawling but promising work entitled "The Complex," which is dedicated to "the wounded child in all of us" and is loosely based on the dilapidated L.A. apartment house all the way out on La Brea, in an area known as the Jungle, where he and Hattie holed up in the early eighties.

Hattie herself, however, is no longer in his life. She and Fishburne have not spoken in three years. She was not invited to his wedding and has never been to his house. In 1994, she complained to the press that her son had been lost to the "sycophantic and bombastic swirl of the Hollywood lifestyle"; in 1996, she went on "Geraldo" to plead poverty and broadcast a sense of entitlement. It was a performance that she is happy to repeat. "I have not gotten a Mother's Day gift, a Christmas gift, none of that," she told me. "I was the sole investor in his career until he stepped out on his own. I haven't gotten a return. The investment just multiplied—it exploded—and I don't have a return."

"She's projecting it, but in reality *she is* the robber baron," says Maurice Watson, who remembers Hattie envying and appropriating Fishburne's success (along with his earnings) in ways that would be hard to admit for a woman who has written of herself, "Hattie consistently shines as an individual, a mother, and a member of the community." Watson says, "She always wanted to go out, to be part of the in-crowd. She had delusions of grandeur. She wanted to be bigger than she was. She wanted to spend more money than she had. She wanted to be running with the Joneses." One day when Fishburne was in his mid-twenties, he went to the bank to withdraw some money. "I had about ten thousand dollars in the bank, and the teller told me that I had only five thousand," he says. When he protested, the teller explained, "Yeah, well, your mother came and took half the money." "She shouldn't have been spending my money, but she was," Fishburne says. "That was the moment I went, 'O.K., this ends.'"

Although Hattie stopped overseeing Fishburne's career in 1984, she can't stop merging her story with his. She gives seminars for parents who want to get their children into show business. ("Laurence Fishburne's Mom will share the steps she took in guiding her son's career from toddler to teen to Academy Award Nominee," a recent press release announces.) In 2000, Fishburne made a stab at reconciliation. He invited his mother to meet Torres at Musso & Frank's, an old Hollywood hangout. "She was completely narcissistic, obviously uncomfortable with the size of her son, with the size of his life," Torres says. "He was so unapologetically happy. It pissed her off." Fishburne took Hattie to meet President Clinton; she also accompanied him to the premiere of the James Bond film "The World Is Not Enough"—a title that proved almost comically prophetic. But Hattie soon reverted to her old, transgressive behavior. "She sent me this tape," Fishburne says. "It had all this mood music in the background. She was speaking in dulcet tones and reminiscing about the old days when she and I were thick as thieves and shit. It was really something that she should have sent to an old boyfriend, not me." He remembers telling her, "I can't be involved in this. I can't live this life with you anymore. I can't be everything and anything you want me to be. I'm a grown man." Now, he says, "I'm waiting for my mother to really be ill, where she can't take care of herself. Then I'll go take care of her."

Fishburne had got married for the first time at the age of twenty-three, to Hajna O. Moss, a dancer and casting director who was a member of the Bahamian royal family. Moss was tall, articulate, and, according to Graham— who refers to her as Fishburne's "mother Part II"—"organizationally controlling." He says, "She had chutzpah that would flatten Capitol Hill and presence that would bend the glass on a CitiBank teller. For me, it was like watching Cruella De Ville." Moss got Fishburne out of his Jimi Hendrix mode; she toned up his language and his wardrobe. "Damn, she knew how to shop," Graham says. "It definitely benefitted his career, the same way that his mom did. But all she wanted to be was rich Mrs. Fishburne. But she wasn't rich enough to be happy, and she wasn't warm enough to be desired." Although they had two children—Langston, in 1987, and Montana, in 1991—and Fishburne adopted Moss's five-year-old nephew, Terrill, they divorced in 1995.

Afterward, according to Graham, Fishburne was "terrified of being trapped again." His relationship with Torres, a Cuban-American who had established herself in Broadway musical theatre, was rocky at the beginning. In their first four years together, they broke up twice. "We had started this wonderful love affair," Torres says. "All the elements were there except commitment." Fishburne had just got divorced, and had, according to Torres, acquired "a bit of a stable." "The last thing he wanted was to get involved," she says. "He didn't know how to function inside a healthy relationship. There was a bit of a saboteur involved." While Torres was in New Zealand playing a warrior princess in rubber hot pants for the TV show "Cleopatra 2525," Fishburne began to "come to terms with the buttons that were installed in him by his mother—the build-me-up-shoot-me-down dynamic he sought in partners," Torres says. After their second breakup, she says, Fishburne "went and sorted himself out."

At opposite ends of their red Viking stove, Fishburne and Torres worked at separate culinary tasks. Fishburne's department was collard greens; Torres's was short ribs. The next day was Thanksgiving, and the short ribs were a supplement to the twenty-three-pound turkey they were preparing. "This is all about cookin' off the bone, baby," Fishburne said, before slicing parsnips for a pasta dish that he eventually passed over the large wooden counter to his three children, who had just flown in from the East.

Four months is the longest that Fishburne has ever gone without seeing his children. Nonetheless, not long ago Langston, who is now sixteen and already a published poet, handed his father a two-hundred-and-thirty-four-page memoir entitled "Diary of a Nomad." "He's gonna have to take space just like everybody else," Fishburne says. "I've done everything I can do. Me pretending to be smaller in the world is not gonna help my son get any bigger." He adds, "I said to them, 'Does it sometimes aggravate you and piss you off that I'm famous?' They said, 'Yeah.' I said, 'Well, guess what? Me, too, but that's just the fucking way it is, it's a by-product of what I do.'"

The question of how the world regards Fishburne came up after I incidentally mentioned that I would be spending the next day at the home of Gordon Davidson, the artistic director of the Mark Taper Forum, with whom, it turned out, Fishburne had a bone to pick. Around the time that Fishburne emerged as a star, in the early nineties, he reclaimed the gravitas of his full name, Laurence Fishburne, but Davidson apparently still addressed him by his eighties moniker, Larry. "Tell that motherfucker my name is not Larry!" Fishburne said, his head swinging from side to side like a dashboard figurine. "My motherfucking name is Laurence! Since you're having fucking Thanksgiving at his house, tell that motherfucker to cut that shit out. And his fucking wife, too. I love him. I've known him all my life but, *God damn,* they make me mad with that shit. Fucking ten years I've been calling myself Laurence! Every time I see this motherfucker, he calls me Larry."

"You were Larry to a lot of people for a very long time," Torres chimed in.

"That is who I was—and it's not who I am," he snapped. "I didn't ask to be billed as Larry Fishburne. That was my name for my friends in my neighborhood as a kid. That's my nick, like Fish. But my professional name, the first gig I ever did, my whole name is 'Introducing Laurence Fishburne III.' In 'Cornbread, Earl, and Me,' my first film, that's how I was billed. If you look at 'Death Wish 2,' you will see that I am billed as Laurence Fishburne III. So, yeah, if I ask somebody to call me Laurence, and they continue to call me Larry, no, I don't like that shit one little fucking bit at all. Sorry. And that ain't got nothing to do with me not knowing my fucking place. That's my fucking name."

In the middle of Fishburne's tirade, the phone rang. He picked it up and, to general laughter, shouted into it, "*Stop fucking calling my house!*"

He continued, "What fucking astonishes me is that people are under this impression that they're not disrespecting me, they're not slighting me at all—they just feel they know me. I understand the nature of what I do is to be publicly available and to reveal the intimate details of my character. I get that. But the fact of the matter is that I have publicly gone on the record and said, 'Yeah, I prefer to be called Laurence.' I decide who I am, what I want to be. You don't get to choose. I don't give a fuck how much money you pay! I don't give a fuck how many movies you watch! Fuck you! This is mine. This right here. Mine. Next in line, these ones right here"—he gestured at his kids. "And Bingo"—his black-and-white English pointer. "And if you don't like it you can fucking get in line to suck my dick! Fuck you!"

He paused, then added, "Anyway, I just thought, maybe, you could pass that on to Gordon."

At the end of the evening, Fishburne said that he wanted to show me something. We climbed into the leather bucket seats of his silver Aston Martin V12 Vanquish, put Mose Allison into the tape deck, and set off for a spin around the two shabby square miles just below his house, which were the backdrop of his early striving. As he pointed out the hotel where he'd stayed with Hattie as a teenager, the church where he'd auditioned for "Two Trains Running," the former Zero Zero Club, where he and other aspiring actors used to meet and get fed, I was still trying to fathom his rant. Naming is claiming. For Fishburne, who says he felt "inappropriately appropriated" in childhood, one of the hardest tasks has been to possess his own life—his talent, his heart, his name.

He stopped the car beside Hollywood High School. Across the length of the large, off-white stucco building were painted portraits, strung like charms on a bracelet, of some local luminaries—Dorothy Dandridge, Judy Garland, Rudolph Valentino, Carol Burnett, Cher, and others. "That's me as Othello," Fishburne said, pointing to the spot between Lana Turner and Cantinflas. "Isn't that great?" He stared at the building for a moment in silence. Then he said, "You know, that makes me feel good, 'cause I walked all over this motherfucker, from Western Avenue to Laurel Canyon Boulevard. I used to walk this motherfucker on the regular. Couldn't catch a break, couldn't get fucking arrested."

On the way back, I asked him what would have happened if he hadn't been successful. "It wasn't about making it," he said. "It was about doing it. I would have gone on the boulevard and created a fucking show and done it on the street. When I was thirty, I was able to go, 'O.K., if you never get to be the guy that we all would love to be, what then? I can make a living.

That's cool.' There was a guy who used to perform on the corner of Hollywood and Cherokee—clown suit and some strange fucking circus music. I
made up my mind when I saw him. If those motherfuckers ain't gonna hire
me to be in a movie, I'll do some shit like that."

The car roared under us as Fishburne turned on the ignition. Then he
accelerated up toward the glinting hills, past the rundown hotels that are
the forlorn landmarks of his struggle—the Magic Hotel, the Highland Gardens, the Montecito—proof, if more were needed, of his spectacular survival. Five minutes later, Fishburne was home.

ANG LEE

BECOMING THE HULK

FROM LAST OCTOBER UNTIL THE end of May, the director Ang Lee was holed up at George Lucas's Industrial Light + Magic, in San Rafael, eleven miles north of San Francisco, working fifteen hours a day with the eponymous star of his eighth film, "The Hulk." Even by superstar standards, the Hulk is exceptional. He is green and, at the height of his powers, stands about fifteen feet tall. He is also completely computer-generated. The challenge for Lee's three-hundred-person visual-effects team was to make the Hulk sufficiently real so that he could coexist on an imaginative level with the movie's flesh-and-blood stars, Nick Nolte, Jennifer Connelly, and Eric Bona. The challenge for Lee himself was to marry his art-house sensibility to the vigorish of a Hollywood summer blockbuster—the first he's attempted. Behind Lee's desk at his temporary office in San Rafael hung a framed birthday card from the Hulk's creators, Marvel Comics. At the top of the card was a drawing of Lee's unassuming, puckish face with its cap of black hair. "Hulk, you're making me angry. You won't like me when I'm angry," Lee said in a cartoon bubble, repeating the character's famous mantra. Below, the Hulk, with his familiar jutting fore-head and a square jaw that made him look like a tinted Bronko Nagurski, complained, "Hulk not understand motivation."

In his comic-book incarnation, the Hulk had little in the way of motivation. Unlike other superheroes, who are agents for good, the Hulk was conceived as a mutant. Part Gargantua and part Green Man, he could not control his power, which, in any case, was neither good nor intelligent; he simply raged when provoked, smashing his world to smithereens. A rampaging manifestation of self-destructiveness, he was a danger to his sane, buttoned-down other half, Bruce Banner, and even to himself. The character was born in 1962 and came of age in the mid-sixties, when the idea of protean transformation fuelled the drug culture and the rock-and-roll revolution—a fantasy of escape from the oppressiveness of the Vietnam War. Hounded, bewildered, strong beyond his ability to calculate, at once a menace and a marvel, the Hulk was the ultimate adolescent daydream. He was as confused as the next man, but more devastating. On-screen, however, Lee has given the Hulk psychological depth; he has reimagined the Hulk's history as part of the universal struggle between patriarchy, repression, and desire, which Lee has spent much of his career exploring. "Everyone has a Hulk inside," Lee has written, "and each of our Hulks is both scary and potentially pleasurable. In fact, it's the pleasure that's the scariest thing of all."

At first glance, it's hard to imagine a Hulk inside Ang Lee. He is, by Hollywood standards, sensationally calm and self-effacing. Short and wiry, with slightly hunched shoulders, he meets the world, as Nick Nolte says, "with a smile and that gentleness coming at you." Even Lee's wife, Jane Lin, a cell biologist at New York Medical College, says, "He has never lost his temper, really. We could never have an argument." Western drama is built on the escalation of tension; Chinese life is built around the reduction of it. Lee is a curious amalgam of both influences. The Chinese have no word for "individualism," and Lee, who is now forty-eight, says that he didn't even think of himself as an adult until the success of his film version of Jane Austen's "Sense and Sensibility," in 1995, and he didn't see himself as "Ang Lee, director" until the release, five years later, of the sleeper hit "Crouching Tiger, Hidden Dragon"—the highest-grossing foreign film ever made and the first Chinese movie to win an international audience.

Because Lee doesn't exude any of the imperialism of self associated with most directors of his stature, he is sometimes difficult to read. Ted Hope, who was a producer of Lee's first three movies—"Pushing Hands" (1992), "The Wedding Banquet" (1993), and "Eat Drink Man Woman" (1994)—quickly discovered that "part of the role I had was getting Ang to say no." Hope remembers looking over at Lee during the filming of a scene in "Pushing Hands": "He was clearly unhappy. I asked him what was the matter. 'The dress.' 'It's a brown dress. You said you liked the brown dress.'

'Yes, I liked the brown dress.' 'Then what's the matter?' He goes, 'Well, I liked the blue dress more.' 'Why didn't you say that?' Ang said, 'Well, you just asked me if I liked the brown dress.'"

Lee doesn't hector; he doesn't bluster; he doesn't insist on his own superiority; and he's not materialistic. He still drives his first car—a 1995 Mercury minivan—prefers sweatsuits, jeans, and sneakers to more elegant attire, and lived, until 1997, in an eight-hundred-and-twenty-five-square-foot three-room apartment in White Plains, New York, where he and his wife slept in the same room as their two sons. (He now lives in Mamaroneck, in a four-bedroom house with seven rare breeds of chickens at the bottom of his garden.) In fact, there is nothing conspicuous about Lee's behavior but his talent. "He has the most quiet footprint, a tremendous humility," Hope says. "He once said to me, describing his process, that movies pass through him."

Still, because Lee likes to find his films as he is making them, he requires from others a special quality of collaboration and from himself a special quality of attention. "Ang is as concentrated as any director I've ever worked with," Nolte says. "He keeps the actor constantly churning. Ang always wants to go beyond and find something new." Emma Thompson, who starred in "Sense and Sensibility," explains, "The quality of listening makes you want to do your best to surprise him, because he's allowing you that space. It's the silent equivalent of somebody like Robert De Niro, whose mumbling makes one lean forward. You don't necessarily see this great intelligence on the surface, but as soon as you come toward it you receive the strength. Ang could always throw us off balance physically, as well as with his words. That's what all creative people need. They need to be pushed off their runnels."

When Lee first met with Nolte to persuade him to play the overreaching scientist David Banner—who murders his wife and turns his son, Bruce, into a literal extension of his own Faustian power—Nolte asked Lee why he wanted to make the movie. "He said, 'I can't make a comic book, but I can make a tragedy,'" Nolte recalls. Lee sees the Hulk as an embodiment of "the unconscious—it doesn't have a logic." He says, "The Hulk is the aggression and the fear and the unknown drive you have in life, which are hiding in the dark, which are not how you want to see yourself." In Lee's case, those turbulent forces translate into only one thing: filmmaking, which he calls "my devil side." For Lee, the making of movies is at once a thrill and a danger, an unsettling explosion of energy, in which greatness and goodness are always at odds. The enterprise tempts him away from normal life and from his family, in pursuit of his own selfish fantasies. It imposes a brutalizing loneliness; it also transforms him into a dictatorial person whose behavior he otherwise would not recognize. In this sense, he says, "The Hulk" has allowed him to visualize his alter ego. "Creativity is the hidden inside—the beast," he says. "To me, the whole process of making the movie is a process of Hulking-out. Any stretch is unnatural. It's nasty because to grow muscle you have to break old muscle. To reach something bigger than who I am, sometimes I cause pain and injury. And I have to hurt myself. It's like Hell. I felt on the verge of exploding—going through a depression—just to reach something. That to me is the experience of 'The Hulk.'" Lee, who in daily life doesn't have "a risk-taking bone in my body," adds, "It's scary, but if I don't touch that scary part I don't feel I'm doing my best. I don't think people should pay their ten bucks to see my worst."

"The Hulk," which has a novel approach to continuity editing and an ingenious multi-panel mode of story-telling, is a significant stylistic stretch for Lee. According to James Schamus, the co-president of Focus Features, who wrote the screenplay for "The Hulk" and has collaborated with Lee on six other screenplays, it is "probably the most technologically ambitious movie ever made." Although the split screen is not news to movies, no previous commercial film has attempted so complex an orchestration of panels that are simultaneously telling its story. The screen becomes a jigsaw, an effect that wittily replicates the comic-book experience. Images emerge, splinter, and dissolve, and these narrative fragments both drive the plot forward and generate tension. "You see both sides without intercutting," Lee says. "It allows the actor to breathe and to perform undisturbed by editing."

Lee, who is often described as a master of genres, is actually a mixer of them. In "Crouching Tiger, Hidden Dragon," for instance, he combined the light-hearted sensibility of kung-fu movies with the more reflective Taoist way. In "The Hulk," he plays a similar game with American culture. The film is a cinematic equivalent of three-card monte—a brazen act of prestidigitation, able to get away with much more than first meets the eye. Lee is creating both "kick-ass action" and art; he is merging the intellectual depth of drama and the surface sensationalism of cartoons; he is attempting to make both a myth and a bundle, or, as he puts it, "a delicacy of fast food."

In Lee's office, the influences that he was trying to merge onscreen faced each other from opposite walls. On one side were some of the inspirations for his cinematic palette: de Chirico for the colors and shapes of the Southwest, where part of the movie is set; Maxfield Parrish for the sky tones; Rousseau and the Hudson River School painters for the sense of scale; Picasso's Dora for the montage of tension; and Cézanne for everything else. On the other side, interspersed with moody comic-strip panels, were the swirling patterns of William Morris and Jackson Pollock. "The internal look," Lee said, inspecting the amoeba-like shapes of the Morris pattern. "The Hulk made me want to work with scale. But what's happening to him is something dim and small. It's in his cells. I found that these paintings look a lot like molecular things and also they have a cosmic look."

Like the Hulk and Bruce Banner, Lee inhabits a world of physical and emotional contradiction: big-small, clumsy-masterly, outsider-insider. Taiwanese by birth, he has lived in the United States since 1978 but has never applied for citizenship. He sees himself as "watercress floating on the water—I don't feel deeply rooted anywhere." Filmmaking is, he says, his way of "anchoring myself to the world." Through his movies, he can take imaginative possession of the landscapes from which he feels detached. "I have to create that culture to own it," he says. "I try to make something that I don't really belong to and make it work. It's a process of planting myself into it." He adds, "I live in people's imaginations, not the land I'm standing on." In "Crouching Tiger," he invented the China he never knew; in "The Ice Storm" (1997), his adaptation of Rick Moody's portrait of suburban American anomie, he captured the era just prior to his arrival in the United States; in "Ride with the Devil" (1999), a Civil War saga about bushwhackers in Missouri, he explored the sources of Yankee imperialism as part of his effort, he says, "to transform myself as American." With "The Hulk," Lee has "planted" himself at the center of the pop-culture landscape, not only by making his first Hollywood studio movie but also by weaving his own body quite literally into its drama.

Twice a week for nine months, in sessions that lasted up to eight hours, Lee donned a body suit studded with sensors that allowed computers to read and catalogue his movements, and went through the arduous task of enacting the Hulk's every possible gesture and facial expression. Lee had begun by using other actors, but for key emotional moments he took over the job himself. The work had some side benefits. "I got to yell and let aggression out," Lee says. "It was very therapeutic." Frederick Elmes, his cinematographer, says, "Something inside him allowed him to let go. He would actually roar a little bit, look up at the ceiling and scream. There was one point when he did such a good job that the second take was sort of just for him, because it felt good."

When the Banners, Jr. and Sr., face off in the final ferocious battle of "The Hulk," what's at stake is the son's power. "I need your strength," David tells Bruce. "I gave you life, now you must give it back to me." Lee, of course, never dared to fight this way with his own father. "I belong to him," he says. "I am an extension of his life." Lee's father, Lee Sheng, the principal of Taiwan's distinguished Tianan First Senior High School, was thirty-seven, and by the standards of the times rather old, when his first son, Ang, was born, in 1954. (Lee has older twin sisters, Wen and Ken, who are accountants, and a younger brother, Khan, who is a film director and playwright in Taiwan.) Lee Sheng had been raised on the mainland as part of the landlord class, and was the only member of his family to survive the Maoist purges. He escaped to Taiwan and eventually married Shu Zwan Yang, an elementary school teacher, but, Lee explains, "He felt very lonely. He had to start the Lee family again." He adds, "In his generation, there was a lot of insecurity, because they'd seen everything disappear and people get killed. He wanted me to be useful, respectable, do something solid."

The family had a cook, a gardener, and a housekeeper, so the main requirement of Lee's childhood was study. "In Chinese culture, the only way to rise above your class is through study," Lee says. "Everything is the book, the book, the book. I'm the creative type. How can I focus on a book, on what people tell me to do?" The absent-minded Lee sometimes forgot his school bag on the bus, and once at lunch, he recalls, "I was so spaced out I fell back in my chair, literally tipped over." Lee Sheng was a stern, didactic presence, whose household was built on the Confucian bulwark of filial duty. He generally took his meals with the family in silence. "He'd finish in five minutes and leave the table," Lee says. "You'd be praying he wouldn't talk. If he talks, it's about something you'd have to be worried about." According to Lee, his father had "a big temper." "I'd really get on his nerves," Lee says. "What would happen? A yell, a smack, whatever. I'd get scared. I'd behave. Then, after a while, I'd drift away again." He continues, "The way I grew up, you take orders until one day you're old enough to give orders. That's how it works. We don't communicate. We don't debate. We don't explain." Inevitably, in this climate of obedience and obligation—"There was no love of art or creativity, not to mention the entertainment business"— Lee grew up feeling "repressed, inert, shy." Bounded by his bedroom's blue walls and his window, which overlooked a bamboo chicken coop, he took refuge in kung-fu fantasies and directed adventure scenes in his head— scenes, he says, that never had "myself in action." On Saturdays, he occasionally saw movies. At one film about lovers who can't speak their feelings for fear of their fathers' disapproval, Lee recalls weeping so loudly "that the other people in the row, who had also been crying, would suddenly get quiet and wonder who was making the noise." When Lee took his college-entrance exams, he says, he suffered a kind of psychological block. "I was too frightened, I think," he adds. "I almost blacked out." He failed, and then failed a second time. To this day, he has a recurring nightmare: "I always dream of taking some sort of maths exam. I wake up sweating." Afraid of failing the exam a third time and being forced to do his military service right away, Lee took up what his family considered the lowliest of nonacademic options. At eighteen, he entered the Art Academy of Taiwan, in Taipei, as an acting student. He had always seen himself as being like his mother, a perception with which his galled father seemed to agree. "She's very good-tempered, reliant, subordinate, and nervous," Lee says. But onstage, to his surprise, Lee was a different person. "I was actually good at it," he says. "I made sense. When I stood onstage, I felt very tall. I wasn't shy." He adds, "I got results. I was the best actor in the school. I won national prizes."

In 1978, Lee applied to the undergraduate theatre program at the University of Illinois and was accepted. (To convince his father of the wisdom of this move, he suggested that he would return to Taiwan as a professor, with "at least a master's degree.") But in America he soon discovered that his haphazard command of English was a major obstacle. "Every word I would check," he says. "It was quite painful. I would take ten hours to read a script that everyone else read in an hour." Lee realized that he wouldn't be able to act under these circumstances, and he switched to the directing program. He studied plays by Brecht, Pinter, O'Neill, and Tennessee Williams, whose words, he says, "talked back to me." He goes on, "I only understood about half of what was going on, but just the look of Western theatre struck me in a big way. You exert your feelings. You outcry. You use drama to do the bangs and through that purge your feelings. It was a big culture shock to me. You've got to verbalize conflict onstage. I got very good at it."

During his first week on campus, Lee went on an outing to a Little League game in Gary, Indiana, with a car full of Taiwanese exchange students. "They were from good colleges and doing science, agriculture, and medicine, and I was still a transfer undergrad in theatre, which is almost laughable," he remembers. On that bus, Lee met his future wife, Jane Lin, an independent, outspoken graduate student in microbiology (on whom Lee later based aspects of the fierce, intrepid character Yu Shu Lien in "Crouching Tiger"). "I never pursued a woman," Lee says. She came and talked to me. She's a good listener, and she has the smallest ego of anybody I know. I was a shy guy, but I was a future director—I had that ego thing and I wanted to express it. I couldn't find anybody to listen to me. And there she was, interested in what I did." Lin also remembers their meeting. "I could be a chair. I could be a bucket of water. It doesn't matter, he just talks—about everything," she says. "I fall asleep, I wake up, he's still talking." Lin soon became Lee's primary source of emotional support. She remembers that, after directing a production of Ionesco's "The Chairs," in which the husband ended up sitting in his wife's lap, Lee would often sit in hers. "It was kind of a jest, but very comforting," says Lin, who is five feet four to Lee's five-seven. "I'm strong, and he used to be very, very skinny."

After two years at Illinois, Lee decided that he wanted to direct movies, not plays. In theatre, he felt, it was acting, not directing, that "carries the scene." Onscreen, however, the moving image could bridge the impasse of language. "I see making movies as a part of acting—both are about expressing yourself, exposing your inner feelings, provoking other people's emotions," he says. In his spare time at the academy in Taipei, Lee had made two Super-8 films, one an eighteen-minute silent movie about a kite, for which he was cameraman, director, and editor. "The editing machine was just a splicer. I had no viewer, so I estimated," he said. "It was quite innovative—it had a free style." Those films got him accepted, in 1980, at New York University's film school. "Things were much easier there," he says. "I was the top student right away." Lee's second-year student film won him a scholarship; his thesis, "Fine Line," a romantic caper about the clash of cultures in Little Italy and Chinatown, proved his ability to handle different genres (and featured the film debut of Chazz Palminteri). Lee dismisses it now as "an exercise" in which he "didn't have anything to say." By the time he graduated, in 1984, he had come to the unhappy conclusion that "there was no way a Chinese speaker could make a movie in the States." As he recounts in Stephen Lowenstein's book "My First Movie":

> I decided to go back to Taiwan. . . . But before I went I wanted . . . at least to show the film ["Fine Line"] at the school's film festival. I realized later that it was a big deal because a lot of people were from outside film school and a lot of Asians were watching. Anyway, I was packing up all my stuff. . . . I got a phone call and they said, "This guy from William Morris is looking for you." And I said, "William who?" Anyway, an agent said, "Why don't you stay here . . . ?" "There's no way, I'm gone," I said. He said, "You'll be working, blah, blah, blah." The Hollywood type. The next day my film won the Best Picture and Best Director of that year. . . . And my baby was only a month old.

In 1983, Lin and Lee had decided to get married, for the benefit of Lee's father. "That was the year his father retired," Lin says. "Chinese always like to have double happiness." Lin's mother, however, was disappointed at the prospective match. "She said, 'Why did you pick this one, with all the other nice boys around—engineering and regular people?" Lin recalls. "I said, 'I earn my own living. I can choose whoever I want.'" Lee worked two incidents from his wedding day into the comedy of "The Wedding Banquet": the hasty, matter-of-fact ceremony at City Hall, and the drunken groom getting his new wife pregnant on their wedding night.

Their union, in the early years, proved to be a marriage of inconvenience. Haan was born in 1984. Lin, who had never even held a child before, struggled to care for him on her own and finish her Ph.D., while Lee, caught in development hell, shuttled between Illinois, New York, and Los Angeles. In 1986, the family went to stay with friends in Chappaqua so that they could be together while Lee was hunting for work in New York. But the situation was far from ideal. Their room was cold. They worried that they were disturbing their friends, who didn't have children. "We felt trapped," Lin says. Lee recreated that sense of isolation and tension in his first feature, "Pushing Hands," in which a retired Tai Chi master, who was persecuted by the Red Guard, comes to live in his son's suburban American home. "Let me tell you," the father says to his son, whose American wife suffers her father-in-law's cohabitation with palpable irritation, "compared to loneliness, persecution is nothing." Every day, after Lin left for work at a lab in Valhalla, Lee walked a mile and a half to a tennis court in Pleasantville—"just to hit, hit, hit," Lin says. "It was nothing to do with tennis." When Lee went to the West Coast on one of his development junkets, Lin felt deserted; she briefly considered divorce.

In 1986, they finally got their own apartment, in White Plains—the first floor of a two-story mock-Colonial, looking out over a rolling sward of grass and a cluster of trees—and the surface of life improved. The family slept together in one bedroom; Lee wrote scripts in the other. In the evenings, they'd stroll through the neighborhood to a farmhouse where George Washington had stayed and from the plateau survey the sprawling ribbon of city traffic below. "We had a very simple life," Lin says. "We were happy about little things." But Lee could not get to the next step in his career. "At film school, we had experience of short films," he says. "It took me years to realize that feature films—the structure, the character development—are a very different ballgame." He wrote scripts and his agent

got him work as a production assistant, but his attention to the details of
other people's movies was slipshod, and he was not rehired. Lin supported
the family, while Lee became a sort of househusband. He played with his
son. He cooked. He wrote occasional articles for Chinese newspapers. And
he tried to decide what to do. "Everything had been turned down," he told
Stephen Lowenstein. "It was just awful. I pretty much sank to the bottom."
He explains, "If I'm not making a movie, I'm like a dead person. Jane basically let me be. She lived her own life, and if I went too crazy, and it looked
like I was freaking out, she'd take me to Kentucky Fried Chicken"—one of
his favorite places to eat. "All those sleepless nights," Lin recalls. "For a long
time I thought that was how we would be for the rest of our lives. He's just
going to talk about these things, and a movie's never going to be made. I
decided you cannot judge a person by whether or not he works."

By the time their second son, Mason, was born, in 1990, Lee was
thirty-six and had little to show for his endeavors. He had twenty-three dollars in his bank account. A few months earlier, in the hope of winning a
sixteen-thousand-dollar screenplay prize set up by the Taiwanese government, he had dashed off a first draft of "Pushing Hands" and included in
his submission a script he'd written some years before—"The Wedding
Banquet"—which he had put aside, because "it was Chinese so they
couldn't make it in America, and it's gay so it couldn't be made in Taiwan."
In late 1990, he got word that the screenplays not only had won the competition's two top prizes but had also earned him the support of the new head
of Taiwan's Central Motion Pictures, who offered to put nearly four hundred thousand dollars toward the making of "Pushing Hands."

Two weeks after winning the contest, Lee walked into the New York offices
of Good Machine, a company that Ted Hope and James Schamus had
recently founded to produce low-budget movies. The first thing Lee said
was "If I don't make a movie soon, I think I'll die." "It was clear when Ang
left the room why he had not made a movie in six years," Schamus says.
"The idea of flying this guy to Los Angeles for a story meeting—forget
it. When he left the office, I turned to Ted and said two things. One was
'Boy, this guy can't pitch his way out of a paper bag.' And two: 'He wasn't
pitching a movie, he was describing a movie he'd already made. He just

needs somebody to realize it.'" Schamus goes on, "It wasn't as if there was magic in the room, but there was enough. At the end of the meeting, I said, 'This guy's a filmmaker.'" The encounter changed all of their lives. Lee had finally met the collaborators who had his measure.

"Part of James's role"—while working with Lee on screenplays—"was making sure that what was in Ang's head was on the page," says Hope, who filled a similar role on the set as Lee's assistant director for "Pushing Hands." Schamus was able to translate, as well as negotiate, American manners and idioms. "Being a foreigner, you look dumber, your speech is slower," Lee says. "People who have a lot of money to throw around, they feel unconfident because you don't look confident. I just wasn't American enough." Schamus, with his knowledge of film culture, the film business, and film writing, was a triple godsend. Where Lee was angular and contained, and, in social situations, could seem almost dull, Schamus was round, buoyant, and full of ideas, which spilled out of his head in a rush of literate words. "Even if Ang had grown up as an American kid, there is something in his psychic constitution that would have been difficult for him to translate," Schamus says. "While the rest of us are dealing with things on a manifest level, the conversation that's going on in Ang's head is on a plane that is completely latent. It stays below the surface, but it's very powerful." Lee will often say, "Let me think about that for a moment," and then do just that. He ponders either with his head down and his hands clasped together on his chest or while holding his right hand against his cheek—a position that Emma Thompson calls his "apogee of distress." "There is the strategy of the entire movie in his head," Hope says. "Ang's aware of the little nuances and gestures of both what we've shot and recorded and of how he anticipates covering the scene."

Lee's first three films—his Chinese trilogy—explore the dilemma of translation between the East and the West. The screenplays themselves, as Schamus writes in an introduction to two of them, "were written in Chinese, then translated into English, rewritten in English, translated back into Chinese, and eventually subtitled in Chinese and English and a dozen other languages." The Lee-Schamus process is a testament to the trust between the two men. "I go into my hole to write," Schamus says. "I emerge to give him pages. But there's very little of that standing over my shoulder. He will let me roam and screw up. What he wants to know, as I'm writing the stuff, is why. Why are we making the movie? What's so interesting about that? What's the theme? The topic? He trusts we'll get there. But he also knows that he will not be able to make a good movie unless he has the answer to those questions." In the case of "The Wedding Banquet" (which was the most profitable film of 1993, based on budget-to-box-office ratio, surpassing even "Jurassic Park"), Lee kept sending back Schamus's pages, insisting that the psychology of the characters was not Chinese enough. "Finally, in frustration, I'd simply give up and write the scenes as 'Jewish' as I could make them," Schamus writes. "'Ah-ha,' Ang would respond on reading the draft. 'Very Chinese!'"

"When I stayed home a lot," Lee has said, "I thought about the old Chinese teaching regarding the essence of life: the only thing you can count on is that everything will change. That gave me a feeling of what I wanted to say about life. It's about people's adjustment to change. And for a Chinese person the biggest change is the value of change itself." He went on, "You become a Westerner and you betray your parents. Something you feel unable to deal with: total guilt." In each of Lee's first three films, a patriarchal figure is propelled progressively closer to the West. In "Pushing Hands," the emotionally dispossessed Tai Chi master struggles with the Western notion of family; in "The Wedding Banquet," a Taiwanese former general and his wife, in order to have a grandchild, reach a sort of stalemate with their married gay son, who lives in New York; in "Eat Drink Man Woman," the father figure—a master chef with three adult daughters, who longs to marry the girl next door—is himself infected with a Western hankering for self-fulfillment. For all three, Lee chose the same actor, Lung Sihung (who died while Lee was shooting "The Hulk"). "When he's not speaking, you feel the pain in his face," Lee said of Liung. "Inside he's getting weaker, but he has to hold up that face so that order will keep going in society. He plays up to his role, but he's losing his grip with the young people." The trilogy, Lee says, "was about me, me, me."

After so much fallow time, Lee made his first five movies in five years. And as his confidence grew he repeatedly raised the bar of his narrative challenges. In the trilogy, he went from a modest two-character drama to ensemble dramas; next, he progressed from a British period piece—"Sense and Sensibility"—to "The Ice Storm" 's medley of eight story lines in suburban America ("It might as well have been science fiction to me," Lee said). In "Ride with the Devil"—a critical flop, in which beautiful action set pieces are undermined by an ambling narrative—he struggled with the dilemmas of the Civil War South. Then, having done his Western, he did what can only be called an Eastern: the Chinese-language action epic "Crouching Tiger, Hidden Dragon," for which he discovered what he calls "an abstract form of filmmaking, where the images and editing are like a dance and music." By incorporating character and story into the conventions of kung fu, Lee took martial arts out of the realm of special effects and into the realm of the mystical. In "The Hulk," he takes what he learned about visual effects in "Crouching Tiger" to a new level of complexity and expressiveness. "Ang has been very clear not to define himself, both in teens of the genres he picks and the characters the audience may sympathize with," Hope says.

Still, there are certain motifs that crop up throughout his œuvre. "All the leading men in my movies are indecisive," Lee says. "All the women characters are very decisive. That's my experience." He goes on, "By nature, I'm indecisive. I get pulled both ways." Lee incorporates this personal limitation into the drama of his characters: the father torn between cultures in "Eat Drink Man Woman," the husband torn between women in "The Ice Storm," the young bushwhacker torn between violence and family in "Ride with the Devil." Lee's directing method is also tantalizingly open-ended. "His desire and his meaning are always left a bit open to discussion," Hope says. "Some directors are very much about the image; others are about performance. Ang is involved in all aspects of the movie—cinematography, production design, editorial, music. This lack of specificity caused everyone on the crew to always be reaching."

"In my culture, you're part of the group," Lee says. "You have to find harmony, so you repress, repress, repress. So far, repression is my biggest source of creativity. Repression—release. Repression—acceleration. That's a good story." This sense of psychological constriction is handled by Lee most brilliantly in "The Ice Storm," where nature provides an uncanny metaphor for the emotional collapse of the characters. But Lee's first study of the connection of repression to landscape came in his fourth film, "Sense and Sensibility," which he made for less than sixteen million dollars. Emma Thompson, who wrote the screenplay, which won an Academy Award, and who played Elinor Dashwood, the pragmatic elder daughter, was sold on the idea of using Lee as her director after watching "Eat Drink Man Woman." "It very much connected to Jane Austen," she says. "It was sisters with a difficult father talking to each other. At one point, the eldest sister says to the younger, 'What do you know of my heart?' I gasped. It's actually the same line in 'Sense and Sensibility' Exactly the same line." Still, Lee's distance from the English language—and from that watershed moment in British history when patriarchy and capitalism collided—called out of him a more fluid visual expression. "There's a sense of landscape as character that I think would have escaped me," Thompson says. "He was always looking for exactly the right field, exactly the right place for us to sit, which expanded the conversation so that narrative and landscape bled into one another." Lee says, "I didn't have to do that when I did Chinese films, because it's all about words—the things I want to say. But because of the language barrier I couldn't really talk with the English actors that much."

"Ang would always come up to you and say something unexpectedly crushing," recalls Thompson, whom Lee urged not to "look so old." His first note to Kate Winslet, who played Marianne, the spirited younger sister, was "You will do better." Hugh Grant, who played the shy Edward Ferrars, nicknamed him Fang and, later, the Brute. At the wrap party, Winslet and Thompson and other cast members rewrote the Rolling Stones' song "Angie" and serenaded their director: "Ang Lee / I still love you / Remember all those nights we cried." Now Lee can laugh at the memory, but on the set the clash of cultures confounded everyone for a while. On the first day of shooting, Lee was filming Thompson and Grant as their characters, meeting for the first time, strolled in a garden. Lee wanted to film it in long-shot to convey an atmosphere of expectation. The actors tried it, and then suggested shooting the scene from a different angle. Lee took umbrage at what seemed to them a normal query. He was awake all night, and I was awake all night, both of us feeling dreadful," Thompson says. As she wrote in her diary, "In the event his idea was much better than ours, but that we should have had an idea at all came as a genuine shock, and he was hurt and confused." In Taiwan, I am emperor," Lee said afterward. "Here, I am President."

Lee's emphasis on framing and background is not unusual, given his origins. "Westerners and Asians literally see different worlds," Richard Nisbett, a social psychologist, writes in "The Geography of Thought." "Modern Westerners see a world of objects—discrete and unconnected *things*. . . . Modern Asians are inclined to see a world of substances—continuous masses *of matter*." On each project, Lee submerges himself and his actors in the deeper context of their story. He assigns homework for almost all his films. Before the making of "Sense and Sensibility," as Thompson noted in her diary, he asked for "character studies" and offered a list of questions, "mostly addressing background and 'inner life.'" (When Winslet handed in a twenty-page analysis of Marianne, he told her that it was "wrong, all wrong.") To prepare himself for "The Ice Storm," Lee amassed a huge dossier, which the cinematographer Frederick Elmes calls "an encyclopedia of what the early seventies were like: Where was the war at? What was Johnny Carson wearing? What was on television? What were the hair styles?"

For "The Hulk," Lee examined molecular growth, blood cells, galaxies, and, as Dennis Muren, Industrial Light + Magic's senior visual-effects supervisor, says, "how there's some connection in the universe that makes everything work: a kind of yin-yang thing he wanted to get into the story." Lee also collected twenty-four boxes of rocks—"their texture shows the flow of time, they remind you that the universe is kind of a big pot of soup," he says—as well as lichen, starfish, and jellyfish, whose shapes were intended to help his collaborators imagine the Hulk's dissonant interior. "He made us feel the rocks and lichen and asked us what we felt," Nolte recalls. "Ang spins a cocoon that is so complex that the actor can't find his way out—he has to live his way out."

I met up with Lee in Los Angeles at the end of May, on the scoring stage at Twentieth Century Fox—a nondescript barn of a building whose only distinguishing feature is a topiary hedge trimmed in the shape of a bass fiddle. He was in position at a behemoth soundboard beside the composer Danny Elfman, a veteran of fifty-five films, who had turned out "The Hulk"'s edgy hundred-and-seven-minute score in a record thirty-seven days. The hundred-piece orchestra behind a glass panel in front of Lee had spent the previous eight days recording, and many of the musicians, along with Elfman, were drinking wheat-grass shooters with their orange juice for a hit of New Age energy. When I got there, they were scoring a scene—projected above them on a large screen—in which a series of Army tanks chase the Hulk across the desert. Elfman, like an infantryman calling up ordnance, was dropping Eastern timpani, Bombay strings, and Mongolian chants into the score. "We use a lot of drums, because the drum is the most primal," Lee said.

By the beginning of June, the fine-tuning of the music, the tweaking of imagery, the shuttling between L.A. and San Rafael, and the fifteen-hour days were over; after two years of work, Lee delivered the final print to the studio and went home to his family—to what he calls his "angel side." "When I first decided to be a filmmaker, I thought it was my way of acting," he says. "Then it became my ultimate expression. Now it's just the texture of my life. It's not so much expression anymore. It consumes me." As a result, Lee sees little of his wife and family. In a diary passage, Emma Thompson describes standing beside him during the shooting of "Sense and Sensibility" as he looked out mournfully over an estuary: "After a moment, he said, waving towards the water, 'Tide goes in, tide goes out, tide goes in, tide goes out—and still no sex.'"

This spring, with the thirteen-year-old Mason in tow, Lin paid a visit to the set. She sat at the back of the projection room while Lee talked and gave strict notes to the artist handling the multi-panel screen. Lin, who her husband says "has a problem with authority," had never seen him in director mode. Afterward, she told Lee, "If I worked for you, I'd kill you." "She's probably right," Lee says. "I'm too picky. But in life I'm not picky at all. It's like I don't know what to do. If I don't make movies, there's nothing you can respect me for." When he's on the job, he calls Lin once a week; on school holidays, his sons visit him on the set. On the scoring stage, as he and Elfman worked up the moody accents under the film, Lee paused long enough to call Haan at Brown University, where he is a freshman. "It's Babi," he said to an answering machine. "Have a great birthday. It's six o'clock." "I'm a strange dad," he acknowledges. "For six years, I laid a very solid emotional foundation to our relationship, which I bank from for the rest of my life. Now I don't see them, but the foundation is there."

On the set, Lee says, "my job is telling people what I want, but when I get home it's back to life—what she wants." "My biggest job is bringing him down to earth," Lin says. "It takes more and more of an adjustment for him. He knows he has to get real when I'm around." At home, Lee is cast, he says, in the role of "the third boy in the family—the naughtiest one." "He gets yelled at more than the kids," Lin says. "He feels very secure being yelled at." He is resentful when Lin works late at the lab. "I try to get used to it," he says. "But when I'm done working I need a lot of nurturing from her." Lee claims to be very "lacklustre" when he isn't working. "I don't have a hobby," he says. "I don't have a life." His main activity is cooking for the family. For Lee, as for the father in "Eat Drink Man Woman," cooking is a gesture of affection; the boys, he says, prefer his food to the junk she gives them," and the only way "I can show my emotion is to feed them." For her part, Lin considers cooking "a waste of time" and sometimes doesn't even arrive home in time for Lee's feasts. "They don't wait for me anymore," she says. "Otherwise I get upset. I think that's a violation of my rights."

"The Hulk," with its technical complexities and its blockbuster potential, has kept Lee away from his family even longer than his other films. He is accustomed to art-house openings—a few prints in a few theatres in New York and L.A., "and gradually building up from word of mouth." "Crouching Tiger" cost twelve million dollars to make, and Lee had to contribute his salary to get it done. "The Hulk" is another matter: its budget was about a hundred and fifty million, and the initial print order was for fourteen thousand copies. "Size does matter," Lee says. "I've experienced things I never experienced before—the marketing. It's just another world. They're marketing everything that's green." From garbage bags to skateboards, more than a hundred and fifty items will be issued with a "Hulk" logo on them. And, to appeal to the teen market, Lee agreed to have the song "Set Me Free"—performed by several former Guns 'N Roses members with Suicidal Tendencies' Dave Kushner and the Stone Temple Pilots singer Scott Weiland—play over the final credits.

So at the end of a long day of scoring he found himself making a courtesy call at Conway Studios, on Melrose Avenue, where the band was being filmed performing the song. As Lee's car rolled through the studio gates into a sort of hallucinogenic tropical oasis—with fairy lights decorating palm fronds and candles lighting the brick path to the recording bungalow—he confessed under his breath that this would be his first visit to a rock recording session. While he waited for the band to arrive, Lee, who is a sports fan, sat in a leather chair in the control room watching an N.B.A. playoff game; at the station break, an advertisement for "The Hulk" came on the screen. Eventually, a collection of thin, tattooed, long-haired men of a certain middle age swaggered in. "So how's it going?" a frizzy-haired rocker with leather pants, sneakers, and what looked like a key chain attached to his nose asked Lee. "I hope you're gonna get the song out there," he added. "Gonna sit in with us? Maybe play some cowbells?" Lee smiled and turned to me. "That's Splash," he said. "Slash," his assistant said. While the members of the band performed the song four times with their backs to Lee, and Weiland tried to situate himself as close as possible to the handheld camera, the sound engineer stood at his console, like Little Richard at the piano, his long hair juddering to the drummer's ear-splitting downbeat. Lee seemed unfazed. The next morning, at the scoring studio, where Elfman was quietly making adjustments to the sound, Lee suddenly pushed his chair back, waved his arms, and started bouncing to the music like the Conway Studio engineer. "You're, like, boring," he said to Elfman.

On a private jet shuttling him back that afternoon to a sound-mixing studio at George Lucas's Skywalker Ranch, Lee put his feet up on a seat and considered his career. "Moviemaking is never as good as what you imagine," he said. "Any good idea that's floating in the air—that's the best. Then you have to bring it down so people can see it, fix it on celluloid. You have to make the most of that celluloid fixture." To Lee, "shooting is like buying groceries and the real cooking is at the editing table." The customers require a story and a satisfactory ending, and Lee, as he pointed out, "has to deliver the goods." "But to me it's more about sequences," he said. "Certain feelings. A certain taste. That's more important than telling the story." He went on, "You make a movie for moments, and you need an excuse to put those moments in—you need structure." His films abound in those ineffable moments: an elaborate Chinese meal being prepared in "Eat Drink Man Woman"; Marianne running up a rain-swept hill in "Sense and Sensibility";

the motif of reflections in "The Ice Storm"; the treetop fight in "Crouching Tiger"; the Hulk hanging forlornly onto the fuselage of a jet as it flies into the stratosphere. These are sequences that still give Lee the sense of wonder and innocence and truth that he calls "the aroma." He wasn't sure where he'd go in pursuit of his next moment, but one story he was thinking of was Houdini's. "People come to see him die," he said. "That's very appealing to me. Big showmanship, big escape. Showing people you're not bound by anything. It's inspiring." The plane started its bumpy descent to the Oakland airport. Lee drifted away for a moment, then he looked over at me. "That's a big part of art, what art is," he said. "You strip down. It's yourself that people can see. They have to see you take the risk."

DAME EDNA EVERAGE

PLAYING POSSUM

MARCH 8, 1989. IT'S 3 P.M., BUT the marquee above the Theatre Royal Drury Lane, the oldest and most venerable of London's theatres, has already been switched on. Passersby as far away as Covent Garden can pick out the sign's blinking red neon message: "DAME EDNA'S SECOND COMING—SHE'S BACK BECAUSE SHE CARES."

In England's rich and vicious eighties, "caring" was high concept that became high parody. Margaret Thatcher, caricatured on the cover of *The Spectator* as a Dame Edna look-alike, complete with pink diamante glasses, assured the nation that the Tories cared. "Labour Cares" was the theme of the Opposition. And Dame Edna, always up to the minute, was repeating her 1987 revue, and raking in approximately a hundred and sixty thousand pounds a week from selling out the Drury Lane's twenty-two hundred and forty-five seats, because she, too, cared. "I mean that in a very caring, nurturing way," Dame Edna was fond of saying after delivering a particularly low blow. The maneuver was in keeping with the vindictive style of the times, and so was the title of Dame Edna's 1987 show, "Back with a Vengeance!" By the late eighties, revenge on liberalism was such a blatant part of the English political climate that maliciousness—Dame Edna's stock-in-trade—could be uninhibitedly flaunted. And Dame Edna was nothing if not uninhibited and illiberal.

Dame Edna had announced herself to the critics and the newspapers weeks before the opening of the 1989 show—"Back with a Vengeance! The Second Coming"—and had done it in her own inimitable style: "My gynaecologist, my numerologist, my biorhythmologist, my T'ai-Chi instructor, my primal scream therapist, and my aromatherapist all tell me that I will be at the height of my powers as a woman from March 9, 1989, for a strictly limited season." The press release, featuring a Russian Constructivist logo and a clenched fist full of gladioli, added, "It's not so much a show, more a private audience. And since I'm writing my autobiography this could just be one of the last chances you have of seeing me before my millennium comeback. DO YOURSELVES A FAVOUR—See the Turn of the Century *before* the turn of the century." This was not a conventional press release, but then Dame Edna is not a conventional person. Dame Edna is, in fact, a theatrical phenomenon: the only solo act to play (and fill) the Drury Lane since it opened for business, in 1663, with Beaumont and Fletcher's "The Humorous Lieutenant." *The Observer* named Dame Edna "one of the idols of the 80s," and the public keeps faith with her. The 1987 "Back with a Vengeance!," which ran nine months and played to capacity, had the third-highest advance in the history of London's West End—exceeded only by "Phantom of the Opera" and "Chess." For the thirty-one shows in Dame Edna's 1989 season, the box office had six hundred thousand pounds in advance sales the day before opening. Television had won Dame Edna an even wider popularity and a new theatregoing audience. In the autumn of 1987, a seventh of the British Isles, or about eight million three hundred thousand people, representing 48.7 per cent of the network share, tuned in to "The Dame Edna Experience" in prime time—at ten-thirty on a Saturday night—to watch Dame Edna, the supremo of narcissists, treat the celebrity guests on her TV talk show like audiovisual aids.

But Dame Edna's influence on the imagination of British culture is best registered by how she has been incorporated into some of the most cherished English institutions. Dame Edna has opened the Harrods Sale, turned on Regent Street's Christmas lights, played a cameo role in the long-running radio soap opera "The Archers," and twice been a radio guest on that surest barometer of British success "Desert Island Discs." Dame Edna has sung in the Royal Albert Hall, when two thousand people in two nights heard her cantata "The Song of Australia." A street has been named after her in Moonee Ponds, the suburb of Melbourne from which she hails. She is one of four Australians whose waxwork effigies are on display at Madame Tussaud's. And the College of Heraldry has drawn up Dame Edna's coat of arms, which bears the motto "I Share and I Care," with the heraldic symbols of crossed gladioli, a funnel-web spider, a blowfly, and the Sydney Opera House. "Dame Edna has been notionally advanced to GBE, so that she qualifies for armorial supporters," the *Times* of London reported in 1982. "They are a shark and a possum, both wearing butterfly glasses."

Dame Edna has also blitzed the commercial world. Between 1981, in a previous season at the Drury Lane, and 1989, Dame Edna's billing, while always monumental, underwent a subtle shift, from "housewife/superstar" to "megastar." She is now, like the celebrities of whom she is a parody, a multinational corporation of one, who franchises every last particle of her persona that the public will buy. And it will buy a lot. Dame Edna is a spokesperson for an airline and an electrical-appliance company. Her piercing singing voice, which sounds like an outback Jerry Colonna, is on tape cassettes doing both disco versions of rock-and-roll standards and her own golden oldies, like "Niceness," "The Night We Burnt My Mother's Things," and "Every Mother Wants a Boy Like Elton." There are mugs ("A Dame Edna Everage Beverage"), badges ("I'm Into Edna"), and even imitation Dame Edna eyeglasses. These yellow plastic replicas of Dame Edna's "face furniture," complete with a star cluster sweeping up and over the rims, cram the joke-shop window across the street from the Drury Lane, while a behemoth green neon version of them flickers on the billboard above the theatre entrance.

Dame Edna's name is synonymous with surprise, and even with shock. As her former sobriquet "housewife/superstar" implied, Dame Edna is a celebration of contradictions: hilarious and malign, polite and lewd, generous and envious, high and low comic. But the most sensational of all Dame Edna's contradictions is that she is a he.

Dame Edna is the creation of Barry Humphries. Or, as the letterhead of his yellow stationery has it, "Barry Humphries is a division of the Barry Humphries Group." This is true. Dame Edna has taken on a visibility and a reality for the public which vie with, even subsume, Humphries' own public persona. A star is the impresario of himself, but Humphries is the impresario of his selves. The small print at the bottom of his stationery says, "The recipient is advised to preserve this memorandum as it could well become a very extremely valuable collector's item." This, too, is true. The fifty-seven-year-old Humphries is a prodigious comic talent. His co-presence in Dame

Edna—a character so real to the English public that her autobiography, "My Gorgeous Life," is being sold by his publisher, Macmillan, on its nonfiction list—incarnates the essence of the grotesque: the sense that things that should he kept apart are fused together. This style—what Baudelaire called "the absolute comic"—also creates in an audience a paroxysm, a swoon, "something profound, primitive, axiomatic, which is much closer to innocent life and absolute joy."

I know the feeling. At Dame Edna's 1981 show, "An Evening's Intercourse with Barry Humphries," I was blindsided by one of her startling observations and fell off my seat laughing. I can't account for the next two minutes of the show. I was on the floor.

Afterward, I determined to write about Humphries from the wings. I still have notes from our first backstage meeting, when I sat with him between acts and we talked as I watched an urbane Australian man of letters transform himself into Dame Edna, whom he has been sporadically impersonating since late 1955. "There's something of the clown, something rather ritualized about the character," Humphries said, applying his carmine "lippie." "It's a clown in the form of an Australian housewife. It belongs a bit to the pantomime-dame tradition, though it doesn't exploit the pantomime dame, which is generally a rather sturdy man. The joke of the pantomime dame is the tension between the female of the clothes and the stocky footballer's legs and boots. The drag queen is the other extreme, really a man on the one hand mocking a woman and at the same time trying to titillate the audience. Edna is somewhere in between—closer, really, to character acting: a man playing a woman and making points about life."

In the years since that first interview, Humphries has become more famous (the marquee announces "THE ALMOST LEGENDARY BARRY HUMPHRIES"), and Dame Edna's frivolity more majestic. But as I walk through the safety doors onto the vast Drury Lane stage, where the technical run-through is noisily in progress, neither the actor nor his creation is to be found. Backstage feels drab and mundane, but the props, scattered about the stage like so many jigsaw pieces on a gargantuan table, promise something bright and extraordinary. An Australian flag stretching the width of the proscenium is being battened down to be flown up in the labyrinth of catwalks and ropes. A cherry picker—a crane with a basket, which will lift Edna fifty feet above the stalls to sing her finale straight into the eyes of her balcony fans, whom she refers to as "the paupers"—is shunted off into the shadows. The basket itself, which usually hoists more earnest citizens, like firemen or telephone repairmen, has been turned into a kind of surrealist sculpture: its sides are now a dress of white organza, and its base is disguised with red, white, and blue crinoline and a pair of Edna's red size-9 high heels. Edna's magic wand, an electrified plastic gladiolus into which a microphone has been rigged, rests on the side of the basket.

The lightboard has been set up in the center of Row J. Behind it, slumped in conversation on the greenish-gold seats, are two men: Humphries' producer-manager, a no-nonsense Australian named Dennis Smith, who joined forces with Humphries in 1979, when he was about to launch "An Evening's Intercourse"; and Ian Davidson, a comedy writer, whom I recognize from my 1981 visit to the Drury Lane. Davidson's name has come up in the credits of almost all Humphries' comic activities since the late sixties, when he directed some of Edna's sketches for "The Late Show," the BBC's unsuccessful attempt to catch the receding wave of satire before it washed out. A modest, quiet man who began as an actor, and, in the mid-sixties, performed with Alan Arkin and Barbara Harris in America at the improvisational Second City, Davidson is one of three men billed as providing "acceptable additional jokes."

"Periodically, Barry says, 'These topical lines are getting a bit tired, better have a think about them,'" Davidson explains, pulling away his *Evening Standard* to reveal a pad on which he has jotted a few droll notions for his friend. "Then we have a phone call about them. But Barry rings other people as well. It's not a sort of solo position I have, although quite often I do get things in." He was whispering comic ideas to Humphries back when I interviewed him in the middle of his 1981 Drury Lane season. "I like to hear what the public are saying at the interval," Davidson told me then, while Edna was slipping into the tennis outfit she was wearing that year. "I stumbled upon a quarrel between a couple. She was accusing the man of sighing. He'd obviously bought the tickets. She was drunk and took exception to the show. 'You're sighing.' 'I never sigh.' 'Don't be so combatative.'

She put in an extra syllable. I told Barry. He thought it was funny, and that night Edna said, speaking of her own husband, 'Oh, Norm. I used to take Norm to the theatre, but he didn't enjoy it. And when I said, "You've been sighing," he'd say, "Don't be so combatative."' Barry's got this sort of total recall. He just threw it in during a little lull. I went back after the show, and Barry said, 'Two people have had an unforgettable night.'"

A BBC television crew appears in the Royal Box, to the left of the stage, and begins setting up its equipment. Smith checks his watch. "She's late."

"She's probably on the phone," Davidson says, jotting something down on his notepad.

"Got anything?"

"Something for Les," Davidson says, meaning another Humphries character in the show—Sir Les Patterson, the well-hung Australian cultural attaché and author of "The Traveller's Tool," who is the star of "Les Patterson Saves the World" (1987), Humphries' latest venture into feature films. Sir Les, with his "enormous encumbancy," has his own special way of opening Dame Edna's revue, and Davidson has come up with an idea in keeping with the full moral authority of the character. "'Catch-69,'" he says. "'If you do this thing, you're wrong. If you do that thing, you're wrong. It's a Catch-69 situation.' That's a Les possible. If you get a funny idea, it could be used for Les or for Edna. Or it could end up as a notice in the foyer."

The show's P.R. agent, Lynne Kirwin, looks out into the auditorium from the corner of the stage, "Edna's just coming," she says, as if the falsetto voice somewhere up and to the left of the lights being tested in the Royal Box could leave any doubt.

Davidson says, "We always talk about Edna as though she existed. 'Edna could say this,' not 'You could say this.' As a character, she is separate from him."

Dame Edna stands against the balustrade of the Royal Box while the TV crew presses microphones and recording machines up under her double chin. In high heels and hairdo, Edna is surprisingly large: around six feet four, with wide shoulders and very well-shaped and well-shaven legs—a kind of amazon of outrageousness. Her dress, a gaudy sunburst of colors, is matched by lensless glasses scalloped today with what look like variegated coffee beans. She stares out at the theatre dress circle, in front of which are the names of literary and theatrical giants, emblazoned in gold leaf: "Byron," "Dryden," "Garrick," "Sheridan," "Kean." "Dennis!" Dame Edna cries, in the high-pitched voice that is her calling card. "Wouldn't it be nice if Edna's name was added to those in front of the dress circle?" Dennis smiles and makes a note.

Dame Edna turns back to the task at hand, which is to talk to the TV presenter Cathy McGowan—herself a media star in the sixties, when she headed a popular music show, "Ready, Steady, Go." The interview starts, and Dame Edna, a master of media manipulation, goes to work. The character is in the voice, and its command never wavers. The mouth may twitch in mock anxiety at a probing question, the timbre may lower in a send-up of intimacy, but the swagger in Edna's falsetto is resolutely consistent.

"I feel I know you, Cathy. . . . I do. That fresh little face has looked at me in black-and-white and color. And your natural coloring is gorgeous. . . . It is! And what a survivor you are, aren't you? As fresh and lovely as you were in those old Swinging Sixties days. You were a famous television star then and I was just an ordinary Melbourne housewife. And look at me now . . . ha, ha! The young adore me. I can't analyze it. I don't analyze these things. But I struck a note with young people. There are a lot of Ednaboppers and WannabeEdnas. Kiddies copy me slavishly, Cathy . . . as they did you in the old days. Remember the whole of London was filled with little Cathy look-alikes, wasn't it? Remember?"

"No," Cathy says, a little nonplussed to find the ball suddenly back in her court. "Can I ask you about the outfits you wear? Your clothes? I don't really recognize the designer, Dame Edna."

"No," Dame Edna says, her voice slipping into its confidential mode. "I don't think designers should be too recognizable. That means an extreme of style, and you can only wear it about once and it goes out of fashion. I like to wear something a bit like Her Majesty the Queen—a close personal friend." She turns to the camera—"Hello!"—then back to Cathy: "She's watching. She just rang me to tell me that. . . . Actually, she faxed me. I've got a little fax in my purse. I'm one of the very few people with an in-purse fax."

"What did she say in the fax?"

"I'm not allowed to say. Our friendship would be at an end. But it was intimate. I can tell you that."

"Dame Edna, thank you so much for inviting me to the Royal Box."

"That's all right. This is the Royal Box. Where members of the Royal Family and very selected friends of mine come and watch my beautiful shows. And there's a lovely anteroom off it where they can have 'sambis.' Beautiful sandwiches. 'Sambis' is an Australian word for sandwiches. An old Aboriginal word. (It's not a very difficult language.)"

The lighting man is laughing so hard at Edna's flight of fancy that a lamp drops out of his hand. The crew sets up again. Dame Edna continues in full confidential flow: "There's a gorgeous mahogany little toilet there, too. Would you like to see that afterwards? Yes, many, many people have made themselves comfortable there."

Even after the camera is lifted off its tripod and the lights are packed away, Dame Edna is still holding forth in the Royal Box. In character, Humphries radiates what Charlie Chaplin, mourning its absence in his own music-hall performances, called "that come-hither thing." Dame Edna enjoys the exhilaration of the liberty she takes. Her pleasure is infectious. She's regaling the assembled about her special Australian ointment for stretch marks. "Ever seen a kangaroo with stretch marks? It contains an extract of a kangaroo's spleen. . . . It does. You don't use too much of it. Princess Diana actually uses it. She said she was starting to develop a pouch. So follow the instructions."

Dame Edna seems amazingly actual. Whether watching her on TV or face to face, a person soon loses the sense that this is a man-as-woman, and accepts her as real. (So real, in fact, that Edna is impersonated at drag parties.) This sense of actuality is due in part to the rich coherence of her story, which Humphries has built up in public over the years, and in part to his own performance, which is so relaxed and vivid within the parameters of her monstrous character. Dame Edna compels belief. (She won't reply to questions addressed to "Barry.") By maintaining Edna's persona, Humphries keeps the people around him playing his game. For both performer and public, it's an exercise in improvisation, but in this battle of wits the public is unarmed.

Dame Edna walks slowly down the back stairs toward the stage. She's a little ungainly on her pins, like an athlete in cleats on the concrete walkway from locker room to field. The stage is empty except for the drum kit of the three-piece band that accompanies the show. This is the first time since 1981 that Dame Edna has been on the Drury Lane stage—her 1987 show played the Strand—and she is all too aware of its history. "Guess what, possums?" her press release boasted. "I've just hired the most famous theatre on the planet." The boxes loom high and close above her. The space itself is expectant. Seats, lights, boxes, aisles all point toward center stage, where Dame Edna moves around, getting the feel of the Drury Lane's size and atmosphere. Dame Edna has a heavy-hipped, awkward, almost royal gait. She does not mince; her step has a thrust to it. "I like to acquaint myself with the empty auditorium," Humphries told me in 1981. "I make strange sounds, rather the way whales or dolphins do. I do a bit of vocal bouncing." Tonight, Dame Edna just comes to the front of the stage and starts confiding to no one in particular. "All you do is stand on the stage and talk to the people as though you were just talking on the phone," she says. "Just have a chat. . . . People make such a fuss about it. I hate shows, don't you, where you go and they're not talking to you, they're talking to each other. It's very rude."

From the shadows of the stalls Davidson answers back.

Dame Edna reacts. "Extremely rude," she says, "pretending the audience isn't there. . . . Imagine if you rang someone up and they were talking to someone else all the time?"

Dame Edna does some more vocal bouncing and then looks down toward the lightboard, where Dennis Smith is standing. "How's the box office?"

"People were lining up until three-thirty."

"We should bring them coffee," Dame Edna says, strolling over in my direction. (I'm in the wings.) "Who are the people in the news, Ian? Winnie Mandela. Has she been in the news? What's that film Dustin's done?"

"'Rainman'!" I shout, obsessed, like everyone else, with getting Dame Edna tuned up for the challenge of opening night.

"'Rainwoman,'" Dame Edna says, sharpish. "I was offered the part."

Davidson lobs something up about Roy Orbison's death. "Little Roy,"

Dame Edna says. "One of the nicest albinos I ever knew." Dame Edna paces the stage in silence and then looks out toward her producer, who has moved to the front row. "What time are we starting the tech?"

"Seven-thirty."

"Perhaps I should have a nibble now. Come into the dressing room." Dame Edna starts off the stage, and is met by Dennis Smith. As she passes me in the wings, she says to her producer, "Look at this mysterious figure."

At the start of the technical rehearsal, the BBC newsreader John Humphreys comes up on a screen that has dropped down in front of the Drury Lane proscenium. His grave and measured voice, which over the years has brokered many a world calamity to the citizens of Britain, is broadcasting the latest jolt to the national psyche. "Sad news, I'm afraid," he says, putting down the phone at his elbow which keeps a BBC newsreader in instant touch with his correspondents on breaking stories. "We've just had confirmed reports that one of Australia's most famous men has died. Mr. Norman Everage, husband of world-famous actress Dame Edna Everage, passed away peacefully in London just about an hour ago. Norman Everage was a shy, modest man. He distinguished himself as a soldier in the Second World War and married Edna May Beazley in the forties. They had three children: Bruce, Valmai, and Ken. However, soon after Mrs. Everage, as she then was, made the first of her highly successful public appearances, her husband developed a urological disorder for which he's been undergoing treatment for a quarter of a century."

Norman Everage never made an appearance in one of Dame Edna's shows, but Dame Edna had turned his prostate into legend. "Norm's prostate has been hanging over me for years," she confided onstage and in her autobiography, as the rolling joke of her browbeaten mate and their family changed with the times and with the rise of Edna's star. In "An Evening's Intercourse with Barry Humphries," Dame Edna told how Norm had to have his hands strapped to the sides of the hospital bed and was learning to knit with his mouth. "He's into oral socks," she explained.

Now another BBC reporter, Sue Cook, is pictured outside "the world's first prostate-transplant unit," interviewing doctors, nurses, and Dame Edna herself. The effect of seeing representatives of the real world incorporated into Dame Edna's fantasy is unnerving. But it's a confusion that Humphries relishes. For Dame Edna's autobiography, Humphries has chosen an epigraph from Benedetto Croce: "All history is fiction, just as all fiction is history." And Dame Edna makes a fiasco of history. Once, looking at a picture of Dame Edna amid the Royals which stood on his dressing-room table, Humphries said, "That's a joke in itself." And so it is. Dame Edna's mere presence at public occasions calls the reality of society into question.

In the early days, Edna sometimes had to thrust herself into the paths of the famous, like Australian Prime Minister Sir Robert Menzies, for whom she waited with a photographer until he appeared outside London's Savoy Hotel. "I'm one of your electors," she said as he snubbed her. "You're doing a fine job." But, as the souvenir program celebrates in snapshot, the famous now flock to Dame Edna. She is shown variously meeting and greeting a gallimaufry of the celebrated: the Queen Mother, Princess Diana, Joan Collins, Joan Baez, Bob Geldof, Zsa Zsa Gabor, Larry Hagman, Charlton Heston, Joan Rivers, Jeffrey Archer, and Mary Whitehouse, Britain's self-proclaimed moral guardian, whose righteousness Dame Edna both voices and lampoons.

At the end of the BBC broadcast, the newsreader looks out at the audience and says, "We have confirmation that Dame Edna has cancelled all stage performances. No money will be refunded. And that's the news tonight."

The screen flies up. The musicians are soon in place, ready for Humphries to start running through the material. The pianist puts a pad beside her on the bench to jot down any tasty one-liners that Humphries may improvise and want to put into the act. Humphries strolls out onstage wearing the head mike that fits under Edna's wig. He's in blue jeans, white socks, and sandals, an altogether unlikely Edna. He speeds through the prose portions of his act in double time: "And so and so and so and so and so. . . . I feel a song coming on!" In Edna's falsetto, Humphries launches into the boffo opening, a hymn to frivolity's refusal to suffer:

> A minute ago
> I was locked in my room.
> My life seemed pointless and hollow,

Where before it was warm
With the presence of Norm,
And I thought "Where he's gone I must follow."
I looked at the Valium, I considered the stove,
I weighed up the stern moral issues.
But the strength inside me grew
When I was almost through
My last box of Kleenex tissues.
So I hope you'll all applaud my great achievement.
I am here tonight in spite of my bereavement. . . .

When Dame Edna sings about the triumph of fame over grief, her big-heartedness always admits the spirit of revenge, an impulse that is never far from the aggressive wellsprings of comedy. It's a game that Humphries, too, has been known to play with his public. He told the Australian Press Club in 1978, "In Melbourne I used to like sitting in a little Greek restaurant called Cafe Florentino at about eight-ten in the evening and seeing old Melbourne Grammar boys, contemporaries perhaps of our Prime Minister"—and himself—"hurrying with their wives down the stairs in order to attend one of my performances which I had absolutely no intention of starting for another three-quarters of an hour. The advantage, of course, of being a solo performer is that they can never start without you. And I think that is probably one of the few advantages, except it keeps me off the streets and fills my evening entertainingly."

Now Humphries stops the song to adjust the arrangement with the band: "Be nice if we could add a note there. A little Kurt Weillish note: 'And now you know/I'm too much of a pro/to let *yoooou* down.'"

After the song, Humphries descends into the stalls and sits talking with us as the crew gets the next set in place. He is a more reserved presence than the ebullient Dame Edna. Edna's voice is tight and sharp, but Humphries' voice is breathy and light. Where Edna is garish, Humphries is suave. Where she is direct and downright rude, he is oblique and well mannered. Edna is unaware of what she projects, and her lack of awareness empowers the public to laugh at her; Humphries is knowing, and his know-ingness keeps those around him at a distance and on the defensive. His smile is tired tonight, but the furrowed laugh lines around his mouth and his high, fleshy cheek-bones give his face a dramatic—even youthful—definition. His eyes, when they focus on you, are bright and warm, and convey a very definite sense of authority.

Dame Edna's biases are there for the world to see, but Humphries is much harder to fathom. As one would expect of a comedian who treads so gracefully between insight and outrage, Humphries is a man of intelligence and taste. Dame Edna says the first thing that pops into her airhead, but Humphries listens. He is reflective, choosing his words carefully and well. Humphries has talked of a feeling of "allegiance to the fellowship of music-hall artistes," but his articulacy separates him from the old-timers whose glorious tradition he is carrying almost single-handed into the twenty-first century. Buster Keaton had two days of official schooling; Charlie Chaplin learned a new word a day; Bert Lahr built up his vocabulary by doing cross-word puzzles. But Humphries, whose act combines lowbrow antics with a highbrow aesthetic, is both well educated and well read, as the range of images and references in his conversation displays.

A stuntman and a stuntwoman are having trouble wiring themselves up for Humphries' most outrageous effect—the spectacle of paupers plummeting from a box seat. So Humphries turns back to me and begins talking. "My German Expressionist touch," he says of the stunt. "I like to produce this in the theatre, and I like to combine it with comedy. I was in the film society at university, and I deliberately disinterred a lot of German Expressionist films. I liked the kind of spooky, rather frightening effects that some of these actors produced in the movies. I very much liked the sense of melodrama and—what are they?—the *frissons*. I don't know why I liked shocking people. I think it just gave me a sense of identity. I guess it gave me a sense of power, too, because I felt rather powerless and swamped by— well, the dullness of Melbourne. Although I'm very fond of it, Melbourne is a transcendentally dull city. I was rather puritanical in those early days, and moralistic. Anxious to *show* people. Edna was conceived as a character to remind Australians of their bigotry and all the things that I found offensive. She was a rebuke. She was a silly, bigoted, ignorant, self-satisfied Melbourne housewife. They're still around. They're still there. Now they just wear a different uniform. They drive Volvos and occasionally swear. No one before me in Australia had looked at the suburbs and said, 'Here is the stuff of comedy.' It's only when Edna took on a life of her own, when she was invested *with a life*, that she turned the tables on me, in a way."

The stuntman yells down that they're ready, so Humphries hoists himself up and goes back onstage to work through "The Gladdy Song," which is the segue out of his coup de théâtre. "Now let's try and throw a few gladdies up to the paupers," Humphries says in an uninflected Edna voice, not lingering to act the words. "'I don't think I can. But I will . . . uh . . . uh . . . uh. . . .'" Humphries mimes the backhanded flip with which for a quarter of a century he has been heaving what Edna calls the Australian national flower at the audience. The drummer does a rim shot as each imaginary gladdy lands in the audience.

"What about me, Dame Edna?" the stuntwoman, sitting on the balcony railing, calls, waving.

"Oh, I don't think I can. Uh . . . uh . . ."

"AAAAAAAH!" The woman tips out over the box, dragging the stuntman with her. They dangle above the empty stalls like rock climbers rappelling a cliff.

"Can you see them?" Humphries asks, as the woman swings on wires and a halter concealed by her dress, "Will enough people see that?"

"Everybody and his dog will see that," Dennis Smith says.

The stuntwoman and the stuntman are hauled back into the box, and Humphries continues running the lines. "You all right? What a miracle there was a rope ladder up there, paups! Heaven be praised."

"We love you, Dame Edna!"

"Oh, you move me when you say that, lemming. Wouldn't it be ghastly if that happened every night?" Even in rehearsal, the line gets a laugh from the crew.

"On first night at the Strand, they dropped out of the top box like that," Ian Davidson says. "Someone from the stalls—an intrepid man—ran up on the box below and climbed out on the ledge to help the woman. Thereafter, they had to have someone standing in the corridor to stop anyone trying to make a brave rescue. The man was terribly brave. The box wasn't as high as this, but it was still damned high. I can't imagine any other comedian who would have such a stunt take place in an auditorium—have such amazing, riveting attention taken away from him in that way. It all rebounds to Edna's benefit, but even so . . ."

The smoke machine starts working, and the cherry picker moves onstage, "I see. That's good," Humphries says. "Tell me, have you got nice color on that? Are there flashing lights? Great blasts of color?"

Humphries, whose first ambition was to be a painter, thinks visually, and his shows make striking stage pictures. In the past, he has tried to shoot gladioli into the balcony with a cannon, fielded people's shoes from the stalls in a butterfly net, pulled a rip cord on his dress that turned its front into a Union jack. But in having Dame Edna rise fifty feet above his audience at the finale of "Back with a Vengeance!" Humphries has topped himself. "It's a parody of the Assumption as though painted by Murillo or perhaps a late-Venetian master," he says.

Humphries locks himself in the basket as the crane begins to work through "Shyness," Edna's last song. As he has instructed, the cherry picker moves him slowly downstage and then thrusts him out and up over the stalls. Just the sight of Humphries suspended in air makes those of us in the audience laugh. The machine judders. Humphries grasps the rails. "There's terrible lurches down there," he says in his own persona, and the word "lurches" reverberates in the sound system. "Hello, paupers!" Humphries says in Edna's brightest falsetto. "I feel like Edna Poppins up here. I do. I hope I don't do anything involuntary. Be it on your heads if I do."

Even without costume and disguise, Humphries in Edna's voice whips up the tired crew and the scattered audience as the band builds to the song's climax. And when Dame Edna says, "Was it good for you, too, possums?" down below all of us shout "Yes!"

A strange lassitude fills the theatre the next day, in the final hours before the opening, Humphries' dresser, Katie Harris, has turned a costume trunk into a table—a kind of altar of artifice, on which many of the disembodied features of Humphries' characters are on view. The table holds Dame Edna's natural wisteria wig, her rings and diamanté bracelets, Sir Les's fluorescent-green socks and his brown-and-white platform shoes, whose soles are stamped "Made from genuine dead kangaroo." There is also a box of black-and-white publicity postcards of Humphries in bow tie, with one eye hidden under the brim of his fedora and the other eye glaring up at the viewer, "I look like a minor Surrealist painter in that," he says.

Humphries, who has described himself as "an Aussie arriviste," is a dandy. He has a deep knowledge of fin-de-siècle Europe and the aesthetes who made a romance of individualism. Over the years, Humphries has affected the dandy's advertisements of impertinence and leisure: the monocle, the walking stick, the silk polka-dot cravat or bow tie, the long hair. In his Dimitri Major tailored suits and his Jermyn Street shirts, he cuts a fine, colorful figure. Through Dame Edna, Humphries allows the audience to share and to excuse the dandy's thrill at bad taste and his aristocratic pleasure in giving offense. Through Dame Edna, he vents both the dandy's insolent superiority and his rebellion against the rigidities of the workaday world, using wit to bend the world to him. Through Dame Edna, Humphries' progress in English and Australian society has been impressive. Even Prince Charles, an Ednabopper of long standing, comes occasionally to Humphries' house in Hampstead for dinner.

Humphries takes his mail and sits down at his dressing table, where his makeup and brushes have been laid out as meticulously as instruments in an operating theatre. Aerosols of hair spray and deodorant, pots of makeup, a polishing pen for Edna's nails, a bottle of Lea & Perrins Worcestershire Sauce (the finishing touch to Sir Les's ruffled tuxedo shirt) are ranged against the back mirror. At his right hand is a small palette for blending the makeup; at his left is Sir Les's snaggletoothed denture. A white towel has been placed in the center of the dressing table, and on it are three sable brushes and two Hudson's Eumenthol jujubes. To the left of the makeup but no less important to Humphries' backstage ritual is the telephone.

Humphries is reading through the stack of mail. A woman in Blackpool writes to complain that she's been upset for two days over Dame Edna's mockery of bereavement. A single parent in Surrey giggles along in Edna's idiom ("gladdies," "possums," "nice"). Someone has cut out an ad for the show and scrawled across it, "Take that shit off your face and do some work you lazy bugger." And Margaret in Bournemouth wants six hundred pounds, to redecorate her flat: "Dearest darling Dame Edna, will you be my Fairy godperson and grant my tiny little wish."

Humphries himself is hardly ensconced in luxury. The dressing room consists of a small changing room and a large, dingy waiting room with a sofa bed, two chairs, and a table on which bottles of soft drinks and mineral water have been set out for opening night. Bouquets from well-wishers have been arranged around the room, but nothing can renovate its drabness. There is not a picture on the wall, not a new lick of paint. The sense of color, texture, fun which so distinguishes Humphries' performances onstage is entirely absent from the gray room, as if all energy and imagination were being saved for the front of the house. But the barrenness and boredom that the dressing room exudes provide the climate that feeds the exasperation that Humphries turns into outrageousness. "I'm always conscious of the desert inside Australia, of the vacuum," he has said. "Sunday afternoon in Melbourne, the exquisite boredom. The exhilarating depression. Neat houses. Somewhere down the street there's a Celica being cleaned; otherwise no sign of life. That appeals to me in a terrible way. But I feel, too, there's a decadence, among all the health and the prosperity." Edna is a product of a subversive imagination that sees itself as "sinking artesian wells into the suburban desert, drawing up composite portraits." The notion pleases him. "I'm in the boredom-alleviation business, aren't I? This art is meant to be an antidote to boredom," Humphries says, speaking as much for himself as his audience.

Humphries has described himself as "self-educated, attended Melbourne Grammar School." The man who would become a dandy of delirium traces the origins of his rebellion to the oppressiveness of the city's poshest educational institution—the one that the upwardly mobile Humphries family chose for their firstborn son, and to which he was admitted in 1947, at the age of thirteen. Humphries was not happy with the choice and has spoken of the move from his friends at Camberwell Grammar School as "a great bereavement." The trauma has never been forgiven by Humphries or forgotten by Melbourne Grammar. In 1953, Humphries was sensationally banned from the Old Melburnians association for his irreverent sculpture

"Old Fool's Tie": a bottle of beer with a Melbourne Grammar tie knotted around it. He was eventually welcomed back, and made an equally sensational return to the fold at an Old Melburnians night in his honor, in 1971: he entered riding on a camel.

Dame Edna owes her paternity in part to Humphries' fierce disgust at the blinkered conformity of the school and its masters, whom he has called in print "picturesque ignoramuses." Humphries says, "I became attracted to the modern school of painting—that is to say, the modern school as it was in the second decade of the twentieth century. The Dadaist movement, and, later, the Surrealist artists, fascinated me very early. I was familiar with the works of Picabia, with the writings of Salvador Dali, with most of the works of the French nineteenth-century writers. I knew all about Cubism, and was, indeed, painting in a Cubist style. So that I was, in fact, very precocious in my reading before I was thirteen." Already a talented painter in oils, Humphries had been introduced, through the influence of a Camberwell art teacher, Ian Bow, to "the exhilaration of eccentricity" and the ravishing thought of "what a marvellous liberating thing it must he to be an artist, to be able to escape from the humdrum world of mathematics, compulsory sport, gymnasium, cold showers, boxing, and all these terrible imperatives of a boys' school." When Humphries was five and his mother asked him what he wanted to be, he answered, "A genius." But Melbourne Grammar put no premium on originality. "It's significant that very, very few people of any artistic sensibility at all emerged from the school after the war," he has said. "But out of a kind of rebellion against the school system I developed certain techniques, which have been very useful in my subsequent artistic life—certain forms of rebellion and anarchy, certain artistic methods."

Humphries also hated the school uniform, which draped his dreamy artistic persona in a navy-blue serge version of a thirties business suit and turned him and the rest of the luckless internees of the school into "double-breasted, tie-pinned parodies of Ronald Colman or the Man from the Prudential." This later seemed to Humphries a self-fulfilling prophecy. "Most of my contemporaries at school entered the World of Business, the logical destiny of bores," he has written. The school's motto was "Pray and Work," but it was to sport and the homogeneity of attitude which games instill that the school seemed dedicated. Humphries was not, and never would be, a team player. "I hated sports. I still do," he says. His aversion to physical exercise earned him the nickname Grannie at Camberwell and Queenie at Melbourne Grammar.

Humphries' sport was frequenting secondhand bookshops—especially one on Bourke Street, whose owner, a Mrs. Bird, called him Mr. Humphries and imbued him with an enthusiasm he still holds for the "curdled late Romantics," like Ann Radcliffe, Monk Lewis, Charles Robert Maturin, Byron, and Mary Shelley. Even rummaging in the dusty shop among stacks of old volumes had maverick overtones for Humphries, because his parents insisted he have new books. "Schoolboys generally didn't go into secondhand bookshops," Humphries says. "One was discouraged from 'dirty books'—that is to say, books that other people had owned. It was a very hygienic society. Hygiene was a great god."

As a child, Humphries dreamed of being a magician. "The big advantage of being a magician," he says, "was that you could make people disappear." But at Melbourne Grammar he discovered that if he couldn't make the school disappear, his laughter could keep the people in it at bay. Humphries found himself in the dandy's dilemma: at once dominated by and attempting to dominate convention. In this delicate situation, wit was the acceptable face of insolence, and his school years were spent in the learning of effrontery. He recalls of his small circle of friends, "We sat in a rebellious and probably rather irritating little group at the back of the class, drawing attention, wherever possible, to areas of ignorance in the schoolmaster. These were considerable, I need hardly say." He acted out what he calls his "dandiacal rage" in caricature both of the teachers and of himself. "I had always drawn, particularly caricatures," he has said. "I used to do caricatures of teachers on the blackboard. So when they entered the classroom they could see themselves up there on the board to the amusement of others. I found I had a gift for amusing my schoolmates, which, in a way, protected me from bullies. If you could make them laugh, they wouldn't hit you."

A renegade reputation requires courage, and Humphries, a churchgoing and well-bred young man, had to summon it up. "It didn't come naturally to me," he says. "One had to impersonate a brazen person. One had to act as if one were courageous." He was emboldened by the sure knowledge that "I had absolutely no desire to be like *them*, whatever happened—*them* were these boys in school uniforms." Humphries grew his hair long. "By modern standards it wasn't long. But it was certainly long for the school, where they insisted 'Long hair is dirty hair.' I later had that translated into Latin—'*Crines longi, crines foetidi*'—and called it the motto of the school. There was such a strong emotional feeling about long hair. It aroused such primitive revulsion that I knew I was on the right track."

Although he bucked the system, he could not always beat it. He became the subject of scandal and concern when his ruse for avoiding sports was uncovered. Humphries had appeared in soccer gear and had his name ticked off, and had then slipped away to the lavatories, where an accomplice brought him his school uniform to put back on. "This went on for over a year," Humphries says. "One day, there was a tap on the door. It opened, and the captain of the school was standing there. He said, 'The game's up, Humphries.' I'll never forget those words. I was caned. It sometimes pleases me to think that this schoolboy, only a couple of years older than I was, who unmasked me so brutally and punished me so mercilessly, is now a traveller for a cheap brand of port. I think Dame Nature, as Edna would call it, has a way of settling some of these accounts." The humiliation was compounded by the headmaster, who called Humphries into his study and said, "I hope you're not turning pansy?" Humphries says, "I hadn't the *faintest* idea of what he meant, except that it was rather threatening. There was no way to formulate a reply to it."

Humphries' way of dealing with his anger was then, as it is now, to perform a kind of psychic jujitsu—to "throw people" by using the force of their attitude to defeat them. Having been labelled effeminate and made to attend soccer matches in the name of school spirit, Humphries sent up both injustices by sitting with his back to the playing field and knitting.

The older generation of clowns to whom Humphries is a legitimate successor took their urgency from poverty; Humphries took his urgency from privilege. They wanted a way into the mainstream; Humphries wanted a way out of it. "The word art never entered my head," Chaplin wrote, speaking of his time in music hall, before it did. And Keaton was equally matter-of-fact: "I never realized that I was doing anything but trying to make people laugh when I threw my custard pies and took my pratfalls." The Old Guard were inspired by business, not art. Humphries was inspired by art, not business. Even at grammar school, he felt a. special kinship with the Dadaists and their subversive gestures of unreason. "I was instantly fired with admiration," he says of his first exposure to them, in William Gaunt's "March of the Moderns." "It seemed to me that even though these stunts had occurred forty years before, they still produced a *frisson* that was the kind of artistic performance I aspired to." Humphries wanted to create his own "ferocious Dada jests." He helped to form the Art Club and to start a Dadaist faction, which organized a sculpture exhibition at the school. The forces of authority won the first round against Humphries' aspiring anarchy: the Dada sculptures were judged too subversive and were withdrawn. But Humphries' gift for provocation, so carefully held in check in his Melbourne Grammar days, was unleashed on the world when he took up his infamous residence at Melbourne University, between 1951 and 1953.

"The only Australian who ever understood the Dada principle of *provocation*," Robert Hughes wrote in "The Art of Australia" (1966), was the actor Barry Humphries, who organized two Dada shows in Melbourne and (before leaving for England in the late fifties) performed a number of gratuitous public acts whose ferocity and point might have pleased Tristan Tzara." The Dada exhibitions and the pranks made a legend both of Humphries' desire to shine and of his sense of displacement. "It was important to emancipate oneself from this suburban milieu, because it was so seductive and oppressive," Humphries says. "You thought it was inescapable. It was so disturbing. I had absolutely no idea of what I would do in life. I remember a friend of mine had a printing press. I had a visiting card made with my name on it. He said, 'We better put occupation.' I said, 'Put "Dilettante."' A very effective card to have. In fact, it didn't entertain me very much to be a dilettante. I became a specialist."

The first Pan-Australasian Dada Exhibition, in 1952, announced Humphries' expertise at creating a panic. "I had packages printed up called Platytox—really just sawdust in packages," Humphries recalls. "It was a 'poison' to put in creeks and streams to kill the platypus, which is a very much protected, loved, endearing indigenous Australian animal. In fact, if I were to be given a chance to save a platypus, at some risk to myself, I would probably attempt it. So why have an exhibit that offers a pesticide to destroy these animals? *Because* everything was in its place in Australia. On the package it said in small print that it was also rather good for Aboriginals. Aboriginals didn't exist: in a way, one was led to believe that they lived a long way away and were dying out anyway, which was terribly sad, but there it was. This was all part of the tyranny of niceness and order. I didn't want to *overthrow* order. I just instinctively wanted to give it a bit of a *jolt*, so that people could *see* it."

"Pox Vobiscum" was the motto of Melbourne University's Dada group, which put on the second exhibition, in 1953. Members of the public who strolled into the lounge of the Student Union and were surrounded by the sound of diabolical laughter counterpointed by a record rigged to repeat, from "South Pacific," "And you will note there's a lump in my throat / I'm in love, I'm in love, I'm in love . . ." soon got the splenetic message. Humphries had filled a pair of Wellington boots full of custard and titled it "Pus in Boots." Under the title "Her Majesty's Male," Queen Elizabeth II was shown with five-o'clock shadow. In both exhibitions, the punning titles of many of the works disabused art of its gravity and proclaimed Dada's faith in life as a joke: "Yes, We Have No Cezannas," "Roof of the Cistern Chapel," "Portrait of James Juice," "Christopher Fried," "ErasmusTazz," "My Foetus Killing Me," "Puree of Heart." Humphries created a series of works that rotted and smelled, in order to satirize the notion of genteel art collecting. He produced "Shoescapes" from old shoes, "Stinkscapes" from lambs' eyes, "Cakescapes" from cake pressed between glass to create a kind of Jackson Pollock abstraction. To a local newspaper he explained, "Here are the artistic media which best express the multifaceted image of Australian life— cake, shoes, and tomato sauce. From footwear, custard, and chutney you can create the Old Masters of the future."

"Dada shows its truth in action," Tzara said. Inevitably, Humphries and the Dada group were drawn toward performance. Their Dada revue, "Call Me Madman" (1952), achieved notoriety. The furor was caused not by the blanks being fired over the audience's head, or by the din of the orchestra playing combs, bottles, and gongs, or by the spectacle of Humphries dressed as a nun and singing "I Wish I Could Shimmy Like My Sister Kate." What made the front page of the Melbourne *Sun* was the finale, "The Indian Famine." A missionary sat across a table from his wife, played by Humphries minimally disguised in a dress over his suit. The table was piled high with cauliflower, cake, and raw meat. "It looked like a harvest festival," Humphries recalls. The missionary read aloud statistics of a recent famine. As each horrific figure was announced, the wife laughed and repeated, "I don't care, I've got plenty of food, lots of food. And they've got nothing." Humphries says, "The point was crudely moral in order to dramatize public indifference to these kinds of catastrophes and to provoke respectable undergraduate audiences into some kind of irrational behavior, some kind of demonstrative feeling."

Humphries succeeded all too well. As the missionary's broadcast of statistics grew louder, so did the wife's hysterical laughter. They started throwing food at each other, and some food found its way into the audience. The audience started hurling the food at the actors, who, in turn, threw it back at them. A food fight had begun. "We had an audience of affluent Australian university students throwing perfectly good food about the auditorium while statistics about the current famine were being broadcast over the amplifiers at them—an act therefore of total anarchy," Humphries explains. "The satirical intention is very apparent in all this. It eluded the audience, however, who stormed the stage, after my blood. I remember hiding in the broom cupboard under the stage." The Dada group was banned from ever again using the Student Union theatre.

Humphries also started making a spectacle of himself. He cultivated his myth. "I was entertained by the idea of slightly fictionalizing myself," he says. His tailored suits, his still longer hair, his mauve ink (an affectation acquired from reading Ronald Firbank) heralded the dandy's intention of inhabiting a world of his own. Humphries gathered around him a group of women he dubbed "hoydens" and "doxies," one of whom was Germaine Greer. "He would dress them up as schoolgirls and passionately kiss them in the street," the Australian critic Clive James reports in his essay "Approximately in the Vicinity of Barry Humphries." Until the police arrived, whereupon birth certificates would be produced.

And so began a series of legendary pranks, in which Humphries moved "from a visual vocabulary to a theatrical one." In one notorious escapade, Humphries had an accomplice, John Perry, dress as a blind man and take a seat in a non-smoking compartment of a Melbourne commuter train. As Humphries has described it: "Perry was reading Braille. How anyone in a non-smoking compartment of a commuter train could have mistaken a piano roll for Braille, goodness knows. John was reading a piano roll. He had dark glasses and his leg was in a cast. He aroused an enormous amount of curiosity and pity, I should think, on the long journey into town. So when, at a certain stop, in came a rather garishly dressed, long-haired youth, smoking gold-tipped cigarettes between the wrong fingers, and reading a foreign-language newspaper—very foreign-looking—immediately they looked. First of all, I'd given them plenty of time to feel compassion and admiration for this man. Then in comes another figure, smoking in a non-smoking compartment, reading a *foreign* newspaper, long hair. So another emotion takes over. Then the foreign person looks down at the blind man and, as he's about to get out of the train a couple of stops later, unleashes a volley of foreign-sounding gibberish, grabs the Braille, tears the paper, kicks at the blind man's leg, and tears off his glasses and throws them on the floor. Then he gets off the train. The commuters were invariably transfixed with horror. No one ever pursued me. Mind you, I ran as fast as I could. People tried to comfort John Perry. He would always say 'Forgive him.' It was also very funny to do, and very hard not to laugh. It's a bit hard to say what effect the stunt was meant to have, since it was meant to amuse us, a kind of outrageous public act."

The pranks turned life into "a mini-spectacle with me as the audience," Humphries says. They also gave him a "theatrical thrill," which he explains as "changing people's lives slightly by making them the witness to some rather remarkable and absolutely inexplicable thing that could not happen in real life." It was a dangerous sport, but one Humphries experimented with after he'd dropped his university studies (law, then liberal arts) and joined the repertory theatre on the Melbourne University campus, in the mid-fifties. The actress Zoe Caldwell was part of the same repertory and got caught up in Humphries' masquerade. "He used to do a very strange thing," she says. "He would pretend to be a spastic, a genuine spastic. People would pity him. It's still in Dame Edna—he pushes responses in people. But they're responses we should feel ashamed of. He forces you to feel emotions. I was his sister. That's what he cast me as. It wasn't my idea of a swell night out. We'd go to a restaurant and ask for tea. The waitress would bring the tea, and he'd take the milk and pour it on his head. The girl was trying to keep her patience. Then Barry would pour the sugar on the floor. He did the whole thing, never stopped. Watching people pity him and pity me, I knew what he was after—false sentiment. He wanted to see what reactions people had to disability. Barry forced you to look at the ugly and the monstrous. He was trying it out. The genesis of what he wanted to trap—bogus emotion, denial, what we all do—was there. I think he wanted to trap it and say 'Look, look what you do.' And so he's outrageous. At parties, he used to sing:

> Lasso that spasso
> And beat him till he's sweatin'
> Lasso that spasso
> I'm a'hangin' on to this here cretin. . . .

"People would say 'How cruel,' or 'Oh, Barry!' That's the response he wanted. He was trying to provoke and entrap their sentimentality. I see this in Edna Everage, only now Barry makes people laugh. He didn't make people laugh much at the time. He's now wonderful as Edna because he's so free, as if he's found exactly what's right for him."

"You can come in, John." Humphries is dialling a number, speaking to my reflection in the left-hand corner of his dressing mirror. "They want me to close the Prince's Trust performance. Frank Sinatra, Sammy Davis, Jr., Kiri Te Kanawa, and Liza Minnelli will be on the bill, too." He puts down the telephone and turns to face me: relaxed, excited, already watching Edna's persona go by. "I have to come on late, because of my show. I suppose I'll do 'My Public' and change the lyrics. But what about them? I don't know too much about them!"

"Well, Sammy Davis is black, one-eyed, and Jewish."

Humphries' eyes drift away into thought. He mumbles a snatch of song:

"I'm better off than Sammy." And then, with a clap of high-pitched laughter, he turns back, beaming: "'I may be overtired and fluish / But at least I'm not one-eyed and black and Jewish.' Dare I sing that? They'd never allow it on television!"

The phone rings. "Hello, Stephen." Humphries launches into a description of a dress he saw in a Parisian revue which he wants Stephen Adnitt, his designer, to copy. "It had mirrors on it. Actually around the neck. A kind of V neck or yoke of mirrors. They were rather chunky tiles, almost. . . . No, but you can imagine what happened when the lights hit them, because they were separate and moved with the fabric a bit. They sent these rays straight out into the audience."

Edna began life, in the mid-fifties, dressed from. secondhand-clothing shops. And as she has progressed in confidence and class, so have her costumes. Humphries' ever-changing satire on modern manners is inevitably a satire on modern fashion. Over the last twenty years, Dame Edna has become a clotheshorse of many colors. She herself explained the transformation to London's *Sunday Telegraph in* 1987: "As late as the early 1970s, I was still really dressing like a tourist, buying off the peg in Oxford Street. I wore a tweed overcoat which may have come from C. & A.; white vinyl Courrèges-style boots, a hangover from the 1960s; and a felt hat in autumnal colours." But since the late seventies, when she declared herself a superstar, Dame Edna has been in the vanguard of fashion, exploiting the punk leather look, the denim look, the tennis look. For her cantata "The Song of Australia," she wore a dress that opened in front to reveal the Australian coat of arms lit up, flashing a kangaroo and an emu holding a shield. Offstage, a stagehand pulled a string, and a cape unfolded behind Edna like wings, adding decibels to the applause. After Princess Di attended the Cannes Festival in a puffball dress, Dame Edna had one made up, complete with a Windsor Castle hat bearing a flag that could be run up on the turret, and little corgis on the brim. Dame Edna has also attempted (and failed) to crash the Royal Enclosure at Ascot wearing a behemoth hat in the shape of the Sydney Opera House, with a shark-infested bay as the brim.

"And, Stephen," Humphries says, "also remember on the bill are Liza Minneli, Sammy Davis, Jr., Frank Sinatra, Kiri Te Kanawa—I have to excel them *all*."

Dennis Smith and the stage manager, Harriet Bowdler, come into the dressing room. Humphries sings Smith the lines about Sammy Davis, Jr. "In superb taste," says Smith, who bears a handful of opening-night telegrams and a memo about the charity performance.

Humphries goes into the bathroom to freshen up. The pre-opening orders to the ushers from the Drury Lane stage sound through the loud-speakers in Humphries' dressing room. "They've adjusted the speakers," Bowdler says. "Barry gets most upset if we play a theatre and the show relay doesn't come back to the dressing room. He likes to hear the audience."

"He often says 'Listen to them,'" Katie Harris says, scuttling into the dressing room with Sir Les's padding.

Bowdler says, "'Is it a nice crowd?' he'll say. 'Who's out there?' He likes to know people are waiting. Sometimes he just needs to know they're waiting."

Humphries comes out of the bathroom and sits on the edge of the sofa bed, which has been made up in the waiting room. "I think I'm going to have a ten-minute nap, John." He pulls down the coverlet. "It'll go all right tonight, don't you think?"

"Your attention please, ladies and gentlemen. Contrary to the television broadcast you have just seen, we have received word that a world-famous woman is speeding to this theatre under police escort in the Ednamobile. The management have little doubt that if this proves to be Dame Edna and that she has indeed decided to keep faith with her devoted public and give you a show tonight the generous-hearted men and women of good will in this audience will give this courageous woman and widow a standing ovation rarely witnessed in the annals of the British theatre."

A crash of cymbals. A spotlight. And there, at the front of the stalls, is Dame Edna, in her widow's weeds. "Hello, possums!" she shouts, waving and smiling and vaulting up the stairs to the stage in her slightly bowlegged gait. "Hello, darlings. Hello, possums." She beams as she crosses the stage.

"I'm glad I stepped onto the stage now, possums. I am. I am. When I first heard that Norm had been axed by the Big Rupert Murdoch in the sky, I phoned up my shrink in L.A. Dr. Marvin K. Schadenfreude, M.D. I share him with little Elton John, little Michael Jackson, and big Sylvester. I said,

'Doctor, what am I going to do?' And he said, 'Let it all hang out, Edna.' I said, 'That's what Norm did. And look where it got him!' He said, 'Time is a miracle healer. Only Time can heal.' And he was so right. Because that was—what?—four hours ago. And already I'm feeling *marvellous*. I am."

He was born John Barry Humphries, in the Melbourne suburb of Kew, on February 17, 1934, the first of Eric and Louisa Humphries' four children. Although it would be wrong to consider Edna merely Humphries' alter ego, it would also he wrong to consider her just "this woman you inhabit," which was Graham Greene's description. Edna originated as a totem of Humphries' sense of displacement both from his milieu and from his parents. "I invented Edna because I hated her," he said. "I suppose one grows up with a desire to murder one's parents, but you can't really go and do that. So I suppose I tried to murder them symbolically onstage. I poured out all my hatred of the standards of little people of their generation." As a comic caricature, Edna allowed Humphries to turn the infuriating fears of his parents against them.

Edna is, among other things, a son's disturbing view of his mother. Edna talks but never listens. She asks questions only to double-bind her interlocutors. She is a queen of control. "You're tired. You're overexcited," she says, turning fiercely on her infantilized audience. "There'll be tears before bedtime!" What Edna claims about herself and what the audience perceives about her are different matters. She is "approachable" and devastating, "nice" and devouring, "caring" and callous, "intimate" and detached. She contains a son's envy of his mother's power to be at once the agent of joy and the means of eradication.

Louisa Humphries looked on her son with bemusement. "Where did you come from, Barry?" she used to say to him when he was a child. "We never knew where you came from."

"My mother would very frequently express surprise at me, which reinforced my adoption fantasy," Humphries says. "My father became very successful. I didn't see a great deal of him. He was always very, very busy." Humphries pictures Eric Humphries—a third-generation builder, whose father immigrated to Australia from Lancashire—as surrounded by the drawing boards, set squares, drawing pins that were the tools of his trade and the source of the increasing wealth that helped him move from Oldsmobile to Buick and on to Mercedes in the fifties. "My mother was a distant figure as well," he says. "I think she had a period of illness. I think she was sent away for a bit. It might have been as little as a fortnight, but it seemed months to a child."

The Humphries family lived in a two-story neo-Georgian cream brick house in Camberwell, the most fashionable new suburb of Melbourne, on the Golf Links estate and looking down Marlborough Avenue. Outside, in the spacious world of herbaceous borders and rolling lawns, Humphries sensed an "unneighborly feeling." His parents didn't fraternize much with the neighbors. "It was thought not altogether 'nice' to know people very well," Humphries says about the general "lack of intimacy," which also prevailed in the world inside his house. By the age of six, Humphries was withholding his deepest hurts from his parents. "I was puzzled even then by the mysterious lack of rapport which seemed to have grown up between parents and child."

The incident that prompted this recollection was a schoolyard quarrel at the detested South Camberwell State School ("I still drive past in order to see if I can revive my hatred of the school: I do so without any difficulty"), which Humphries briefly attended before entering Camberwell Grammar. "Once, a whole crowd of bullies set upon me in a corner of the arid and ashen playground, because I had a toy submarine they envied," he recalled. "They'd seized handfuls of gravel to pelt me, and in self-defense I threw a handful back at them and was immediately reported for throwing stones to Miss Jensen, the woman in charge of our class. Miss Jensen preferred to take their testimony against my own, and she threatened to take me to the headmaster. Waiting to see the headmaster, I was placed in a corner of the classroom, in front of everyone, with a note on my back. 'I am a bully,' said the note. 'I am a bully.' So I was subjected to this humiliation, and after that I broke down and confessed that in fact I had been culpable— when, of course, I knew I hadn't really—to avoid the ultimate vengeance of a confrontation with the headmaster. This filled me with very uncomfortable feelings for many, many years. I've often thought to this day of taking some form of revenge upon Miss Jensen if she is still alive, some kind of incomprehensible vengeance to find her in some place of retirement and inflict upon her some mild punishment, some bewildering punishment. It would make me feel better."

Humphries found impersonating Edna "very therapeutic and liberating." He says, "I was finally more comfortable as Edna, because I was more heavily disguised. I could relax in the character. It was like a girl who suddenly discovers she has a career in prostitution. On the one hand, she suddenly thinks, Oh, I've got a job. And, on the other hand, Well, actually, it's a job my parents aren't going to be too happy about."

Humphries' parents were vociferously disapproving of their son's vocation. "A man does all he can for his kids and what does he get for it?" was the beginning of one of Eric Humphries' familiar litanies, which his son put verbatim into one of his lesser caricatures, the successful businessman Colin Cartwright. "Things were going well for *him* professionally," Humphries says of his father. "Then, suddenly, I seemed to be what Vance Packard called the 'slip generation,' the one who was going to blow it all. I shared his anxiety but didn't let on. What, indeed, would I be? I was tortured with wondering. It certainly couldn't be anything I was good at or enjoyed—it had to be something else." At first, his parents boycotted his shows, and, even with his success, Louisa refused to see her son perform his priapic Sir Les Patterson. "Only later did my father come," Humphries says. "He went to a theatre in Melbourne. The box-office lady said to me, 'Oh, your father's such a nice man.' I said, 'When did you meet him?' She said he'd come in that morning. He wanted to buy all the tickets in the theatre and give them to his friends. He was very surprised to learn they were sold out. He was convinced no one would come."

To his mother Humphries was, according to him, "guilty of letting down the side, a frequent crime." An elegant woman, Louisa was adored and spoiled by her husband, whose preoccupation with his business left her ruling the roost at home. "My mother wasn't a particularly warm woman," Humphries says. "She had artistic qualities that were *all* suppressed." Louisa was judgmental and could make her disapproval felt. When Humphries told her he had met the Queen after a command performance at the Palladium, she replied, "I hope you were wearing a nice *suit*."

Humphries wasn't. "She had a very oblique way of paying you a compliment, always very recondite," Humphries says. "It didn't seem necessary to inform her that I was wearing a dress." But, even before acting and Edna, Humphries had difficulty in making his mother see him for himself. She once asked him to return the gift of a pair of earrings he'd bought her, "This was a very wounding experience for a child," he says.

The problem of being properly accepted remained an issue between them in his adulthood. Humphries tells of returning from London to Melbourne to show off to Louisa his newborn son Oscar, the first child of his now dissolved third marriage, to the painter Diane Millstead. "She had not met her grandson," he recalls. "As I arrived home, I noticed my mother listening to the transistor radio. I came forward to present my son to her, and she was cautioning me, 'Listen! Listen!' It was a typical Australian disk jockey on a phone-in program. He happened to be talking about me. Was I good for Australia or not? It was generally felt that I was doing Australia a great disservice by my impersonations—particularly that of Sir Les Patterson, this anachronistic figure. My mother was saying, 'Sh-h-h . . . sh-h-h . . . listen!' People were ringing up and saying things like 'Well, I haven't seen one of Barry's shows, but from what I've heard it's a disgrace.' This disk jockey by impugning my patriotism was inflating his own reputation. My mother said, pointedly, 'You see That's what they think. That's what they think of you!' I was so incensed that I should come home and my mother should be listening to this rubbish, and not dismissing it, instead of greeting me and her grandson, that I went into another room. I telephoned the radio station as Edna. I got through using the voice of Edna. I said that this was Dame Edna and I was on a brief visit to Australia and I was listening to the program about Barry Humphries and I heartily agreed with these women. I said, 'Not only do I agree with what these women said about Barry Humphries but I happen to know that Barry Humphries' mother thinks *exactly* the same.'"

Dame Edna is out of widow's black now and into iridescent celebrity red. "Eat your heart out, Tina Turner!" she shouts, unveiling the short, fringy dress in which she hymns her dead husband, her public, and her professionalism. The audience is in a party mood. Someone hidden in the shadows of a box throws a chartreuse-and-yellow card, and it lands with a clatter at Edna's feet. She kicks the missive offstage, and Harriet Bowdler retrieves it. "I LOVE YOU," it reads. "Hays, known as 'Hayseed' from Kentucky. 1st bloke in 1st box on left."

Edna, too, is talking of love: "I love to hear laughter. I call it Vitamin L, what an essential part of our spiritual diet it is, isn't it, possums? Norman and I—oh, how we used to love to laugh. We were always playing little jokes on each other. And it's not easy, is it, playing jokes on institutionalized loved ones. Huh. But every April Fools' Day we had a little jest with each other. I remember last April the first . . . hah! . . . We pretended to Norm . . . hah! . . . he was going to he discharged from the hospital. Ha, ha! Isn't that gorgeous? You could do that with a loved one. The matron helped, too. She packed his little case so he could watch her doing it out of the corner of the mirror above his page-turning machine. He's had 'The Thornbirds' open at the same page for the last seven years. (Who hasn't?) Anyway, they got him into his dressing gown, and he shuffled down to the front of the hossie, where they had an ambulance ticking over. And just as Norm was about to fall into the ambulance . . . hee, hee . . . *it whizzed off down the driveway!* Ah, ha, ha! . . . He fell flat on his face in the gravel. And all the doctors and nurses leant out the windows and said, 'April Fool!' . . . Ha, ha! . . . I wish Norm could have laughed at that. . . . Oh dear . . . oh, but I'm a lucky, lucky woman, because I was born with a priceless gift. 'What gift is that, Dame Edna?' I hear you saying. . . . The ability to laugh at the misfortunes of others. . . . And, you know, that keeps me cheerful twenty-four hours a day, it does!"

Edna frequently criticizes Humphries in public and in the press. (In her autobiography she writes, "BARRY HUMPHRIES. Still my manager, but under solicitor's thumb. His contributions to our show getting smaller by the year.") And Edna's putdowns about his lack of talent only add to his legend and his mystery. In explaining Edna to the public, Humphries does what all dandies do: he obscures his depths and his roots. "If England is the Mother-land and Germany is the Fatherland, Australia is certainly the Auntieland," he told his friend the actor-writer John Wells. "I had a lot of aunts, all very nice, but they were there, all the time. So I was pretty good at giving an impersonation, certainly, of a kind of synthesis of these women. And also of their obsession with domestic detail, seeing the whole world, really, through the venetian blind of the kitchen window: seeing everything in terms of household arrangements, cleanliness, all that stuff. These people who managed to live comfortably and happily in such a narrow world that they could get by without ever having read the Muirs' translations of Kafka, that they could he perfectly happy and well entertained without dipping into 'Cardinal Pirelli.'"

There were few books in the Humphries house. "My mother was a great student of *The Australian Women's Weekly*." Humphries says. The family's tidy and comfortable home was as free from dirt as it was from the infection of ideas. "There were just standard books," Humphries recalls. "'The Family Doctor,' an encyclopedia bought from a travelling salesman. Very few novels. My uncle—my mother's brother-in-law—had been in France during the First World War. He had a lot of books and gave me some. My father bought me whatever books I wanted, although a copy of D. H. Lawrence was seized by my mother." Humphries also had two great-uncles who painted. "They did very large pictures of the River Nile at sunset and of lions in their lair," he says.

It was not only the deadly tedium of the Melbourne suburbs that so powerfully affected Humphries but the silence inside his own house. "It was quiet. Only at my insistence was a gramophone obtained," he says. "I started collecting records seriously as a boy." Music partly answered Humphries' "hankering for somewhere else." He says, "In the early Melbourne days, sitting in Camberwell wondering what I was going to do when I grew up, I was mostly listening to English music: Vaughan Williams and Delius in particular, romantic 'pastoral' music." The family's brown Bakelite radio also abetted Humphries' yearning for "moister climates," by bringing him into contact with British music-hall comedians and the notion that people told jokes for a living. This discovery occurred when Humphries was about ten, and laughter seemed to hold out to him a power comparable to his fantasy of being a magician and making people disappear. Humphries says, "I wanted to exercise power over people. I wanted to control their access to me." In a mock novel about "an androgynous and eldritch child" named Tid,

Humphries wrote, in 1961, "Tid's main thing was trying not to be seen. You can't imagine how hard this job was. . . . He just wanted ladies and men to accept the fact that he wasn't there." At the end, Tid becomes king. Humphries wrote, "Tid hides in the world and is king of it."

"It's true," Dame Edna says, scanning the front rows. "There are such a lot of lovely young folk here to see me. The young *adore* me. And please, youngsters, remember everything you see tonight. Will you promise Edna? Please? Your grandchildren are probably going to want to know about this experience. They are. This could be your only interesting anecdote."

Dame Edna sees herself as the world's role model. She is, she says, into "M"s, including matrimony, motherhood, and monogamy. Dame Edna has always been true to Norm in her fashion. As she sang in "Why Do I Love Australia?":

> Why do I love Australia?
> Why does it grab me so?
> Life was so sunny and informal
> When my husband Norm was normal
> And my career was in embryo.

Dame Edna treats her children with the same combination of sentimentality and neglect. "I think my famous softness really took a big leap forward when my first bubba came along," Dame Edna writes in "My Gorgeous Life," and she recalls returning to her roots in Moonee Ponds and going through the postures of parenthood while looking at the pencil marks of her children's heights still on the doorframe. "My lovely hazel eyes prickled with tears as I looked around."

Humphries himself is a much married man. In *Who's Who* he does not acknowledge his first marriage—to a classical ballerina, Brenda Wright, in 1955, when he was twenty-one. He married, he told the press, "much too young," and in 1959, after he was divorced, he married another dancer, Rosalind Tong, whom he'd met during the run of a children's play he co-wrote and starred in—"The Bunyip and the Satellite." Humphries' second marriage, which produced two daughters—Tessa, in 1963, and Emily, in 1965—lasted nearly twelve years and ended with Rosalind's leaving a packed suitcase for Humphries at the stage door. Humphries told the Sydney *Daily Mirror* in 1982:

> I was enjoying all the razzle dazzle of success. After leaving the theatre at night, instead of going home, I'd find myself going to a pub, then on to a club or party. I got to the stage where I hardly bothered to look at my watch.
>
> I don't reproach Rosalind at all for what she did. I reproach myself. We were together for nearly twelve years, and when it was over, I was deeply unhappy for a long time.

For a few years after his divorce from Rosalind, Humphries declared himself a bad matrimonial bet and swore off the institution. "For a long time I was an impossible person to live with," he told English *Vogue* in 1976. "I'm fine as far as work is concerned, but I'm bad at other things, like returning phone calls and making breakfast. The traditional wife has her uses—but I wouldn't want to live with anyone who wanted to be just a wife. Anyway, after unsuccessful relationships, one gets a bit tense, a bit wary."

But in 1975 Humphries met Diane Millstead, whose paintings he had admired in a Melbourne gallery, and in 1979 she became the third Mrs. Humphries. "Diane claims I used to be a terrible womanizer before I met her," Humphries said in the *Mirror*. "I prefer to say I was very, very fond of female company." The marriage produced two sons—Oscar, in 1981, and Rupert, in 1982—and its share of headlines. At the beginning of their marriage, Millstead referred to Humphries in the press as "the sex symbol of the Eighties," but when the marriage ended, in 1989, she was calling him "a champion mattress tester." In June, 1990, Humphries married Lizzie Spender, the actress-playwright daughter of Stephen Spender.

"Isn't it a spooky thought," Dame Edna says, pursuing the idea of family and children, "to think that one day in the twenty-first century your little grandbubbas will he huddled around your gnarled and knotted kneecaps? You'll be leaning on your Zimmer frame and they'll look up to you and they'll say, 'Oh, Nana, Nana, tell us again that lovely story of the night, that historic night at the Theatre Royal Drury Lane (now a supermarket) . . . tell us about the night you went to see Saint Edna.'"

Dame Edna scowls at the audience for laughing at the notion of her as a canonized model of nurturing self-sacrifice. "Please! Don't laugh. I've had a tipoff. I can't tell you who told me, but he's Polish, single, and lives in Italy. That's *all* I can say." But later, after her monologue has meandered through accounts of her "regular exploratories" and her Swiss financial advisers, Dame Edna returns to her latest claim for herself as a mother. "I'm an upmarket Mother Teresa. I am. I am. And Mother Teresa comes to see me, too. Every time she comes to London. She comes to London once a year, for the Harrods Sale. It's not—no, it's not for the merchandise. She just loves sleeping in the street. She *loves* it. She said to me, 'Edna, those Knightsbridge gutters have got the edge on Calcutta.' She came backstage with her little program, holding a little gladdy she'd caught. And I said, 'Did you enjoy it, Tess, tell me?' And she said, 'Edna, I came out of your show feeling another woman!'"

Dame Edna is spinning a yarn about a letter she has received from a woman in Shepherd's Bush who has been to one of her shows. "She said, 'I was the woman sitting in the first six rows that you chose that night . . . as you always do . . . choose a woman . . . to do the nude cartwheels onstage.'" Dame Edna paces the stage and looks down into the front rows. "And now the mood has completely changed, hasn't it? I don't know what you'd call it. Blind terror, I think, don't you? I think these yups want to be up with the paups, don't you: *I think they do.* But don't you be nervous. Please. Supposing I chose, for argument's sake, YOU! In the third row—as I almost certainly will. Hello? What is your name? You. Yes. Yes. What is your name?"

"Emma," says a middle-aged blonde, faintly.

"Hello, Emma," Dame Edna coos. "Have you done much nude-cartwheel work? Don't worry, Emma. We've found audiences prefer an amateur nude cartwheelist, they do! They have a way of falling over which is vulnerable and—well, strangely appealing. So don't be nervous, Emma. Don't scratch your eczema, Emma. Because you will not know that you're doing these cartwheels, Emma. Do you know why? You'll be in deep shock,

Emma. You will. Because whenever we women are very, very frightened, our bodies do a funny thing. We secrete an enzyme at the same time. So you'll not only be in your birthday suit endeavoring to do cartwheels, and failing. But you'll be secreting an enzyme at the same time. I hope that's reassuring."

Dame Edna began as a less strident voice from the back of the Union Theatre Repertory Company touring bus taking "Twelfth Night" on one-night stands through Victoria in 1955. It was Humphries' first year as a professional actor, He was twenty-one. Having dropped out of Melbourne University two years earlier, he had been earning his living by working at E.M.I. as, variously, a wholesale record salesman and a breaker of recently obsolete 78s. "This latter chore," he says, of days he spent in a windowless room in an "inane frenzy," destroying piles of Mahler, Sibelius, Debussy, and the Ink Spots, "produced a more acute form of nervous exhaustion than I had experienced in my less compulsive Dadaist activities, though it bore an ironic resemblance to them." Humphries' Duke Orsino, on the other hand, was less than smashing. "He wasn't a swell leading man," says Zoe Caldwell, who played Viola. "Clearly, he didn't concentrate. He couldn't stay in a role. You thought, He can't possibly be an actor. But I knew he'd be something. He had such an extraordinary mind. As Orsino, his legs were too thin. When he came on, he got a laugh."

To entertain themselves from one country town to another, the cast sang songs, told tales, and recited verse. Humphries' party piece was Edna, who had "the unmistakable voice of the genteel Melbourne housewife," he says, and who was also "a flashback, really, to my earliest university days and late school days, when with a group of friends we formed a Melbourne Dada group . . . in which we attempted to ridicule the fellows who we felt were terribly stuffy—and, indeed, we were quite right in thinking so." Edna allowed Humphries to show off his gift for caricature and his desire to shine. "I found that I had a good falsetto voice, and I invented a character to go with it—a female character, because, you see, every night, when the curtain fell on 'Twelfth Night,' the local lady mayoress or the ladies' committee would invite this distinguished cast from the city of Melbourne to what was called a bun fight: cups of tea and wonderful cakes such as only Australians seem able to make—plates of lamingtons and iced vovos and butterfly cakes all stuck together with cream and cocoa. They used to give little speeches about how wonderful 'Twelfth Night' was. I had a knack of anticipating some of the ladies' speeches very, very well as my funny little character in the back of the bus."

Edna was encouraged by the company's resident writer-director, Ray Lawler, whose "Summer of the Seventeenth Doll," in the late fifties, was the first Australian play to win international fame and, along with Humphries' characters, sound a new theatrical note of Australian self-awareness. Humphries recalls, "When it came to be time for the annual revue, 'Return Fare,' which Lawler was directing, Ray said, 'Why don't you write a sketch for that character you did in the bus: What's she called?' I plucked a name out of the air; 'Edna,' I suggested, since I'd once had a kind of nanny called Edna, of whom I was very fond. I said, 'Her name is Edna, and she comes from Moonee Ponds.' I thought, I daren't say Camberwell, or my mother will think it's based on her. Indeed, Edna is more of a Camberwell character than she is a Moonee Ponds character. Moonee Ponds was a suburb of Melbourne I'd never been to, at the time. . . . 'Well, if I write a sketch for this character,' I said, 'who will play Edna? Will I do the voice from offstage?' Ray said, 'You do it yourself,' 'Can't Zoe be Edna?' I asked. He said, 'No, you be Edna. Do it like a pantomime dame.'"

On December 19, 1955, Edna Everage made her stage debut. She wore no wig, no eyeglasses, and no makeup "She had shortish brown hair, which was in fact my own longish hair combed down," Humphries says. "She wore a hat, a voluminous skirt, flat shoes, and sockettes, and carried a rather large handbag. She looked somewhat gauche and nervous and spoke in a high, genteel, less vigorous and confident way than she speaks now. She was, after all, someone who had merely strayed from the kitchen onto the stage." The sketch was called "Olympic Hostess"—a title as up to the minute as Edna's palaver. The 1956 Olympic Games were to be staged in Melbourne, and already there were advertisements in the local newspapers asking for fifteen thousand beds to put up the athletes. In the sketch, Edna attempted to offer her Moonee Ponds home for the Games, an opportunity not so much for hospitality as for house-pride. "There were not many tradi-tional jokes in this piece," Humphries has written. "The real jokes turned out to be her lovely home itself."

> There's our bedroom, one—then there's the lounge and din-ing room. If you open the double doors—little Kenny—that's my youngest—always calls them the reindeer doors because of the sandblasted reindeers on the glass—if you open the double doors it's a lovely big room. We pushed back the Genoa velvet couch and rolled back the burgundy Axminster squares for Val-mai's twenty-first, and the young people had the time of their lives.

"You could hear the whoosh of laughter," Humphries says of the audi-ence's rapturous shock of recognition. Even the cast was surprised by the sketch's impact. "No one had really talked about Australian houses before," Humphries has said. "Since my father was a builder, and the creator of a number of substantial Melbourne houses, in jazz moderne with manganese bricks, or Spanish Mission with the barley-sugar columns and little grilled windows, I was interested in houses. I found that I'd discovered something I could write about, not by putting the telescope to my eyes and trying to write something in the manner of Coward or Alan Melville, but by just looking through the venetian blinds onto my own front lawn. So Edna was born, Edna Everage as in 'average,' husband Norm as in 'normal.'"

Until Edna's debut, Humphries had been "the boy in the rep who was worst at learning his lines and was getting smaller and smaller parts." Edna's success made him the star of the revue. Humphries ended up getting an eighteen-month engagement in revue at the Phillip Street Theatre in Sydney. "I found, to my great pleasure," Humphries says, "that the 'Olympic Hostess' sketch was popular there and that Mrs. Everage was by no means unknown in New South Wales." But Humphries had no ambitions for the character. Having discovered her, he promptly put her in mothballs. Edna made her Sydney debut in 1956, in "Mr. and Mrs.," but she didn't appear onstage in Melbourne again until 1958, when she was seen first in Peter O'Shaugh-nessy's "Lunch-Hour Theatre Revues" and later in the "Rock 'n Reel Revue."

"In Australia, before me, most comic stereotypes were kind of rural people, hayseeds, hillbillies," Humphries says. "There seemed to be no Australian comedians who actually tried to reproduce *as accurately as possible*, without the use of jokes, or even funny names, something intrinsically funny in the way that *most* people really did live. In refrigerators. In appliances. In the problems of parking the car. It was just a sort of fresh interpretation of ordinary life. Whereas before, when you were identifying with Lucille Ball or Bob Hope or the Marx Brothers, you had to go through a very quick series of transpositions. First, you had to translate from the American into the English or Australian idiom, and *then* get the joke." In Edna's case, the joke was at the Australian front door.

Edna was the doyenne of philistine denial. She feared the penetration of anything: germs, ideas, certainly sex. "Although my childhood was in the midst of—at the very heart of—niceness and decency and cleanliness and comfort," Humphries has written, "I perceived the little dramas of Australian suburban life: the war against stains and creepy crawlies and the mysterious Outback; the knowledge that we didn't really live in Bournemouth or Wimbledon, but on the ghostly periphery of Asia with no traditions or even ghost stories to palliate our fear." Edna barricaded herself in the trivia of daily life. She gave her listeners detailed baking recipes. She lectured the audience on home hygiene: "A drop of disinfectant in your kiddy's schoolbag could save a lot of heartache. A Pine-O-Cleen rinse makes your rubbish bins safe to live with." She hymned the contents of her medicine chest: "Calamine lotion. Milk of magnesia. Laxettes. Aspros. Band-Aids (flesh-tint). Bicarbonate of soda. Golden eye ointment. Raleigh's Ready Relief . . ." Her fear of infection betrayed a mind without a thought—with just the echo of brand names and the rhythms of their advertising slogans.

For Humphries himself, there was no advertisement like self-advertisement. Edna gave Humphries the license to make a spectacle of himself. And he did. "Barry Humphries is, perhaps, the most gifted clown in Australia," said Humphries' bio in the 1958 program for the "Rock 'n Reel Revue." By 1959, Australian society had taken both the character and her creator to its heart, and that summer Humphries set off to test his talent in the more competitive arena of English theatre. Dame Edna, in her chapter about the Australian leave-taking in her autobiography, recalls that Mother Teresa subsequently told her that true happiness comes from renunciation. "I began my Life of Renunciation years ago," Dame Edna writes. "I decided to renounce Obscurity." It was a big roll of the dice for both Edna and her creator. Humphries' arrival in London was noted in one paragraph of the *Evening News* with the headline "A STAR HERE?" "That question mark haunted me for years," Humphries says.

"Excuse me," Dame Edna says, breaking off her monologue in "Back with a Vengeance!" to take the twenty-two hundred and forty-five paying customers sternly into her confidence. "*Paupers, stop leaning forward. I've told you a squillion times!* There was a tragedy here the other night. We've kept it out of the papers, but I have to tell you what it was. A pauper woman—a paupess, actually—plummeted . . ." Having invented a word and reinforced it by alliteration, Edna continues to dazzle the audience with her effortless juggling of pun, innuendo, and irony, which unobtrusively plants in the audience's imagination the notion of someone falling out of the balcony. "She was leaning forward—it's so steep up there—she was leaning forward to get a chockie off the lap in front of her. At least, that's what we *assume* she was doing. She was fumbling for a hard one, Emma, when she came out. She wrapped *her* chops around the back of a seat, the toughest hard one she's ever experienced. They had to put her in a plastic bag and take her away. I laughed. . . . I laughed compassionately. I did."

"A number of people prophesied success for me who saw me on my home ground, where I *knew* I was funny," Humphries says of his move to London. "There's nothing better than seeing a comic who thinks he's funny. If he's not entirely sure that what he's saying is amusing, or if his anxiety gets the better of him, he's not doing himself justice." And anxiety was the mood of Humphries' life as he struggled to get a theatrical foothold in London. "Barry was absolutely broke," says his compatriot Ian Donaldson, a professor of English Literature and also an Old Melburnian, who hung out during the early, insecure years in the louche atmosphere of Humphries' Notting Hill basement apartment, with other artistic Aussie expats, like the painters Arthur Boyd, Sidney Nolan, and Francis Limburner. In order to audition by day, Humphries took a job in an ice-cream factory by night. "I didn't work there very long, but it was my only experience of factory work," he says. "It was a hellish experience, and sort of Dadaist as well. At first, I was working on a conveyor belt. It was Chaplinesque. Because of my maladroitness, I was put with the morons. I wasn't *allowed* to work on the conveyor belt, because I kept dropping the ice creams. I was put in a room where a group of us sat around an enormous plastic drum throwing damaged ice creams into it. I felt I smelled rather of raspberry ripple when I went to auditions."

Five months after arriving in England, in June, 1959, Humphries landed a small part. He played the madhouse keeper in "The Demon Barber," a musical about Sweeney Todd, at the Lyric, Hammersmith—far from the West End. Humphries' own characters fared less well. His desiccated Melbourne ghost, Sandy Stone, made a brief appearance on British television upon his arrival. "I don't think anyone made anything of it at all," Humphries says. Edna seemed to arouse even less interest. If his prospects appeared to be dim, his intellectual life took on a new amperage. He seized his London days with manic energy. His appetite for England and all things English filled his unemployed hours. "He was extraordinary," Donaldson says. "He fitted in immediately. He knew London. He knew about various writers and artists who we thought were dead. He said they were living in basements and attics. He knew the right pubs to drink in, the right people to talk to. He established this extraordinary network—still not getting employment but becoming known and being seen as someone of extraordinary knowledge who was also entertaining."

"In London, it was a question of finding a voice that people could actually hear and wish to listen to," Humphries says. London seemed like the Big Table at which he was not allowed to sit. "People are talking and you're outside" is how he characterizes the feeling. "You sort of tune in. You think, I want to come in on this, but I have to wait until the moment."

Humphries goes on, "I've suddenly discovered that England is really a province of Australia. And so I needn't have been frightened all those years ago. If I'd gone straight in . . . But I wasn't ready." Although he soon got work in the West End, appearing as Sowerberry in Lionel Bart's "Oliver!" (1960) and, later, in his "Maggie May" (1964), he did not get much satisfaction. "I think Barry's mood in London when I met him was bad," says Peter

Cook, who was then at the height of his celebrity both as an entertainer in "Beyond the Fringe" and as an impresario of outrageousness, who owned substantial shares in the satirical magazine *Private Eye* and was the proprietor of the Soho comedy club The Establishment. "I feel sure that he was certain he was very talented. I don't think he liked being in a minor part in 'Oliver!' Why it took Barry so long to became established—and, indeed, adored—over here, I don't quite know. I think in those early years, he was feeling a bit embittered." Cook, who was a fan of some records Humphries had made—especially those featuring Sandy Stone—but who had never seen him perform, generously threw Humphries a lifeline, asking him to do a three-week season at The Establishment in 1963, for a hundred pounds a week. "Big money," Humphries recalls of his Establishment gig, in which Sandy Stone and a timid Edna made their theatrical debuts in England. "Very big money. As soon as I got there, though, I felt a little uneasy. The shape of the room was long and narrow. The audience wasn't close to me, and it wasn't an experienced cabaret audience, either. The huge success of satire and 'That Was the Week That Was' on TV had led them to expect a certain kind of humor—very topical and often very witty and very irreverent about British institutions. My kind of rambling regional monologues, which depended for their effect not on jokes or on impersonations of political figures, were really unsuitable for that kind of place. They wanted Harold Macmillan. They didn't want Glen Iris, Melbourne."

In the annals of The Establishment, according to Peter Cook, no turn went down worse. "The stoniest of stony silences," Cook says. "*Nobody* found Barry remotely amusing. There were about three or four people who thought, This is very, very funny. Mainly, John Beeman, John Osborne, and me. I felt ashamed of my fellow-Londoners for not appreciating him." In "My Gorgeous Life" Dame Edna turns this punishing memory of humiliation into hilarity by blaming her actor-manager, Humphries, for the disaster. He, she claims, went on *before* her, and emptied the room. "I had a bit of a weep afterwards," Dame Edna writes. "Barry had gone home in a huff, the worse for a few sherries I'm afraid. . . . This was the lowest ebb in my career, but I have described it honestly and courageously. I was hurt at the time and my confidence was badly shaken, but I decided to have a few tough new clauses written into my contract with Mr. H. I also vowed that if I ever found success outside my native land, I would remember this incident."

And Dame Edna has remembered it. As the title of the present show admits, Dame Edna embraces her celebrity with a vengeance. And, like Humphries, Edna deals with her corrosive sense of envy by becoming the envied. She revels in her distinction in the same way and for the same reason that all the programs of Humphries' twelve one-man shows contain encomiums of his genius and photographs of him with the cultural icons of his era. "Barry Humphries is the first Australian Satirist, he is also one of the funniest men in the World, if you don't think so, then it's your loss," Spike Milligan wrote for Humphries' second one-man show, "Excuse I" (1964), adding, under his name, "(being of sound mind)." On the same page is a photograph of the young Humphries with another licensed trickster, Salvador Dali. Humphries' insistence on his comic and intellectual pedigree belies his long, sometimes hurtful struggle to have it validated.

"Barry first came to my attention at The Establishment," says the New Zealand-born cartoonist Nicholas Garland, who collaborated with Humphries on the sixties cult cartoon "The Adventures of Barry McKenzie," which ended up as two feature films. "The act was a failure, but we were all *enormously impressed* by Barry. We all began talking to each other in this preposterous parody of Australian. He instantly became somebody you rated. He was immediately subsumed into our culture, into our vocabulary, into the way we spoke. But it was a struggle for Barry. The English have plenty of eccentrics, plenty of people pretending to be Oscar Wilde and wearing their hair long. It took a while for Barry to get the measure of this." With a leg up from Peter Cook, Humphries was soon playing with the big boys. He crashed the cliquish Shrewsbury set that ran *Private Eye*, appearing in the magazine's columns both in the Barry McKenzie cartoon and as its astrologer, Madame Barry. He was cutting comedy tracks like "Old Pacific Sea," "Chunder Down Under," and "The Earl's Court Blues." He was doing character work for Joan Littlewood's Theatre Workshop, in Stratford East, as well as appearing in the West End. (He would make seventeen appearances in the West End in the subsequent decade, including a leading role in "The Bed-Sitting Room," with Spike Milligan; a memorable Long John

Silver—"I'm going to take a peep round the poop"—in a Christmas production of "Treasure Island" at the Mermaid Theatre; and Fagin in a revival
of "Oliver!") He was also tapped to join BBC-TV's "The Late Show" wits in
1964-67. Humphries was promising but not established. His frustration
was beginning to show. He was on the page, on the stage, on records, on
TV, and on the bottle.

"I remember Barry at a Boxing Day party doing something that I'd
never witnessed before," says Peter Cook, who enjoyed bending an elbow
with Humphries. "I think you have to reach another level of drunkenness to
achieve it. I did the normal thing of falling down drunk, but Barry upstaged
me by falling upstairs. I don't know how he did it." Between the mid-sixties
and the early seventies, when he swore off the sauce, Humphries drank so
heavily he nearly died from it. By the power of his charm and his humor, he
managed to conceal much of his drunken desperation. "I remember sitting
in a taxi with a Harrods bag on my lap that had a half bottle of whisky in it
and looking at the queue of heroin addicts outside Boots the Chemists in
Piccadilly Circus with contempt," he is quoted as saying in a recent biography by Peter Coleman, of the time he now characterizes as "when I was ill
and mad." "They were addicts and I was something else. I was, if you like, a
genius out of luck. I was a sensitive person. I just drank alcohol like all the
best people, like Dylan Thomas, like Scott Fitzgerald, like Malcolm Lowry,
like John Barrymore, like Tony Hancock. I belonged to the aristocracy of
self-destruction."

"There is a woman here tonight," Dame Edna says, peering over the footlights. "A woman who intrigues me. *You!* In the middle of the second row,
with a little thoughtful look on your face. Hello, darling. Did you see me
peeping at you?"

"Yes," says a thin voice from Row B.

"I saw you peeping at me, too. You'd be a foolish woman if you weren't,
wouldn't you? Swivelling your head like the kiddie in 'The Exorcist.'
What's your name?"

She's Margaret from Hornchurch.

"I don't know Hornchurch very well, but there are some lovely homes down that way, aren't there? Do you live near any of them, do you? Margaret? What type of a home have you?"

"A detached home."

"Oh, lovely," Dame Edna says. "Hear that, paupers? A detached home. It's a foreign language to them, Margaret. Have you made it nice inside? I . . . think . . . you . . . have, Margaret. I think you have. You can redecorate, can't you, Margaret, quite inexpensively. A little bit of emulsion. A little bit of paint. To make a beautiful home, I think that's serious money, as the yuppies would say. And yet . . . you've saved on clothes, haven't you, Margaret?"

Dame Edna likes to disconcert her audience. In previous shows, she has asked for, and received, shoes from the audience for her inspection. She has coaxed four people onto the stage to cook a barbecue and then left the paying customers alone in front of two thousand people while, with consummate daring, she made her exit for a costume change. She has insisted that her audience sit still for a Polaroid picture to remember it by. "You could feel the audience posing," Ian Davidson says, recalling the preposterousness of someone trying to photograph an entire audience. "A little picture would come out, and Edna would say, 'It's not very good of *you.*'" Dame Edna has also pulled a flashlight from her purse and trained it on the critics, trying to make them identify themselves—a job made easier by a sign saying "CRITIC" which dropped down over their assigned seats.

"What color carpet?" Dame Edna is asking Maud from Chingford. "Beige? Good heavens, she's been to the same remnant sale as you, Margaret. Any pictures on the wall? No pictures. No little pictures on the bedroom wall? Sounds delightful. And you're delightful, Maud (You're going to adore this woman when she's onstage in a minute.) Maud has gone beige now! Not yet, darling, no, but *soon*! So soon, that if I were you I'd start tensing up now.

Dame Edna is maneuvering the audience to join her onstage as extras in her epic. "Did you ever see my wonderful show 'The Dame Edna Experience'?" she says. "Emma, did you see it? It was marvellous, wasn't it, Emma? (Emma's getting a bit more animated by the minute there.) Did you see it at all, my TV series? Did you, Maud? Lovely. I tell you what I started doing. I was just talking to friends like Charlton Heston, Larry Hagman.

And then it proved too popular. They said they wanted me to do another series this year, I said *I will*. But I said I want real people. I said this time actually I want nonentities. I want . . . I want women like you, Maud, as a matter of fact. Whose chances of becoming a celebrity are—ha, ha—let's face it, darling, *nil*."

Edna was damed spontaneously, on camera, by the Socialist Australian Prime Minister Gough Whitlam. Happy to hitch his then popular public image to Edna's rising star, Whitlam made a guest appearance in the final scene of "Barry McKenzie Holds His Own" (1974), the second successful film collaboration of Humphries and the director Bruce Beresford. "Did you know the Prime Minister and I once slept together?" Edna says to her nephew Barry McKenzie as they approach Sydney Airport and a hero's welcome at the end of their adventures in Central Europe. "It was at the Opera House, during the second act of 'War and Peace.'" The joke was cribbed from Ronald Firbank's play "The Princess Zoubaroff," but the finale was wholly original, a surprise even to Humphries. Edna came out of the plane and fell into the Prime Minister's arms, and Whitlam said, "*Dame* Edna. Arise, Dame Edna." Thereafter, she was Dame Edna. "In a sense, Edna takes directions from herself, not me," Humphries says. "If the character seems to be developing that way, I generally go with it. I don't allow the puritan conscience to arise in me and say, 'What is she doing being a famous person when she should be back in Melbourne telling them what's wrong with their bathroom fittings?'"

Dame Edna declared herself a superstar. It was a smart career move. The mutation in Edna's character occurred in the mid-seventies, by which time the West had become accustomed to parody display and celebrity rule. Of Edna's evolution into superstar, which gave her a universal focus and turned her quickly into a piece of cross-cultural folklore, Humphries says, "I noticed that Barbra Streisand was starting to make pronouncements on things. They were views on poetry and art. These people who were traditionally philistine were not meant to excel in intellectual pursuits or matters of alternative religions. So Edna caught the wave that her country-woman Germaine Greer had helped to generate, and started doing some fancy surfing. It was originally a conscious parody of what these other people were saying. For instance, Streisand came out and said that her favorite picture was Edward Munch's 'The Scream.' That played right into Edna's hands. She said it was her favorite picture, too, and she'd had it made into dinner mats. Also, when these stars started to talk about being 'very private people,' Edna leaped on that. It was only people who were *fiends* for publicity who ever said it. As she became more famous, she adopted the postures of modesty. So she became a kind of cipher and also a megaphone for the styles and affectations of the period, which changed very rapidly. You had to be very up-to-date."

In the program, Edna identifies herself as Housewife, Megastar, Investigative Journalist, Social Anthropologist, Children's Book Illustrator, Film Script Assessor, Diseuse, Swami, Monstre Sacré, Polymath, and Hard-nosed Literary Agent, specializing in radical women's issues. (Her bio photograph shows Dame Edna posed with the book "Sexual Harassment: A Pictorial History.") "More and more, I find with Edna that you can throw anything into the cauldron, and somehow it's just Edna's new shape," Humphries says. "That's how she's developing today."

"Bring on my talk-show hostesses, please," Dame Edna says, suddenly Lady Bountiful dishing out compliments to the show's four chorus girls, the Lesettes, and promises of BMWs and world trips to the audience.

This is the moment that the audience has feared and been thrilling for, the moment in which Humphries, in a sense, recapitulates in the audience his childhood terror of being wiped out. Such is the power of Humphries' control of an audience and Dame Edna's tyrannical charisma that, no matter how far away they sit, all members of the audience feel a shiver of terror that Dame Edna will choose *them*. Humphries says, "I've taken to holding out these bribes—'Now, my next big major prize-winner is . . .'—if there looks to be a difficult, recalcitrant member of the audience. I prefer the doubtful ones."

"So," Dame Edna says, "without any further ado . . . I feel the excitement mounting. . . . And so I would like to invite to your ovation a very special person that I noticed almost as soon as I stepped on the stage tonight. Let's hear it for Maud from Chingford."

With the entire auditorium straining to see her, and the boom of some two thousand deeply relieved people clapping at the sound of her name,

Maud is finally coaxed out of her seat and up the stairs at the side of the stage into Dame Edna's waiting arms. "Hello, darling. Hello, Maud. How nice to see you," Dame Edna says, giving her a big hug and a big smile. "You delightful woman. You are absolutely delightful. And what lovely, lovely happiness you radiate, too. You do. Hairdresser's this morning, Maud?"

"No," says Maud.

"I didn't think so for a moment. However, never mind." In the moment between the uplift of Edna's compliment and the sting of her putdown, Humphries winks at Maud to disown the laugh and relax her fear.

"Barry's got the audience so well drilled that they all laugh at the same time," Ian Davidson says. "They're a solid mass. And they all turn to their partners to seek confirmation. You can see this. I've sat in the box and watched the audience. Between the moment of laughter and when they turn for corroboration, there is a moment of audience blindness. The audience isn't looking at the stage. You can do things in that moment. Barry usually smiles and winks at his victim."

Maud is ushered, laughing, offstage to be dolled up for the talk show. Dame Edna turns back to her audience. "And now my Hornchurch pilgrim, MARGARET! Here she is!"

But Margaret isn't budging.

"Come on, Margaret. Come on. Wait a minute. What's the matter, Margaret, darling?"

"I would prefer not to come," says Margaret.

"What? Mmn."

"I would prefer not to come."

"No?" says Dame Edna. "But the audience would love you to come. And to be branded a spoilsport would be horrible, Margaret. Wouldn't it be ghastly? Leaving the theatre, people spitting on you. I mean . . . I think the little bank manager next to you is trying to discourage you, isn't he, darling? Is he? You're the first woman who's ever rejected my offer, Margaret. Isn't that sad? I hope it doesn't bring you *terrible luck* for the rest of your life. What is Margaret's seat number? Ah, yes, yes. You would have—you would have won the BMW. Ha, ha. I'm so sorry. Never mind. Some people are killjoys, aren't they? It's a lovely opportunity to meet an understudy. A woman who we've spoken to before and she's longing to come up and join me. And what an ovation she'll get when she does. It's the lovely EMMA!"

Emma, tonight's erstwhile nude cartwheelist, gets a big hand and is greeted by Edna with fulsome praise for her "little outfit." Says Dame Edna, "I think you've paid me a great compliment coming straight from work to my show."

The audience creases up. Humphries gives Emma the wink and rounds on the uproarious crowd. *"Please! Don't be so rude! Have your manners just flown out the window?"* To which the answer, happily, is yes.

"Now let's hear it for Dame Edna's seminal, pivotal, mold-breaking, and revolutionary TALK SHOW!"

In conventional talk shows, the host listens while the guests talk, but with Dame Edna, who assumes that the guests are there for her amusement, the formula is reversed. They have to listen hard while *she* talks. Rarely is she bested. Dame Edna once probed former Prime Minister Ted Heath about his homes and the names of his Spanish staff. "I have a cleaning lady called Purificación," said Dame Edna. "And I have another Spanish helper, called Contracepción."

Said Mr. Heath, sharpish, "How do you get the two to work together?"

TV viewers had the unusual sight of Dame Edna laughing out loud at repartee that beat even her to the draw.

The show tries to exploit Dame Edna's confusion of reality and the credulity of the viewing public. "Most upmarket London penthouses have very highly trained Filipino staff," Dame Edna said in one show, "Mine is no exception. Except the little woman who smilingly Vims my sanitary unit and is my next guest. She's the former First Lady of all Filipinos. Yes. IMELDA MARCOS!"

"Imelda Marcos" entered to studio-audience applause, took a bow, and began walking toward Edna, "She's wearing my shoes!" Dame Edna said in horror, blowing a whistle she had taken from her purse. A barking mastiff bounded across the set and chased the stand-in offstage. In Dame Edna's first series of shows, "Charlton Heston" appeared in a wheelchair at the top of the set's steep and dangerous staircase. "It's just a had sprain," he said.

Dame Edna sent a nurse to help him. "Heston" and the nurse proceeded to tumble down the stairs. So real did the stunt look that Humphries' other guests, who could see "Heston" only on the monitors, were terror-stricken. The real Heston subsequently received thousands of get-well letters until he appeared on the show the following week in one handsome piece. Other public figures have met similar disasters. "Kurt Waldheim" appeared at the top of Dame Edna's stairway only to be dropped through a trapdoor. And "the Duchess of Kent," on her entrance, was snared in a booby trap and swung from her heels as Dame Edna signalled for a station break.

Dame Edna gives her non-celebrity guests a much gentler ride. Dressed as a nun, an Edna look-alike, a punk rocker, and a showgirl, the guests cram onto Dame Edna's postmodern sofa like so many dummies on a ventriloquist's knee. Dame Edna gets them to nod and respond while she pretends to ask for some collective wisdom about her wayward daughter, Valmai. "She shoplifts now, she does," Dame Edna says, keeping her guests captive with the cold intensity of her eye contact. "She goes into some of those Bond Street shops. She steals things. Puts them in her panty hose. Particularly frozen chickens when she's in a supermarket. Of course, the store detectives can smell those barbecued chickens when she goes out. Because she's a human microwave. She thinks she's an art collector. She thinks she's Peggy Guggenheim. That name ring a bell? She collects primitive art. New Guinea sculpture. Do you know much about New Guinea sculpture, Maud?"

"No," says Maud, running the gamut of her dialogue for the evening.

"You're missing nothing, darling. It is grotesque. It's mostly wooden willies."

And, with the notion of penises firmly planted in the audience's mind, it's a quick segue to the Gladdydämmerung that has been Edna's traditional spectacle of mayhem since the mid-sixties. "There's nothing more holy," Dame Edna said in "An Evening's Intercourse," "than massed gladioli." And, from the audience's delight, so it would seem. "It's gladdy time," says Dame Edna, frog-marching her accomplices downstage to the footlights. "There's some glads I want you to throw one at a time *gently* into the audience. Don't forget to let go. The Flinging Nun. It's gladdy time, a very beautiful moment in my famous show. Gladdy time. I mean, what other show . . . Could you imagine Barry Manilow doing this? Or Stevie Wonder?" Dame Edna throws a gladdy over her shoulder. "*Not in a million years! Not in a million years!*"

Dame Edna propels each gladdy higher, until the audience is watching gladioli fly up to boxes three tiers high.

"What about me, Dame Edna?" calls a woman from a fourth-tier box.

There's a drumroll. Dame Edna backhands the gladdy up to her. It falls short of its target. Another drumroll. Another try. The gladdy arches up past the follow spot, The woman reaches for it, and, with an ear-piercing scream, topples out of the box.

People beneath her shriek and scatter as she holds on and clambers up.

"Has anyone got a blanket?" Dame Edna shouts, and then she passes down a blanket from the stage. There is a moment of pandemonium. Panicked theatregoers are cowering by the exit doors. Four stalwart members of the audience hold the gray blanket beneath the woman, bracing themselves to catch her.

"Heaven be praised! There was a rope ladder in that box," Dame Edna says. "Oh, wouldn't it be ghastly if that happened every night!"

Harriet Bowdler, the stage manager, turns to me, "He enjoyed it. They look silly."

"Up, up, up! Hold your gladdy by the end of the stem for maximum gladdy thrust. And when I give the word—there we are, darling—up, up. What a beautiful sight!"

The audience sings "The Gladdy Song" with Dame Edna, and, at her command, stands and trembles the gladdies. The evening is almost over, but not before the proper benedictions and the absolution of applause. The guests are sent back to their seats with appropriate gifts: Camembert, Nivea cream, Steradent, a jar of Vaseline, a pair of Norm's Y-fronts, along with flowers and bottles of champagne. Before Edna's Assumption, there remains the blessing of her disciples. Maud, who is the last to leave the stage, is asked to bow her head. "Isn't it pathetic that this is the highlight of her life?" Dame Edna confides to the audience. And then she waves a gladiolus over Maud's head and recites:

Lucky possum that you are,
You are now a mini-star.
A big fish in a tiny pond,
Thanks to my magic wand.
Timid once, now you are bolder
Since Edna's gladdy
Touched your shoulder.
Go forth now, be kind and true,
Like Dame Edna was to you.

Soon dry ice is filling the stage with smoke, and Dame Edna's apotheosis is in its full magnificent swing. She has saved the most spectacular stage picture for last as she rises on the hydraulic lift high above the audience, singing about her shyness. No one in the audience wants Dame Edna shy. Everyone wants her as loud and vulgar and daring as she always is. Everyone wants her never at a loss, but filling life with the articulate energy of great clowning:

Yet, I must confess that I've felt slightly better since
You've helped me sublimate my grief-stricken reticence.
So . . . now . . . goooodbye.
I've got my act together and my head held high,
So high.
I'm a merry widow with a roving eye,
Yet I get so terribly shy
When the time finally comes for me to say
Was it good for you, too, possums?
And gooooodbye. . . . Good night. Darlings.

The cherrypicker deposits Dame Edna back onstage, and the din of applause and bravos continues over her bows. But she can't sit still for an audience even in its adulation. Dame Edna is twisting to a samba beat, blowing a carnival whistle, waving to her paupers. Her need for attention is no smaller than the audience's need for joy. Dame Edna doesn't want to leave the stage, and the audience doesn't want her to leave it. Even when the curtain falls, Dame Edna is still a presence. A spotlight lingers on her hand, which plays near the floor in front of the curtain. Behind the curtain, Dame Edna is on her stomach, gesturing into the noisy void. She begins by giving the audience a wave—"almost a caress," says Humphries—and ends by almost giving it the finger.

Outside, after the show, people linger under the dark-blue columns of the Drury Lane's portico. Maud from Chingford is exiting with her armful of gladioli. A young man within earshot says, "There's Maud. There's the star of the show."

She nods in his direction and walks slowly down the marble steps into the chill of the London night.

YIP HARBURG

THE LEMON-DROP KID

On March 5, 1981, near the intersection of Sunset Boulevard and Veteran Avenue, in Brentwood, a car drifted slowly across the lane into oncoming traffic. The body of the songwriter E. Y. Harburg, also known as Yip, was found lying across the front seat of the wayward vehicle; his chest had caved in from a heart attack. Harburg was eighty-four. At the time, there were rumors that the car he'd collided with was the former limousine of Richard Nixon, which would have been a piquant irony, given that Harburg was blacklisted in Hollywood in the fifties because of his politics and always took delight in tweaking the nation's follies, including what he called Pentagoonery. This year marks Harburg's centenary, and although his songs are still very much a part of our musical atmosphere (his ASCAP royalties average about five hundred thousand dollars a year), Harburg himself is a forgotten man. He belongs in the pantheon of great theatrical lyricists—Ira Gershwin, Cole Porter, Oscar Hammerstein, Lorenz Hart, and, latterly, Stephen Sondheim (whose favorite lyric lines are "Ever since that day / When the world was an onion," from Harburg's "The Eagle and Me")—but he has become the invisible man of the American musical. Though he collaborated with Harold Arlen on the classic score for "The Wizard of Oz," you won't find his name on "The Wizard of Oz in Concert" or on the three-disk set of "The Ultimate Oz." Unlike his Broadway colleagues, Harburg does not have a coffee-table compendium devoted to his lyrics—a reversal of fortune that puts Harburg himself with the other demoted "big-wheel controversials" he laughed at in "Jamaica" (1957):

> Napoleon's a pastry
> Bismarck is a herring

Alexander's a crème de cacao mixed with rum
And Herbie Hoover is a vacu-um.

But before the wa-wa pedal, before the Fender Stratocaster, Harburg—
who will finally get his due this November, when the New York Public
Library for the Performing Arts mounts an exhibit devoted to his life and
work—was writing songs that moved Americans and gave words to their
inarticulate longings and fears. He called himself variously "a wheeler-
dealer in stardust," "a rainbow hustler," and "a re-evolutionist"; Arlen, with
whom he wrote a hundred and eleven songs, and who died in 1986, called
him the Lemon-Drop Kid. "Yipper is not a blues thinker," Arlen once told
me. "He likes things to be joyous and/or poetic." Harburg liked to take issue
with his times, and he did this by making unacceptable ideas irresistible.
"Words make you think thoughts. Music makes you feel a feeling. But a song
makes you feel a thought," he often said. "Barriers fall. Hostilities melt, and
a new idea can find a soft spot under a hard hat."

Every lyricist has his own thematic obsessions, and Harburg, whom I
interviewed at length in the mid-seventies, regularly discoursed on the
views of the other lyricists in his league. "Cole Porter saw the world as an
élite party," he said. "Hammerstein had a little more humanity. He felt for
people. He *was* as corny as Kansas in August. Berlin saw the world as a hit
song. Ira Gershwin saw the world as a smart song. His thematic attack is
always 'Oh, sweet and lovely lady, be good. Oh, lady be good to me!' He
wants mothering: 'Someone to watch over me.' Larry Hart saw songs as a
means of stopping the pretty girls from rejecting him. His songs always
yearn for a 'hand to hold my hand': 'When the music swells, I'm touching
your hand; It tells that you're standing near.' The height of ecstasy is to have
somebody hold his hand. And me? 'It's only a paper moon, Sailing over a
cardboard sea, But it wouldn't be make-believe, If you believed in me.' And
somewhere over the rainbow we'll be all right."

The theme of freedom—sexual, social, intellectual—runs through
Harburg's œuvre and forms a kind of emotional signature to his work. He
wrote one of the first antiwar musicals ("Hooray for What?," 1937); the first
all-black Hollywood musical for general audiences ("Cabin in the Sky,"
1943); the first musical about feminism ("Bloomer Girl," 1944); the first

stage song about the emerging civil-rights movement ("The Eagle and Me," 1944); and, with his masterpiece, "Finian's Rainbow" (1947), he was the first to mount a fully integrated Broadway musical. Many of Harburg's songs defined their times ("Last Night When We Were Young," "April in Paris," "Let's Take a Walk Around the Block"); and two of them—"Brother, Can You Spare a Dime?" and "Somewhere Over the Rainbow"—became not only the anthems of their eras but global statements. Even at the end of his life, Harburg was updating his old standards to reflect the new civilization that had inherited them. In 1974, he revised "Brother, Can You Spare a Dime?" and published it in the *Times* as "Anthem for a New Depression":

> Once we had a Roosevelt,
> Praise the Lord,—
> Life had meaning and hope,
> Now were stuck with Nixon,
> Agnew—Ford,
> Brother, can you spare a rope?

Harburg suggested to Irving Berlin that he, too, rewrite his standard "God Bless America," to comment on the havoc of Vietnam, and retitle it "God Help America." "Yip's thoughts drift over to Moscow, but his heart is deeply planted in Fort Knox," said Berlin, who wrote the parody ("God bless America / Land I enjoy / No discussions with the Russians / Till they stop sending arms to Hanoi"), but, like many other Broadway high-rollers, did not share Harburg's politics. J. J. Shubert, who, with his brother, Lee, produced Harburg's 1932 Broadway revue, "Americana," declared that "Brother, Can You Spare a Dime?" was "too sorbid [sic]." Bert Lahr (my father), who made a comic classic of Harburg's "Song of the Woodman," told him he was "too foivent." And Arlen passed on writing the music for "Finian's Rainbow" because of Yip's penchant for what Arlen called "propaganda." Hammerstein, however, was gradually persuaded by Harburg's convictions. "At first, he felt the stage was a place only to amuse people," Harburg told me. "When he heard Harold and I were working on an antiwar show called 'Hooray for What?' he told Arlen, 'For God's sake, tell Yipper to leave the pulpit alone.' But after Hammerstein saw 'Finian's Rainbow' he sent me three telegrams—one in the morning, one in the afternoon, one at night. They all said, 'Will You Marry Me?' Two years later, he wrote the antiracist anthem 'You've Got to Be Taught.'"

The musical is—and always has been—America's most persuasive political theatre. It incarnated America's sense of blessing—a buoyant universe where "Something's coming, something good, / If I can wait." Harburg, in his puckish fashion, wanted the musical to be both payday and May Day. He understood better than all his songwriting cohorts the essentially political nature of song.

Harburg sauntered through life with a distinctive youthful twinkle; with his quiff of white hair and his toothy grin he was—even in old age—catnip to women. But darker tensions nevertheless showed through. He was a bundle of twitches: his eyebrows, fingers, and what he called his "restless legs" seemed to contradict the composure of his lyrics. These judderings lifted from Harburg's body when he sang. "Song is a lyricist's autobiography," Harburg said, and the manic playfulness of his songs made light of a life that was hard. The son of Russian-immigrant parents, he came into the world in 1896, as Isidor Hochberg (in 1923, when he got married, he changed his name to Edgar Yip Harburg), and lived to see his brilliant older brother, Max, a scientist, die of cancer at twenty-eight, and his younger brother, Harry, die of a stroke at twenty-nine. As early as 1932, in "That's Life," Harburg was joking about these devastations:

> You go along in the red
> Just when you're getting ahead
> Bingo! You're dead.
> That's life.

Over the years, Harburg's viewpoint became more Olympian, but his cautionary message remained the same: "Life is short, short, brother! / Ain't it de truth? / . . . You gotta rock that rainbow / While you still got your youth."

During Harburg's youth, on the noisy, cramped Lower East Side, he rarely heard music. A German band played occasionally in the alleys between the tenement walkups, and an organ-grinder cranked out snatches of Italian opera for pennies thrown from apartment windows. "Half the time, we were in the dark to save money," Harburg said of life in the family's three-room tenement apartment at Eleventh Street and Avenue C. He gravitated toward the airy southern exposure of the Tompkins Square Library, where he became an avid reader, and the limelight of the Yiddish theatre on the Bowery, where he and his father escaped on Saturdays after synagogue. He told many vivacious tales of Lower East Side street life—the bustle of Hester Street, roasting stolen potatoes on midnight bonfires—but his prevailing adult memory was of sour, suffocating drudgery. Indeed, Harburg and Irving Berlin were the only giants among the Broadway songwriters who actually grew up poor. The rest were middle-class kids whose sense of the Good Life was part of their lyrical optimism. Harburg's high spirits as a songwriter were a kind of reassurance, manufactured to reverse the gravity of what weighed him down. "I never liked to see my father come home from the sweatshop with gnarled fingers. I never liked seeing my mother's panic about where the rent was coming from," said Harburg, whose own day as a teen-ager began at 3 A.M. with a four-mile hike around lower Manhattan to turn off the street lamps and ended, at dusk, with another circuit to turn them on.

Harburg saw his sense of humor as "a survival trait handed down from father to son." Louis Hochberg, who enjoyed funny songs and Yiddish poetry, encouraged the boy's clowning. Most evenings, Harburg sat with his father at the kitchen table as he read from Sholem Aleichem, in Yiddish, over glasses of tea. Louis also read the *Forward*, the *Yidishes Tageblat*, and the Communist *Morning Freiheit*, and looked forward to the seemingly impossible day when the sweatshops would close. So Harburg's lessons in socialism and in consolation began at home. "My parents seemed so helpless in America," he said. "I was disturbed that they didn't speak English. I wanted to make them feel good, because they were so out of place and insecure."

Harburg began getting laughs when he was eleven; he wrote a parody of "I Want a Girl Just Like the Girl Who Married Dear Old Dad" for the bleacherites of the Tompkins Square championship baseball team. But it was in 1910, when he found his seat in English class at Townsend Harris High School, a C.C.N.Y. school with a rigorous curriculum designed for gifted poor children, that Yip, unbeknownst to himself, was finding his future. The rumpled, shy "quick blusher" seated alphabetically next to him was Ira Gershvin (whose family name was later changed to Gershwin by Ira's brother, George). Yip and Ira became fast friends when one day Yip pulled out his cherished copy of "The Bab Ballads," W. S. Gilbert's light verse. "Ira took a look at the book and said, 'Do you know that a lot of this is set to music?'" Harburg later wrote. "I was incredulous. 'There's music to it?'" Ira invited Yip to his family's first-floor apartment in a brownstone at Second Avenue and Fifth Street, which Yip considered "swank." Ira had an allowance and could afford to buy magazines like *Smart Set* and *Vanity Fair*. He also had records and a Victrola. "That first afternoon he played 'H.M.S. Pinafore' for me. There were all the lines I knew by heart, put to music! I was dumfounded, staggered," Harburg wrote. "Gilbert and Sullivan tied Ira to me for life."

Yip never entertained Ira at his house, but he was a frequent visitor to the Gershwins' large, well-heated apartment. Yip also knew Ira's younger brother, George, from the neighborhood. "He was considered a failure, a roustabout, a nogoodnik," Harburg said. "He was a kid who liked to go dancing, wear spats and a bowler hat long before he was grown up." Harburg was present when the Gershwins' first piano was hauled into the family home—a status symbol acquired by Mrs. Gershwin for Ira, who was the good student. "Ira was not only stunned, he was mad," Harburg recalled. "But he could never lash out at anybody. He just muttered under his breath, 'My mother. There she goes again. Always telling me what to do. I don't want a piano!'" Harburg went on, "I remember the piano being moved in through the window. Mrs. Gershwin was very fearful that it not be scratched on the way in. George came running up when he saw the piano. He didn't know it was coming, and he sat down and played a song. He played Irving Berlin's 'You've Got Your Mother's Big Blue Eyes'—a big hit at the time. Ira, Mrs. Gershwin, everybody said, 'George, where did you learn to play?' Two hands, with chords. He saved the day. Ira was off the hook." George told the amazed onlookers that he'd learned to play at the nearby piano store. "He ran errands, and for each errand he was allowed to make three cents. At that time, people didn't have telephones—only stores had them, and the shopkeeper would call a kid from the street and say, 'Wanna make three cents? Go up and call Mrs. Birnbaum to the phone.' George would run, and instead of taking the three cents he'd say, 'Let me play the piano for ten minutes.' He sat down there and figured out the chords and the tune of whatever were the popular songs of the day. The rest is history."

Harburg's first full-fledged song—an attempt at a hayseed comedy turn for vaudeville at the outbreak of the First World War—was written with George Gershwin, who was then just setting his sights on show music:

> When my son Sy heard the Sheriff's proclamashun
> That war wuz on with the gol dinged Dutch
> He enlisted in the Navy to proteck the Yankee nation
> And to show them furreners they ain't damn much.

But Harburg's association with Ira Gershwin over the years is what fed the sophistication of his light verse. At Townsend Harris, the two boys co-edited a column in imitation of Franklin Pierce Adams's "The Conning Tower," where they eventually published their own efforts. When they moved on to C.C.N.Y., signing themselves "Yip" and "Gersh," they collaborated on a column called "Gargoyle Gargles" for the college paper, but Ira dropped out after sophomore year, whereupon Yip edited another column and called it "The Silver Lining: A Chronicle of Our Own Wit and Other People's Folly." One of the follies that he soon had to contend with was President Wilson's preparedness campaign. "What should I fight for? I don't own anything. Let the millionaires fight," he wrote in "Arguments for and Against Preparedness" in 1916; a year later, he sailed for Argentina, saving his skin and acquiring "a global outlook." He learned Spanish, and ended up in Uruguay working for Swift & Company, where, after developing a special can for bully beef, he became a well-paid company big shot. He returned three years later and set up an electrical-appliance business in Brooklyn with a friend. He got the firm off to a profitable start by inventing an ironing board that opened with a flick of the hand and a dryer for baby clothes which could be attached to a radiator. Over the next seven years, the company grew until it was worth a quarter of a million dollars, by which time Harburg was married and the father of two; but he was not happy in the marriage (it lasted two years) or in business, which gave him migraine headaches. He spent most of his workday in the back of the office writing poetry.

Harburg's salvation was the crash, which liquidated his profits and left him with fifty thousand dollars in debts. "All I had left was my pencil," he wrote. He got in touch with Ira Gershwin, who had been putting words to his brother's music since 1924. "Ira, I think I'd like to be a songwriter from here on," Harburg recalled telling him. "Ira said, 'You should have done it a long time ago.'" Ira gave Yip five hundred dollars to get started, and told him, "Get your rhyming dictionary and go to work." In 1929, there were more than two hundred shows on Broadway, many of them musicals and revues. It was a seller's market. "When I lost my possessions, I found my creativity," Harburg said. "I gave up the dream of business and went into the business of dreams."

"I still would say it takes four or five years collaborating with knowledgeable composers to become a well-rounded lyricist," Ira Gershwin wrote in his excellent "Lyrics on Several Occasions." Many versifiers, including Dorothy Parker and F.P.A., were never able to make the transition from light verse to hit song; Harburg made it in three hardworking seasons. His first collaborator was Jay Gorney, who was then in charge of music for Paramount Pictures in Astoria. Harburg wrote thirty songs with him. Gorney provided him with a sense of construction and with connections, and Gorney's then wife Edelaine, a diminutive, sparky woman, provided him with inspiration. "He relied on me, because I recognized his talent when he wasn't sure of it," Edelaine told me, recalling nights when she'd fall asleep on the sofa while the early songs were being pieced together. "I was a good little thesaurus." Harburg eventually seduced his muse; in 1943, Edelaine Gorney became Edelaine Harburg.

Harburg and Gorney broke through with "Brother, Can You Spare a Dime?," which was originally a torch song. "We didn't want to write another 'I love that man' or 'broken love' kind of song," Gorney told me. He recalled walking with Harburg down Central Park West, reviewing their possibilities for "Americana": "A young man in a straw hat, with the rim pulled down so it was hard to see his eyes, shyly approached us. He said, 'Buddy, can you spare a dime?' Well, we had the idea. It was perfect. It wasn't about a woman who'd lost her man but about a man who'd lost his job." Harburg rushed back to his room at the Level Club to write it. "I wanted to see the breadline onstage," he told me. "I was writing the song very fast. I couldn't stop crying as I was writing. About halfway through it, I couldn't go on." He added, "In a lot of songs I write, I cry. I write with what they call in Yiddish *gederim*—it means the very vitals of your being. I feel everything." The predicament of the song called out of Harburg ancient family sorrows, and the song added a new idiom to the American language. It was cartooned, lampooned, and plagiarized. Lucky Strike cigarettes asked, "Brother, Can You Spare a Light?" Radio networks tried to ban it for being "sympathetic to the unemployed." But the song, and Harburg, were unstoppable. Bing Crosby recorded it, and the record made history. Even the Shuberts finally came around. "I'm glad to see you," Lee Shubert said, greeting Gorney a decade later. "Do you have another song like 'Mister, Can You Spare Me Ten Cents?'"

"He would dig, dig, dig—always with that special sense of humor," said the late Johnny Mercer, whom Harburg had hired to work on comedy material for "Americana." "I used to say to friends, 'Wanna go over and see Yip do eight rounds with a song?'" Mercer added, "Yip really taught me how to write. I told him that. He said, 'I taught you how to *sweat*.' He'd get me in that room and he wouldn't let me go. I would sit there with a rhyming dictionary, and we would pun and write away. If we had to write four verses, we'd write eight." Mercer repaid the favor by introducing Harburg to Arlen in the early thirties. During the 1932–33 season, *Billboard* announced that William Shakespeare was the most prolific playwright, Harold Arlen wrote the most music, and E. Y. Harburg turned out the most lyrics. The Broadway revue was still flourishing, and this gave him access to a group of great performers—Bea Lillie, Bob Hope, Bert Lahr, Fanny Brice, Jack Benny, Imogene Coca, Eddie Cantor, Willie Howard, Ruth

Etting, and Jack Pearl among them—who schooled him in the vernacular. In smart revues like "Walk a Little Faster," "Life Begins at 8:40," and "The Show Is On," Harburg brought a new intelligence to the comedy song. Sometimes, though, the Old Guard balked at his sophistication. "You're making it tough for me, boys!" the comedian Bobby Clark barked at Harburg and the composer Vernon Duke over the "tricky lyrics" to "That's Life." But soon applause made believers of them all. No lyricist, except perhaps Stephen Sondheim, has been as funny in song as Harburg. In "Life Begins at 8:40," Harburg and Ira Gershwin joined Arlen in taking potshots at the ménage à trois in Noël Coward's "Design for Living" ("Duets are made by the bourgeoisie-oh / But only God can make a trio") and at erotic literature in "Quartet Erotica," where Rabelais, Maupassant, Boccaccio, and Balzac sing, "A volume like 'Ulysses' / Makes us look like four big sissies!"

In 1934, when Broadway produced only sixteen new musicals, Harburg and Arlen joined the theatrical migration West. "Dear Relaxin' Daddy," Harburg wrote to his famously lethargic friend Ira Gershwin, "we have gone Hollywood with twenty-one guns." He went on, " We have bathrooms with barbecues, copper fire-places, pine-wood music rooms, tangerine trees, everything in fact but the Gershwins. . . . Harold falls into the lap of these luxuries with greater ease, due probably to the fact that he hasn't been preaching communism as I have." But Harburg soon got into the swing of things. "From San Pedro to Fresno," he wrote in "Californ-i-ay," "No maiden there says 'No.'" There are home movies of Harburg playing tennis and doing the hula by his pool; he even became a health-food fanatic and was once caught by his stepson, Rod Gorney, pouring orange juice on a favorite peach tree.

Nothing seemed to die in Hollywood's exotic climate except the creative spirit. "We had a tough time starting," Arlen said. "But we ended with a good batting average." Harburg found words for an Arlen melody that George Gershwin disliked, and turned it into what Arlen called "one of the most beautiful lyrics of my time"—"Last Night When We Were Young." On the other hand, Harburg disliked Arlen's melody for "Over the Rainbow." "Harold played it like a symphony. I didn't get the hang of it," Harburg said.

His first reaction was "That's for Nelson Eddy, not a little girl in Kansas." He dismissed it as "a piano exercise," but when he called in Ira Gershwin (who had since come West, too) and asked his opinion, Ira liked the melody, and the song soon earned Harburg his only Academy Award. Dreaming and destiny were forever linked in the nation's collective unconscious by the Harburg lines "And the dreams that you dare to dream / Really do come true." There was no reference to a rainbow—a word that is now nearly as central to American popular song as "I" is to Romantic poetry—in L. Frank Baum's fable "The Wonderful Wizard of Oz": Harburg put it in. To Harburg, the rainbow, as a visual bridge between Earth and the galaxy, was a symbolic link "between man and the heaven of his imagination." He said, "I've laid great store in man's imaginative ability, on man's ability to be bigger than death, bigger than life in his imagination. Man's imagination is what takes him out of his misery."

By 1943, Harburg had grown disenchanted with being what he called "a metro-gnome for Metro-Goldwyn Nightmayer" and trying to please the movie audience. He returned to Broadway, and there, in a series of original musicals of which he was co-author, he set the lyric to work dissecting injustice and economic paradox in the Land of Plenty. His first post-Hollywood hit was "Bloomer Girl," which dealt with women's rights and the Underground Railroad; it consolidated the advances in musical form and content that "Oklahoma!" had made the previous year (and used the same choreographer and ingénue) but was also a brazen assertion of Harburg's playful Realpolitik:

> Freedom needs a sweet song
> Sweet song's gotta be
> Freedom gits a sweet song
> And back of that song is little old me.

Harburg was fond of quoting the philosopher John Dewey's observation that if you could control the songs of a nation you didn't need to care about its laws. In the age of radio, catchphrases soon became credos. Adver-

tisers understood this, and so did Harburg. He tried to make liberalism pre-
vail not by reason but by rhyme—his own kind of "subliminal advertising."
He saw "The Wizard of Oz," for example, as a metaphor for the New Deal.
The lyrics, he said, were "rhymed chronicles" of the dicta of F.D.R.'s "sunny
leadership." The Scarecrow's expression of longing for knowledge—"I
would not be just a nuffin' / My head all full of stuffin'"—was his translation of "Let us have freedom from want. Time for learning and for the arts."
F.D.R.'s Good Neighbor Policy was translated into the Tin Man's desire for
a heart; and the Cowardly Lion embodied F.D.R.'s "The only thing we have
to fear is fear itself." Harburg, who was a founding member of the Hollywood Democratic Committee, wrote songs for F.D.R.'s 1944 Election Eve
broadcast, and also contributed songs to the war effort—"The Son of a Gun
Who Picks on Uncle Sam" and "And Russia Is Her Name." (The latter came
back to haunt him when the movie "Song of Russia" was cited by Robert
Taylor during the HUAC investigation of the film industry as Communistic,
despite the fact that at the time the lyrics for it were composed Russia was
America's ally.)

The subliminal impact of Harburg's songs came from their ingenious
construction. He was meticulous about syllabic emphasis, and this made a
song's logic irresistible:

> When a rich man doesn't want to work,
> He's a bon vivant.
> Yes, he's a bon vivant.
> But when a poor man doesn't want to work,
> He's a loafer, he's a lounger, he's a lazy good for nothin'—
> He's a jerk.

Harburg also had an extravagant gift for internal rhyme. For example,
"Happiness Is (Just) a Thing Called Joe" begins, "It seems like happiness is
jes' a thing called Joe / He's got a smile that makes the lilac want to grow."
Even the name Glocca Morra, for that lost Irish paradise of Finian and his
daughter, Sharon, was invented by Harburg for the famous ballad "How Are
Things in Glocca Morra?" with an eye to its subconscious appeal. "I took the

words from the German. *Glück*—'luck.' *Morgen*—'tomorrow.' Lucky tomorrow," Harburg explained. "It sounds good to you. You like the word 'Glocca Morra' because, whether you know it or not, you connect it with good luck."

Song answered Harburg's sense of omnipotence, which was easier to take in music than in person. "The same old tailspin as before—can't sleep, has palpitations, etc., etc., and is generally a mess," Edelaine wrote to a friend about Yip's agitation while doing a play. According to Fred Saidy, who was the co-author of "Finian's Rainbow," "Flahooly," and "Jamaica," Harburg was a whirlwind of enthusiasm as a writer. "He flits. He bounces. The one thing Yip needs is the freedom to spout without inhibition," Saidy recalled. But Harburg's creative process didn't translate well into the rehearsal process. He took over the direction of the highly successful "Bloomer Girl," and he infuriated his collaborators. "The worst!" said Agnes de Mille, who had to cut eight minutes of her Civil War ballet. "He was the worst! A: Yip does not know how to direct. B: He knows less about getting along with people in rehearsal hall than anyone I've ever seen." The composer Burton Lane waited three months before agreeing to work with Harburg on "Finian's Rainbow." "On lyrics, Yip will take criticism and change if he respects your judgment," Lane said. "But make a criticism of a line of dialogue and, because he's insecure in that area, he'll take your head off. If I had agreed to the project immediately, I'd never have got the changes I thought were necessary in the script." Lane, who produced a classic score, was introduced by Harburg at auditions as "my pianist." Lane said, "Yip always resented the reviews the music got." Harburg felt he'd hummed the tunes into Lane's ear; he even tried to ban Lane from the cast recording of their smash hit. Lane, who didn't talk to Harburg for two years after that, never collaborated with him again. As for "Jamaica," Harburg and Saidy were banned from the theatre after their ambitions for the story, which was originally written for Harry Belafonte, were frustrated: the show became a cabaret star turn for Lena Horne. "Take heart," Harburg wrote to the actor Ossie Davis on "Jamaica"'s opening night, which Harburg himself boycotted. "The ink in the pen of the poet is warmer and more plentiful than the blood in the veins of them as lives off us."

But Harburg did only two more Broadway shows: "The Happiest Girl in the World," which ran ninety-seven performances in 1961, and "Darling of the Day," which closed after thirty-three performances in 1968. After that, he and Broadway were quits. "I would sum up my own situation as being hopeless and helpless," he wrote in *The Dramatists Guild Quarterly*. Any journalist who went to talk to Harburg or any friend who lingered too long by the piano at one of his songfests got an earful about the new singers— "kindergarten Kierkegaards," he called them—who had more or less put his kind of song out of business. Harburg tried to study the new songs and even to write them. When I knew him, a book of Bob Dylan's collected lyrics was on his coffee table, along with the works of the Gershwins and Burton Lane. Harburg was even known to buy a teen-age friend fifty dollars' worth of rock records each time he visited, in order to argue with him about that music and to fathom what the younger generation heard in it. What Harburg heard was the death rattle of the culture. "They communicate only emotional intensity. They're crude. It upsets me," he said. "You're living in a savage world, and when you listen to the shrieks and savage cries in the songs you know it." He added, "Songs now are a reflection of fright. It's the fright of no hope, no stability. When we began writing songs, we felt life was good. The world was beautiful, and we were enjoying it. Death was at the end of the adventure, but we didn't worry about that. These kids are worried. They're on their deathbeds, and they're teen-agers!"

Until the end of his life, Harburg continued to write and sing his buoyant songs. "I like the mischievous feeling of getting on top of something I fear," he said. "If it gives me courage, it'll give others courage." Harburg knew he was a forgotten man, but his words ("And the dreams that you dare to dream . . .") are part of this century's ozone, part of the litany of our lives. He once said, "The song is a magical thing. Its power is its invisibility. A book, a play, a painting must be sought. The song seeks you. It is ubiquitous and sinewy. It pursues you every minute. It's your shadow. You're sitting in a dentist's chair. There it is. Or in the elevator. Or the supermarket. Or a car. You may catch the song from somebody else. Its ideas may infect you. It is a very haunting thing." He could have been speaking about himself. He was everywhere and nowhere, which is the fate of the sprite. Harburg, who set his wit against all injustice, gallantly tried to laugh even this one away:

Mozart died a pauper,
Heine lived in dread,
Foster died in Bellevue,
Homer begged for bread.
Genius pays off handsomely—
After you are dead.

BAZ LUHRMANN

THE RINGMASTER

THE AUSTRALIAN DIRECTOR BAZ
Luhrmann is an impresario of himself; inevitably, for a protean talent, he is
known by many names. At the entrance to his temporary base of operations, in a wood-beamed loft on Wooster Street, in New York, he lists himself as "C von G." It's an abbreviation for Count von Groovy, a nickname
conferred on Luhrmann by his cohorts, in acknowledgment of both his
sometimes grandiose pursuit of the extraordinary and his image as a swami
of style. His more common moniker, "Baz," which Luhrmann, who is forty,
started using in the seventies—he was christened Mark—is also intended
to add a defiant lustre to a lifetime of self-invention. "I imagined I needed a
fabulous name, an exotic name," he explains. "I was always theatrical. I was
mythologizing my own existence from the age of ten." His long-time associate director, David Crooks, agrees. "He likes to see himself as a sort of
director cum rock star," he says. "He is the consummate actor. It's very rare
that he just takes off all his façades."

Luhrmann has been in town to oversee a production of Puccini's "La
Bohème," which he first staged twelve years ago, at the Sydney Opera
House, for sixteen thousand dollars, and which will open December 8th, in
a six-and-a-half-million-dollar Broadway version. His company Bazmark
Inq—which has its headquarters in a rambling Victorian mansion known as
the House of Iona, in Sydney's seedy Kings Cross area—employs about
twenty people, including an archivist, but Luhrmann is the source from
which the energy flows. He is the visionary, the director, the huckster who
pitches the product. "He is the fire," says Luhrmann's wife and partner,
Catherine Martin, whose job it is to give his imaginings material form.
(Last year, she won two Academy Awards, for the costumes and for the set
design of his film "Moulin Rouge.") Luhrmann, who has a leading man's

good looks and a mane of carefully layered and tinted hair, claims to see "no separation between work and life." For the last thirteen years, he has contrived to be always either in rehearsal, in production, or on the publicity trail. "Work is the prayer," he says. He is, first and foremost, an entrepreneur of astonishment. "It's not enough that you move through the world— you must change it to suit your expectation," he says. The root of his romanticism, he adds, is "a belief that things are better, more incredible, more wonderful than they actually are."

Over the last decade, Luhrmann has produced three flamboyant films that turned into box-office hits: "Strictly Ballroom," "Romeo + Juliet," and "Moulin Rouge." His movies are distinctive for both their speed and their sharpness. He says, "You've got to create some sort of experience where the audience goes, 'Gee, I feel aggressed, oppressed, but I'm excited.' It cannot be passive." He adds, "Stories never change. The way we tell them must change, so that we can reënliven the ears and the eyes of the audience." So far, his audiences have been outspoken. "Strictly Ballroom," which is reported to be one of the Pope's favorite movies, merges the David and Goliath and Ugly Duckling myths in a high-spirited and genial musical about competitive dancing. Luhrmann's deconstruction of Shakespeare, which updates "Romeo and Juliet" to the Miami gang wars, was controversial but won high praise from such actors as Sir Alec Guinness, who admired its "powerful visual imagery." Luhrmann hit rougher water with "Moulin Rouge," his attempt to reinvent the Hollywood musical; the film is an acrylic version of the fin de siècle in Paris, souped up with cartoonish characters and an eclectic pop score. The response, as noisy as the movie's soundtrack, was divided about evenly between those who called it genius and those who called it a mess. Collectively, the films, which Luhrmann refers to as "tweeners," for their ability to appeal to the art house and the multiplex, have grossed three hundred and forty-three million dollars, and they were recently released in a DVD boxed set as "The Red Curtain Trilogy"—a reference to the theatricality of Luhrmann's cinematic language. He has also moonlighted as guest editor of Australian *Vogue*. In 1999, he produced the spoken-word single "Everybody's Free (to Wear Sunscreen)," which went platinum in the United States and Britain. And in

2003 he will embark on what he calls his "next big gesture": a film of the life of Alexander the Great.

Bazmark Inq, which Luhrmann founded in 1997, is a sort of artistic holding company for his overheated imagination, with divisions for film, live entertainment, music, and publishing. The company's office is a hive of workers with whom Luhrmann has "a chemical connection," and whose storytelling talents maximize the impact of his work. Bazmark's coat of arms—an emu and a kangaroo—signals a certain lightness of spirit. Its motto—"A life lived in fear is a life half-lived"—broadcasts daring. Part Barnum and part Diaghilev, Luhrmann is also something of an imperialist. He controls the look of every poster, every sign, every piece of information connected to each of his shows, because, as he says, "you're already in the show, even before you've bought a ticket." In the age of the multinational corporation, he aspires to go beyond fame to trademark. "He does want the whole world to be affected by Baz Luhrmann," Crooks says. "To be in people's minds, to make them aware of the Bazmark product." He adds, "He's a humble person in a ruthlessly aggressive way."

When I met Luhrmann in San Francisco in September, "La Bohème" was having its last studio rehearsal before moving from the Presidio Army barracks, near the Golden Gate Bridge, to the Curran Theatre. (It would run for six weeks there, and then travel to New York.) Luhrmann has a quick, conceptualizing mind, and it's sometimes hard to follow him as he bushwhacks his way through a tangle of articulation to a new thought. But with actors on the rehearsal floor he is kind, clear, and to the point. He is intense but measured; he rarely yells. His way of registering irritation at the cacophony of cell phones in the vast rehearsal room, for instance, was to say to the assembled, "Would I be wrong in saying there is one too many telephones on today?" (His company runs the same way—in accordance with a book of protocols that Luhrmann has developed, "The Bazmark Way," to keep his artistic domain fair and efficient.)

His work is presentational; his direction, like a brass rubbing, attempts to make vivid and exact the outline of action. "You should actually be able to turn the sound off and follow the story," he says. To his Rodolfo, who on an impulse had carried the frail, consumptive Mimi to her garret chair and dumped her into it, he said, "Lead her into the chair. Like, 'I'm not trying to impose myself on you.' Find what that tells you. This is really a big moment. Stop and listen. Make it a big moment. When you're dealing with Mimi, she is the only purpose for you." Rehearsing the beginning of Act IV, when Colline and Schaunard arrive onstage with their paltry repast of bread and a single silvery fish, Luhrmann spent nearly an hour making a proper spectacle of the scene. "You're showing each other, but you're really sharing it with us," he said of Colline revealing his small catch. Here he imitated Colline flapping the fish matter-of-factly in his friend's direction, and said, "At the moment, it looks like fish, fish, fish, fish. There's no story." He added, "Just lean back in the chair and really connect with the fish moment." By the time he'd moved on to the next bit of low comedy, the fish business had been polished to a shine. "I'm the mechanic," he says. "I'm making the mechanism so the audience can have an experience."

Luhrmann maintains that he is "culturally blind." He says, "I refuse to be drawn into the belief that there is high culture and low culture. There are just things that travel through time and geography." (He, of course, hopes to be one of them.) He often invokes as icons of popular entertainment Shakespeare, Puccini, Molière, and Mozart, whose "absolute direct connection with the audience" he tries to emulate. Shakespeare, he says, "was singularly driven by the popular environment and by commercial realities. He knew he had to come from a personal place but then decode it, in a way in which the child, the adult, the Queen of England could read it." He adds, "That forced a form of genius."

In order to reach across classes and ages with his own flashy intelligence, Luhrmann chooses simple, mythic stories, which he can update in order to make their subliminal emotional essence accessible. "My mission is to make people feel first, so they can think, as opposed to making them think so that they can feel," he says, adding, "Psychological work is a fairly recent fashion. We actively reject the idea of psychological depth in character. We have overt archetypal character, overt archetypal story, so that you can have an exalted experience that is individual to you. My job is to vibe the zeitgeist and work out a way of releasing the power of the story."

Luhrmann's productions reflect the thin air of contemporary atmospheres. They conjure a garish, whirligig world that is almost giddy with a combination of doom and delight. The eclecticism of a media-saturated civilization comes through in a collision of fragments, filling the screen with print and image. Luhrmann's organizing principle is, he says, "collage, really—it's basically drawing from any source to make a bigger statement." Martin and Luhrmann create "pitch books" for each of their projects, in order to map out a visual ground plan and explain it to actors and producers. In a book for "Moulin Rouge," the hero, Christian, is captioned, "He's multi-talented, he's a genius, he's got the modern technique." Design, not depth, is Luhrmann's dominion. He mines the surface of his stories. Inevitably, therefore, "Romeo + Juliet" overlooks the poorly managed verse; and "Moulin Rouge," on first viewing, for me, anyway, was all surprise and no outcome. In order to find a simulacrum for the momentum of turn-of-the-century Paris, Luhrmann paced the movie to "the absolute extreme edge of what we felt the tempo could be and be comprehended." I found the film, with its constant quotations from classic musicals and its cinematic jaggedness, confounding. The old musicals were about flow and the feel of humanity; "Moulin Rouge" is about interruption and the feel of technology. What you get is sensation without joy. In subsequent screenings, this approach—no pauses, no paths, no future—seemed to me a bold attempt to elevate a claustrophobic style to the level of metaphor. The smash cuts, cross-cuts, zooms and sudden focus, the idiosyncratic soundtrack, the juxtaposition of tragedy and comedy all help to create a roaring—some would say maddening—cinematic language that nonetheless personifies the hellish interior space of contemporary life: what the art critic John Berger, speaking of Bosch's vision of hell, calls "the clamour of the disparate, fragmentary present . . . a kind of spatial delirium."

Luhrmann finds a special visual vocabulary for each event. In his "La Bohème," the opera is sung in Italian and performed in its entirety, but the story has been updated to Paris in 1957. And he has chosen to work against the typical operatic casting, by hiring young, attractive singers, who are believably sexual, to tell the story of starving artists and doomed love. (There are three sets of star-crossed lovers, because eight Broadway performances a week would be too vocally demanding for one couple. "I feel like an acrobat in a Chinese opera who spins plates on the tip of a stick,"

Luhrmann has said.) To free the production from its traditional naturalistic sedateness, Luhrmann has set the interior scenes in what looks like a revolving Rubik's Cube, pushed around by stagehands who are always visible to the audience, and he makes the supertitles a prominent scenic element by putting them inside the proscenium, not above or below it. "There's no curtain," he explains as the artist's garret is rolled onto its marks. "You walk in. People will be working onstage, singers warming up. Noise. The stage manager—if I can get the lass to embrace it properly— she'll be miked. You'll hear all her calls. She'll just go, 'Stand by,' and there'll be silence. The conductor will come on. She'll say, 'Thank you.' And—*bang!*—we'll go. You're on. So the curtain is created by the performance." (This has been slightly modified for the Broadway production.)

The maneuver takes the odor off the opera's romanticism. Far from diminishing the power of the music, Luhrmann insists, the emphasis on artifice makes viewers more receptive to the emotional weight of the story. "We show them our hands," he explains. "We say, 'Listen, just so you know, we're here to manipulate you and show you beautiful things. Apparently, you want to do this. Now do you want to be massaged?'" Where naturalism encourages a kind of passivity—"looking through a keyhole," Luhrmann calls it—his "real artificiality" draws the audience into the spirit of play. "You have to teach the audience the story as quickly as possible," he says— thus the gigantic neon sign hanging over the set that reads "L'Amour." "This is not a psychological drama where we're hiding plot. We tell you the plot, so that, as you accumulate tempo, you're breaking down and uniting the audience." He continues, "If you compare, for instance the tempo of Pavarotti's 'La Bohème,' which is gorgeous, to Toscanini, who conducted the original production, the original is much faster, because he was telling it to the groundlings—a gusty romp, a fast comic story; ripping along at the speed of life."

Luhrmann, who is expert at staging entrances and exits, made a dramatic entrance of his own on life's stage. He was born in the back seat of a gray-green Vanguard van, in which his mother was being rushed to the hospital. The ringleader of four siblings, he learned the business of show at his family's Mobil gas station, nine hours into the Australian bush from Sydney.

His parents, Leonard and Barbara, had paid twenty-three thousand dollars for a windswept place at a crossroads called Heron's Creek, a conurbation of eleven houses on the edge of the Watagan Forest. Luhrmann likens it to the diner in the film "Baghdad Cafe"—a solitary center of activity in the middle of nowhere. "My relationship with the audience is the same relationship that we had with our customers, that my father drummed into us," says Luhrmann, who pumped gas, waited tables, and ran a tropical-fish concession on the side. "They were our guests. We had to perform. The audience came in every day. We were the Luhrmann Boys. We had to dress up, wear little ties, white shirts, and suits." As cars rolled into the station, they were barraged by a loop of music—the Beatles, the Tijuana Brass, and "Pagliacci"—endlessly repeated over reel-to-reel Akai speakers. Later, his father set up a radio station, and Luhrmann would disk-jockey: "Let's hear that 'Pagliacci' one more time!"

Luhrmann calls his parents "an extremely intense couple, huge characters." Both were dreamers, in their own ways charismatic and self-dramatizing. Barbara, in her later years, became a ballroom-dancing instructor. According to Luhrmann, she "always thought she had a light—she had good access to fantasy." Leonard, who served in Vietnam as the head diver of the Australian Navy's demolition squad and as an underwater photographer, was a series of contradictions: soldierlike and soft; disciplined and romantic; practical and problematic. "I think he could love Baz in a way that his mum couldn't, because he was more true to himself," says the Australian actress Catherine McClements, who lived with Luhrmann and collaborated with him for seven years in the early eighties. Barbara, she adds, was "too busy creating her own life and having her own sort of experiences."

Although the Luhrmanns were just scratching out a living, they were determined to turn out extraordinary offspring. "We were brought up to believe that we were super-special, that there was nothing we couldn't do," Luhrmann says. ("The Renaissance men of Heron's Creek" is how Catherine Martin characterizes the family.) "According to their father, you had to be the best," Barbara says. "Their father never really became top of anything he did. He was a good instructor." Leonard, who died of cancer while Luhrmann was shooting "Moulin Rouge," oversaw his sons' development in an almost military manner. He insisted on crew cuts, which set the boys apart. "This made our life hell," says Luhrmann, for whom hair remains "a touchstone obsession." "We three boys were constantly attacked and ridiculed. If you had short hair, you were uncool, a freak." Leonard also kept them on a regimen of activities, which included horseback riding, scuba diving, farm and gas-station chores, commando training—"He'd drop us in the middle of the bush and we had to find our way home"—and competitive ballroom dancing, which meant a three-hour drive, three days a week. "One of the great things his parents gave him was no fear of mastering physical challenges," Martin says. By the age of ten, Luhrmann also knew how to develop the negatives of the photographs he took with his first camera, a Brownie, and how to operate his father's Straight 8 Bolex moving-picture camera. (Luhrmann made "Strictly Ballroom" without any additional cinematic tutelage.) "There was never a moment of peace," he says of the "almost psychotic" amount of childhood activity. "If we ever just sat down, the sense from my father was that it was wrong. We weren't allowed to eat until dinner. We had work to do. It was absolutely nonstop until we dropped at night. We got up early in the morning, and—*bang!*—you'd do it again." He adds, "My family was a cult."

Luhrmann's mercurial quality and his fertile fantasy life ("I imagine twenty-four hours a day—it's like a storm," he says) seem to derive from the habit of ducking and diving he adopted as a child, in order to evade his parents' control. "Both parents had tyrannical natures," Martin says. Leonard imposed himself; Barbara exerted her power by withdrawing. "Baz, got out of things by being incredibly entertaining," Martin adds. "He was always in his head, maybe because he thought he wasn't fabulous enough. He had to create it." In person and in public, Luhrmann accentuates the positive aspects of his tense, hard-striving childhood. But no one courts fame out of happiness. "There was a lot of shadow, sure," he admits. "We lived daily with death. We lived on a bridge, which on a regular basis caused car accidents that killed people. My job was to man the phone or call the local cop. Violence was around. The level of drama was extreme." But, when pushed to speak about the shadows in his own life, Luhrmann struggles to find language. His long silence surprises him. "I'm never at a loss for words, as you know," he says. What he can't bring himself to acknowledge is that, for part of his childhood—until he was ten, according to his mother—the man whom he now thinks of as "a wonderful father" was an alcoholic, and that by his teen-age years the family atmosphere, according to his mother, was "dreadful." "Their father was too hard, too harsh, almost impossible to live with," Barbara says. Leonard sometimes wouldn't speak to her for three weeks at a time. "Fifteen years. I couldn't take it anymore." Their breakup was violent and traumatic. "It was a horrendous day," Luhrmann recalls. "There were many horrendous days. There was my sister and a lamp shade in a car. And screaming and hitting and yelling. And she was gone."

Luhrmann remained with his father at Heron's Creek, nursing subversive longings for the big city and, he says, "aware that we were perhaps incarcerated in this other world." After about eighteen months, Len remarried; three and a half years later, Luhrmann, then fifteen, ran away. He ended up living in Sydney with his mother and didn't see his father again for seven years. He attended an all-boys Catholic high school, which he found, he says, "a bit of a shock." He rebelled by growing his curly hair long, and he earned the nickname Basil Brush—after a furry fox puppet on British television—which was the derogatory origin of Baz. Around 1979, "as an act of defiance against this derision," Luhrmann says, he changed his name officially to Bazmark. "Baz and Mark are the two sides of who I am," he says.

Luhrmann was not an outstanding student, but he was drawn to acting. (He played Sky Masterson in a high-school production of "Guys and Dolls.") "I can remember walking back from the beach, the heat coming off the road, and Baz talking about great acting and great theatre and great movies, and wanting to be great," the screenwriter Craig Pearce says. (Pearce, who was Luhrmann's best friend in high school, is the co-author of all three of his films.) He adds, "What I was attracted to in Baz was this feeling of being part of something bigger. It was going to happen." Pearce and Luhrmann didn't aspire to be jobbing actors; they wanted to be, as Pearce puts it, "Marlon Brando, Montgomery Clift, James Dean, Mick Jagger, all rolled into one." He says of Luhrmann, "He wanted to be extraordinary and, in a sense, when you were around Baz life *was* more extraordinary." For Luhrmann, acting was a natural direction; he had been role-playing all his life. "In order to avoid confrontation, he would become whatever was asked of him," his mother says.

Luhrmann applied to Sydney's National Institute of Dramatic Art—

"the grand temple of serious acting," he calls it. He was rejected, but on the same day he received word that he'd been cast as a pimp, playing opposite Judy Davis in "Winter of Our Dreams." He was eighteen. He went straight from high school to a full-fledged acting career. He was featured in one of Australia's most popular television shows, "A Country Practice," and had a convincing cameo as a transsexual on another show. For a documentary he conceived about Sydney's homeless youth—"Kids from the Cross"—he shed his suburban looks, went undercover, and slept rough for three months. When Luhrmann couldn't find financing for the film, he took the footage to a television company, which turned it into an embarrassing program that left him "morally confused" and brought him into the unfortunate glare of Australia's tabloid press. "HOW KIDS SURVIVE IN A CESSPOOL—THIS IS SICK" was the headline in one Sydney paper. The result, he says, was "a very, very, very strong drive to be creatively responsible." Prodded also by the fact that "sitting around waiting for the phone to ring was basically killing me," he formed his first theatre company, The Bond, in 1981.

At twenty, Luhrmann was accepted at the National Institute of Dramatic Art. By his own admission, he became "internalized, self-conscious, very intense." He says, "I have always had a natural connection with people. But I think I read that as uncool and not what serious artists did. I was very unapproachable." He cultivated a sense of mystery and danger. "People imagined that he was uncontrollable, that he was scary, that he broke the rules," Catherine McClements says. Luhrmann did his best not to disappoint. To act Chekhov, he studied Russian; to play a Chinese peasant in "Fanshen," David Hare's play about Communist Chinese agrarian reform, he walked around with his books in a pail and put his fist through a window, trying to pull a punch. "I created a character who wasn't me," he says. He explored the postures and attitudes of Elvis, Nijinsky, David Bowie, and Prince. Obsessed by African-American culture, Luhrmann even turned up for one class as a black woman. "He was incredibly convincing," McClements says. "One time, we were listening to classical music. He said, 'You've really gotta forgive me for this.' He went off, and that night at the corroboree"—an aboriginal word for gathering—"he dressed up as an opera singer, with the whole gear, lip-synching way before it became popular. The drag was brilliantly done."

McClements helped Luhrmann develop "Strictly Ballroom," which began life as an acting-school exploration and a metaphor for, among other things, his increasing sense of "creative oppression" at NIDA. "I'm sick of dancing someone else's steps," the hero of "Strictly Ballroom" says, before he finds a way to triumph on his own terms. When Luhrmann entered NIDA, he had an acting career, an agent, his own theatre company; when he left, he had nothing. "He entered drama school as a fantastic actor and through the process at NIDA became worse and worse," McClements says. "He became too self-aware." He felt stalled. He was frightened. "Things weren't going to plan," Luhrmann says. "I had a genuine breakdown." For about a month, he sat paralyzed in the squalor of a ramshackle fishing hut, barely moving or speaking. Finally, one day, he remembers, he walked to the beach, ate a popsicle, and started to read the paper. "I suddenly thought, I'm going to do something—I'm going to put on a play," he says. "I got my old company back and convinced everyone I could do this production 'About the Beach,' a sort of myth set in the beach culture of lifeguards and surfing. From that day on, I was back to being who I was before I went to NIDA."

Luhrmann likes to tell the story of his first screening at Cannes, in 1992, with "Strictly Ballroom." "I remember every second of it," he says. "Nervously hanging up signs: 'Come and see our film.' A very small audience coming to see it, then a standing ovation. Then us being the toast of the town. Twenty-four hours later, another screening being called—you couldn't get in. A security guard leaned over and said to me, 'Monsieur, your life will never be the same again.'" So it has proved. Fame is a live wire that Luhrmann can't let go of. "You can't shake it off at the flick of a switch," he says. "You can't go home. Your home is the public world." Now he lives at full tilt. "If I'm able to run the movie of my life, in my mind it'd better be a good one," he says. "You can't afford any sloppy scenes."

Luhrmann is built for speed. He's thin, lithe, and streamlined, rejecting anything that might weigh him down. His collaboration with Martin has only increased his velocity. From the outset, for Luhrmann, artistic partnership was crucial to creative success. "He definitely needs someone to be in love with him, to be obsessed with him and what he's doing, and to make him feel good about it, " McClements says. "He doesn't want to be alone." Martin was a designer in her third year at NIDA when, in 1986, Luhrmann discovered her and she joined his opera and theatre companies. Her first real memory of Luhrmann, though, came a year later, when they were working together on "Lake Lost," an opera he was directing. "He had two stage managers pushing this rowboat on wheels with two of the lead players inside. I just remember thinking that this man was a fucking genius. It was so beautifully artificial." She adds, "What Baz forces you to do is go through the cliché to a transcendental understanding."

Of their at times volatile early relationship she says, "We connected in a profound way. It was more than romantic love or sexual attraction. It was bigger and more frightening than that. He not only channels himself through the collaboration—he pulls out the best in you." She adds, "He's the magic, but I'm the high priestess." Luhrmann and Martin were married at a Sydney registry office in 1997. In the post-wedding celebration, Martin, who is thirty-seven and known as C.M., literally ascended to her new role on the stage of the Sydney Opera House, where "La Bohème" had played. There, under the "L'Amour" sign, in a notional chapel made of candles, she rose into the scene on a hydraulic lift as the producer Noel Staunton, who now heads Bazmark's live-entertainment division, descended from above in an angel costume, to officiate in yet another Baz Luhrmann spectacle.

In the vortex of his production and promotion schedules, one way that Luhrmann stops time is to keep a diary. The frontispiece of each year's journal, which is about the size of an accounting ledger, is a photograph of his current project; the back cover shows his next one. Instead of writing about his hectic life, he fills the diary pages with a visual record: images and mementos snatched from the blur of hours, which reflect him back to himself. The quick inventory I compiled, as I flipped through his 2002 diary during a production meeting, included:

> January 15: Luhrmann asleep on C.M.'s lap. A letter from Martin Scorsese.
> January 21: The Golden Globe Awards: Luhrmann stands with Nicole Kidman on a red carpet.

Luhrmann and C.M. reclining in deck chairs on their hotel patio. Hair unkempt, unshaven, Luhrmann looks hungover. C.M. holds up an ad in the L.A. *Times*: "3 Winners: Best Picture, Best Actress, Best Original Score."

February 14: A card from Kidman: "She sings, she dances, she dies. . . .Thank you for giving me the gift of a lifetime. Nic"

March 5: Luhrmann with Debbie Reynolds and Carrie Fisher.

March 24: Ticket stubs to the 74th Academy Awards—Center B-1. A photo of Rupert Murdoch holding one of C.M.'s Academy Awards; C.M. stands beaming beside him with the other Oscar.

May 10: India—a map of the state of Kerala.

Years, for Luhrmann, are measured not by days but by work, and his chronicle consists mostly of lists. "When I get hugely insecure, I make lists and lists and lists of things I have to do," he says. The 2002 diary began with a list of "goals." Among them were "Conceive a child" and "ISSUE—I am exhausted and fucked trying to conceive and develop Bohème."

Luhrmann's diary is symptomatic of something essential in his performing nature: he is always watching himself go by. "It's not vanity as we understand it," McClements says. "It's experimenting with himself." "He spends a lot of time looking at himself in the mirror," Crooks says. Luhrmann, who, like the characters in "Strictly Ballroom," was a ballroom-dancing champion as a boy, believes in looking good. He doesn't allow the cast to see him eat, and, before he goes on the rehearsal floor, if there is anyone from the press around, he often spends a few minutes in Hair and Makeup. (The stated Four Pillars of the House of Iona are "Transportation, Communication, Accommodation, and Hair." "Over the years, I've learnt that these four elements are the ones to watch out for in derailing the creative process," he explains.) According to Crooks, "If there's a photo to be done, there's just a little touch of something, a little Aschenbach moment." Still, his self-regard has nothing to do with looking inward. "Only look *out*," he advises. Like his films, he resists psychology. "I put my own character off-limits for a very long time," he explains. Luhrmann recalls listening to Leonardo DiCaprio, who starred in "Romeo + Juliet," do impersonations. "He's a fantastic impersonator," he says. "We're sitting in a circle. We're laughing at his Johnny Depp, Robert De Niro—great. Marlon Brando. And he does another one. Everybody's laughing, laughing, laughing. And I'm going, 'Oh, who is it?'" Luhrmann says, "It was me."

When we sat down to talk alone, during a rehearsal break, on what turned out to be Luhrmann's fortieth birthday, September 17th, he was considering the nature of his self-invention. "Is it that I construct a life that seems to be tremendously well stage-managed?" he asked. "Or is it that my zealous romanticism has caused a very interesting staging of my life? The curtain is coming down on the first act of my life. It's ending with the production I began with, thirteen years ago." He added, "I'm not young anymore. And I'm gonna be old. The new journey is a spiritual one." Later, in front of the cast and crew, who presented him with wine and proffered a birthday cake with a burst of song—"Couldn't we get decent singers to sing me 'Happy Birthday'?" Luhrmann said—he feigned surprise. "I couldn't think of a better way of turning forty than just to be in the middle of doing 'La Bohème.' With such risk out there, with all of you." He went on, "If you turn forty, the thing that everyone talks about is you feel your life's over. I just feel like I'm right in the middle of life. I am very, very privileged. Well, listen, look: I'll tell you what"—here he looked at the cake and then at his watch. "Beautiful, but the show must go on."

Although the three films of "The Red Curtain Trilogy" are devoted to the conventions of traditional narrative and heterosexual love, the camp style of Luhrmann's telling always subverts normality. This contradiction seems to express what McClements calls his "uncertain heart." He seems almost obsessed with the romantic entanglements of others. "For somebody who's not an overtly sexual being, he loves watching people in love," Crooks says. Luhrmann admits that his fascination with "Romeo and Juliet" was about "coming to terms with an impossible love, which could not be, no matter how perfect." When he talks about "Alexander the Great," his preoccupation with love seems to reveal the autobiography beneath the archetype. "I'm thinking of doing a work about a young historical figure who must continually succeed and conquer because of a lack of love, because he is pursuing a phantom love," Luhrmann told San Francisco's *Bay Area Reporter*. "He goes on and on until there can be no more conquering, and at a certain point you've got to realize that that phantom love will never be found."

After "La Bohème" opens on Broadway, and before Luhrmann gets into the heavy lifting of "Alexander the Great," he will do what he always does at the end of an epic undertaking: go walkabout. "I never know where I'm going," says Luhrmann, who ended up in Alexandria on his last sojourn. He will turn up at the airport, he will put his credit card on the counter, and, except for a few calls home during the couple of months away, he will get lost on the planet. "One gets connected to the street, to the world, to life," he says. "I think it's absolutely fundamental because that's the audience." He also reconnects to his own romantic notion of "the wandering storyteller." In this persona, he is a denizen of the underworld, albeit a Prada bohemian, a pilgrim in search of an answer to some longing he can't quite bring himself to define. One night over dinner in San Francisco, talking about Alexander the Great, Luhrmann almost found the words. "He needed love from everyone," he told me. "The love of the army, the love of Hephaestion, the love of Roxanne. I understand without any complication what it is to feel the need."

KENNETH TYNAN

THE WHIRLWIND

A T OXFORD, WHERE HE BECAME A postwar legend, Kenneth Tynan cut a gaunt romantic figure. He liked to characterize himself to the Bright Young Things as a kind of meteor who would blaze across the English scene only to be extinguished before his thirtieth year. "By then," he said, "I will have said everything I have to say." In fact, Tynan's skyrocketing crash-and-burn scenario took nearly twice as long to play itself out. With his reputation for brilliance more or less intact, he died too young, of emphysema, in July, 1980, at the age of fifty-three. At the memorial service, Tom Stoppard turned to Tynan's three children, Tracy, Roxana, and Matthew. "For those of us who were working in the English-speaking theatre during those years," he said, referring to the period between 1950 and 1963, when Tynan's drama criticism was as much an event as the plays he reviewed, "for those of us who shared his time, your father was part of the luck we had."

Critics do not make theatre; they are made by it. Tynan's luck was to be in the right place at the right age with the right credentials, the right vocabulary, and the right impudent temperament to savor the new British theatrical resurgence—certainly the greatest flowering of dramatic talent in England since Elizabeth I. With his hard-won intellectual precocity and his rebellious instincts ("Rouse tempers, goad and lacerate, raise whirlwinds" was the quotation—his own, as it happens—pinned above his writing desk), Tynan was the old Brit and the new rolled into one lanky, well-tailored package. Of the many qualities that made him an outstanding critic—qualities of wit, language, knowledge, style, and fun—perhaps the most important and the most surprising was his profound awareness of death. It fed both his voracity for pleasure—for food, for drink, for sex, for talk ("Talking to gifted and/or funny people," he wrote, is "evidence both of intense curiosity and of jaded palate")—and his desire to memorialize it. "I remember about thirty times between waking and sleeping and always while I'm asleep that I am going to die," he said. "And the more scared I am, the more pleasure and enlightenment I want to squeeze from every moment." For Tynan, writing was a hedge against loss, a way of keeping the consoling dramatic pleasures alive inside himself by making them live for others. "I mummify transience," he announced, at the age of twenty-three, in the epilogue to his first book, "He That Plays the King" (1950), an almost delusional rant, intended as an exercise in what he called "the athletics of personality," with which he launched himself from Oxford into the waiting world.

Tynan fancied himself sui generis. He was his own greatest invention, and he loved his maker. When he told his life story, he downplayed his humdrum provincial Midland origins. "In any real sense of the word I was born at Oxford," he said. "I have no more connection with my early life and with Birmingham"—the city where he was born, in 1927—"than I have with Timbuctoo." He wanted glamour, which was not easy to excavate in the threadbare blandness of postwar England. "No cafés. No good restaurants. Clothes were still 'austerity' from the war, dismal and ugly. Everyone was indoors by ten," Doris Lessing wrote—and that was raffish London, not baggy Birmingham.

The deadliness leached into Tynan's childhood, where the unsolid ground of his family life had a habit of shifting. An older sister had died at birth. His father, the taciturn, successful Sir Peter Peacock, who was fifty-four when Tynan was born, spent two days a week up the road in Warrington, where he was the mayor for six terms, and where, unbeknownst to his son, he kept another family. Peacock had never married Tynan's mother, Rose, a kindly, depressed, modestly educated former laundress, who had aspirations to respectability, and from whose tastes and personality Tynan felt increasingly estranged. In 1958, Rose, unkempt and confused, was picked up by the Yorkshire police carrying a suitcase on which was written, "I DON'T KNOW WHERE I'M GOING, BUT I'M GOING TO THOSE WHO LOVE ME." She ended her life in a mental institution. Tynan, however, wasn't the type to feel shame and self-loathing about having abandoned her there. "I could have postponed her death at the expense of my own absorption in self advancement," he wrote. "I chose not to." As a teen-ager, he turned to the wall the family's déclassé oil paintings of cows in pasture, but his sense of parental detachment was born out of issues deeper than taste. "A cesarean, a bastard and a contemptible object" is how Tynan characterized himself in infancy, in notes he made in 1962, during his psychoanalysis. "A bedwetter, I soiled my mother and she punished me by refusing to feed me."

In the end, like all narcissists, Tynan fed himself. His passion for intellectual distraction fended off what he called "my old meddlesome bugbear, solitude." And although his astonishing intelligence bewildered his parents, they indulged his eclectic enthusiasms. Tynan's mother introduced him to music hall and the "high-definition performance." Together, they travelled to London to see Ivor Novello, the Crazy Gang, Gilbert and Sullivan operettas, Donald Wolfit's hectoring Shakespearean performances. For his ninth Christmas, Tynan asked for and received a hundred books from his parents; on another occasion, they splurged on a monocle for their little showoff, whose large vocabulary was marred by a permanent stutter.

If it was hard for Tynan to be understood at home, he was compelled to make the rest of the world pay proper attention. As a boy, he collected the autographs of such contemporary heroes as Winston Churchill, Neville Chamberlain, and Joseph Kennedy, but he soon became his own star. "As long as I'm not ignored you know quite well I'm perfectly happy," the teen-age Tynan wrote to a friend. At eleven, he appointed a chum at King Edward's School—which he attended on a scholarship—to be his Boswell; at fifteen, he addressed the school literary society on "Art and I" ("a history of the Influences that have Gone to the Making of KPT"); at seventeen, he played Hamlet; at twenty-three, he published his first book of criticism; and by twenty-seven he was the famous, iconoclastic drama critic of the *Observer.* Tynan's life was proof of one of his most famous aphorisms: "A man who strives after an effect not infrequently achieves it."

Tynan's performance of personality—the flamboyant dress (pastel shirts, dove-gray suits, and velvet collars), the mannerisms (cigarette held between the third and fourth finger), and the word horde—embodied the notion of the extraordinary that he'd studied on stage and screen. "Have a new pose: arrogance, bass voice, hanging lower lip. Which reads O-R-S-O-N," he wrote, in a letter to a friend in 1944, just five years before buttonholing the bemused Welles himself to write the preface to his first book. "This sad age needs to be dazzled, shaped and spurred by the spectacle of heroism," Tynan wrote, and certainly he needed it: big magic as an antidote to big hurt. "I was illegitimate and I was made to know it by my father and my family," he later wrote to his first wife, the American writer Elaine Dundy, whom he divorced in 1964, after thirteen tempestuous years of marriage. "I was the boy . . . at whom everyone smiled knowingly and despisingly, and I have pretended ever since to be somebody—anybody—else." Tynan's first published piece of prose, which appeared in the King Edward's School *Chronicle* when he was fourteen, spelled out the credo by which he would more or less live for the rest of his life: "In every community there exists a certain element of the insignificant," he wrote. "The undistinguished person; the person who never argues, never shouts, and whose presence is not immediately noticed. . . . As I watch the useless lives of these people, so foolish, so wasted and so ordinary, I become afraid, and try desperately to forget them."

Tynan arrived at Magdalen College in 1945, and immediately plunged into a whirlwind of public display that included directing, acting, writing, and debating, and only intensified what he called his "superiority complex." "Nothing can ever top the sense of privileged exhilaration I felt then," he said. By his own calculation, his experience at Oxford amounted to seventy-two weeks, three hundred parties, and the equivalent of five full-length volumes of essays. Tynan's tutor was C. S. Lewis, the writer and professor of medieval and Renaissance literature, who taught him how to deploy paradox and how to make his verbal firepower more accurate. "Keep a strict eye on eulogistic & dyslogistic adjectives—They shd *diagnose* (not merely blame) & distinguish (not merely praise)," Lewis wrote on a Tynan essay about early English drama. Tynan learned his lessons well. A stripling aesthete, he prophesied, "My collected works will bulk small but precious." (His subsequent dashing and incomparable oeuvre is currently out of print on both sides of the Atlantic.)

By the end of his three years at Oxford, he was already attacking members of the British critical fraternity and their impoverished sensibilities. "A sham necklace of bitter brevities or false, hollow eulogy will not do for criticism," he brayed, in the first chapter of "He That Plays the King." "The fixed quizzical grin, the bar-fly impressionism, the epicene tartness which most critics affect is no substitute for awe, hate, and rapture." He went on, "What I am saying is that attack, not apology, passion, not sympathy, should lie behind the decorous columns of our drama critics." Criticism, he added, "calls for great flexibility of reaction and above all, great flair and cocksureness." What Tynan was really proposing as the Rx for the parlous state of dramatic criticism was himself.

As a critic, Tynan emerged on the English scene almost fully formed. He was poised; he was knowledgeable. He was also—and always—spoiling for a fight. He inherited a moribund theatrical scene, where, as he wrote, "two out of three London theatres were inhabited by detective stories, Pineroesque melodramas, quarter-witted farces, débutante comedies, overweight musicals and unreviewable revues." He wrote as a man of the theatre, not as a man of the reading room, and his style blasted prolix Victorian waffle from critical discourse. Here, for instance, writing on Shakespeare's "Henry IV" in 1946, is James Agate, the leading theatre critic of his day, whose style Tynan mocked for its "breathless punch-drunk downrightness":

> "England," announces the program. And who is to set the
> first half of this great play in its country and period. Not, one
> thinks, the wan and shaken King, nor yet his priggish, pragmat-
> ical son; and surely the Percys and the Mortimers, Douglases
> and Glendowers have long been piffle before the wind of time.

Instead of the highfalutin, Tynan developed an artful, pungent, sly tone, which might be called "lowfalutin." His pomp had a knockdown wink in it. Of Rodgers and Hammerstein's excursion into contemporary Chinese culture in "Flower Drum Song," Tynan wrote, "Perhaps as a riposte to Joshua Logan's 'The World of Suzy Wong,' Rodgers and Hammerstein have given us what, if I had any self control at all, I would refrain from describing as a world of woozy song."

In print, Tynan's wit and limpid style presented him to the world as a specimen of perfect individualism without wound or worry. "I know nothing of ardour and am not dogged: to write, for me, is not *necessary* as gunpowder *needs* to explode," he wrote in "He That Plays the King." "I do this because I can, not because I have to." Tynan protested too much. He did have a need, and that was to align himself, in a kind of symbiotic way, with the extraordinary souls whose work onstage he tried to match with his own literary performance. "The study of actors should be a full-time task," he wrote, "worthy of the same passionate scholarship which lepidopterists devote to butterflies." His stunning evocations of performers worked a kind of sympathetic magic that bound their glory inextricably to him. Fame, and the celebrated company he kept, gave him legitimacy.

Tynan had a language beyond the usual lit-crit stammer, and it conveyed the subtlety of a craft that was undergoing profound sociological changes. The 1945 Education Act had enabled many talented young people, including Tynan, to get scholarships to universities and acting schools that before the war had been the privilege of the rich. This created a dynamic new pool of working-class talent—actors like Rita Tushingham, Peter O'Toole, Tom Courtenay, Albert Finney, and Richard Burton, who came to the stage with different energies, different behaviors, different connections to British experience, and who in a short time would require a different kind of play. Tynan was on their wavelength. And because he understood glamour and the discipline of planting the idea of self in the public mind and keeping it there, these stars, and others, found themselves deconstructed by him with unusual finesse. "To be famous young and to make fame last—the secret of combining the two is glandular: it depends on energy," Tynan wrote with particular prescience, in an account of Noël Coward's famous nightclub début at the Café de Paris.

Tynan was never shy about shivering the timbers of the English acting establishment. On Vivien Leigh's Cleopatra, for instance: "Taking a deep breath and resolutely focusing her periwinkle charm, she launches another of her careful readings; ably and passionlessly she picks her way among its great challenges, presenting a glibly mown lawn where her author had imagined a jungle." Still, Tynan, who aspired to be a spellbinder, was at his most compelling when he was under the spell of others: Marlene Dietrich "shows herself to the audience like the Host to the congregation and delivers the sacred goods"; Katharine Hepburn is "wide open yet with no breaches in her armour"; Judy Garland, at the Palace, "embodies the persistence of youth so completely that we forbid her to develop. . . . Even in young middle age, she must continue to sing about adolescence and all the pain and nostalgia that go with it. When the voice pours out, as rich and pleading as ever, we know where, and how moved, we are—in the presence of a star, and embarrassed by tears."

Tynan never succumbed to what he called "the critic's scourge: atrophy of love." He was passionate, nowhere more so than in his review of John Osborne's "Look Back in Anger" (1956). "I doubt if I could love anyone who did not wish to see 'Look Back in Anger.' It is the best young play of its decade," he wrote. But theatre is a recalcitrant beast; even with Tynan's prodding, it didn't move quickly in the direction he wanted. At the end of the fifties, he concluded that English theatre was "desperately enfeebled" and that "the strongest and most unmistakable influence on our drama in the last ten years has been transatlantic." In 1958, Tynan took himself off for an infusion of American energy, and was the senior drama critic of this magazine for two years. But, as the sixties wore on, he found himself with less to say about Britain's writers (Pinter, Orton, Bond) and more to say about the establishment of a National Theatre, where the sprouts of their theatrical renaissance could be properly nurtured.

In 1962, having just attacked the newly appointed head of the National Theatre, Sir Laurence Olivier, for his season of plays at the Chichester Festival Theatre, Tynan wrote to Olivier asking to be made the National Theatre's first dramaturge. "How shall we slaughter the little bastard?" Olivier fumed to his wife, the actress Joan Plowright, who nonetheless liked the idea, because young audiences would be "thrilled with the mixture of you and Ken." In a letter inviting Tynan to work as an in-house critic and to help plan the seasons, as well as take charge of all published material, a position Tynan held from 1963 to 1973, Olivier added a postscript: "GOD—ANYthing to get you off that *Observer.*"

The job increased both Tynan's public prestige and his private frustration. Of the seventy-nine plays mounted on his watch, according to his second wife, Kathleen Tynan, "thirty-two of these productions were Ken's ideas; twenty were chosen with his collaboration." This kind of defensive scorekeeping is typical of the dramaturge's dilemma; the successes or failures of the theatre may be of his choosing but not of his accomplishing. Neither odium nor glory falls, finally, to him: both inside and outside the theatre, the critic's role, Tynan knew, was one without risk. "I took the safer course and became a full-time critic," he wrote in his journal. "That is why, today, I am everybody's adviser—Roman Polanski's, Larry Olivier's, Michael White's—and no one's boss, not even my own."

"Such is servility," he wrote in 1972, when Olivier had gone behind his back to ask the director Peter Hall his opinion of a play that Tynan had suggested. And when Olivier accepted Hall as his successor, rather than nominating one of his colleagues at the National, Tynan wrote, "He has passed a vote of no confidence in us all. . . . He has hired us, stolen our kudos, and now shows no compunction about discarding us." The National kept Tynan busy but did not allow him to accomplish his mission. In the theatre's tenth-anniversary year, Tynan noted in his journal that it had "discovered one new playwright (Tom Stoppard) and no new directors." He added, "It's a sad reflection on the way in which I've occupied my time for the past decade."

Over the next seven years, Tynan's sense of regret and self-loathing grew. He heard himself described as the greatest English theatre critic since George Bernard Shaw, but, unlike Shaw, he had no other forum in which to express himself. Renown requires deeds, and where were Tynan's? He tried and failed to float the idea of himself as a stage and film director. He could manage the sprint of a newspaper column but not the long-distance run of a sustained piece of work. None of the books for which he took advances got written. (He got halfway through a study of Wilhelm Reich but dropped it.) The routine of reviewing had palled, and the anomie it had once kept at bay now filtered deeper into his life: "The sensation of vanishing. Nothing registers on me: I register nothing." He seemed unable to claim new, meaningful territory for himself. There were always causes to debate and to keep him in the middle of things: Vietnam, sexual liberation, censorship (he was the first person to break the BBC sound barrier by saying "fuck"). He produced two West End shows, which failed, and a sex revue, "Oh! Calcutta!," one of the top three longest-running musicals of all time. But, as his journal shows, Tynan's self-lacerating spirit was increasingly channelled into sadomasochistic sexual obsessions (he had an appetite for spanking and whipping). More and more, he smiled at the world with cold teeth.

At the beginning of Tynan's career, when he was still inventing himself in "He That Plays the King," he turned his emptiness into a kind of heroic self-advertisement, depicting himself variously as a "soft blotting-pad," a "shell," a "spying-glass," a "chameleon," an "echo." As a critic, he hitched that emptiness to stars and to productions whose energy he absorbed and reflected back. Over time, though, the increasing momentum of his fame led to a sort of disintegration. His emphysema compounded a lassitude that he could neither control nor quite understand. "I used to take Dexamyl to give me enough confidence to start work," he wrote in 1971. "Now I take it to give me enough confidence not to." The frequent high spirits in Tynan's sad tale make his journal all the more poignant. "Was Elaine a trial?" the critic Cyril Connolly asks him about his first wife. "No. More of a jury," Tynan answers.

On his deathbed, he whispered the words "a small talent for brilliance." If he was speaking of himself, his judgment is too harsh. The journal he left behind bears witness to his own advice: "Be light, stinging, insolent, and melancholy." It demonstrates both his brilliance and his struggle to find a place in the world for his intelligence to shine. Unwittingly, in its accounts of Tynan's restless and wayward sexual exploits, it also tracks a larger human theme, which "Oh! Calcutta!" tried and failed to dramatize—what one of Tynan's famous friends, Tennessee Williams, once called the "mad pilgrimage of the flesh."

DAME JUDI DENCH

THE PLAYER QUEEN

IN THE OPENING SEQUENCE OF "Iris," an extraordinary film about the late novelist Iris Murdoch's descent into the limbo of Alzheimer's, Murdoch and her loyal man-child of a husband, the Oxford don John Bayley, are shown swimming like two plump sea lions through the murk of the Thames. They're happy in their underwater playground, which distorts light and form and contains the sediment of ages. They float freely but are always in contact, dodging among the rocks and weeds in joyful, directionless exploration. Water was Iris Murdoch's primal habitat; by no accident, it is also the favorite element of the woman who plays her here, Judi Dench. "There's a wonderful abandonment you feel in water," Dench says. "It's very liberating. It's like the unconscious. You're just floating around there and trusting that you're going to come up to the surface."

This is not the only point of intersection between the two women: the adventure of the unknown, the salvation of the imagination, the promotion of happiness, and a lifelong inquiry into goodness are all themes in the elusive lives of both Murdoch and Dench. Sir Richard Eyre, the director and co-author of "Iris," says that while writing the screenplay he tried to instill his sense of Dench into the character of Iris. "There was never a question of how do you bring Iris and Judi Dench together," he says. "Essentially, the character is Judi Dench-stroke-Iris Murdoch."

Dench, who has played both Queen Victoria and Queen Elizabeth I on film and was made a Dame Commander of the Order of the British Empire in 1988, is beloved by the English public for her quintessential Britishness. "I think that in a lot of people's eyes she is the equivalent of the Queen—she inspires such phenomenal affection," says the director John Madden, who launched Dench's late-blooming film career in 1997 with "Mrs.

Brown."(Significantly, last month the seventy-seven British families that lost relatives in the Twin Towers catastrophe chose Dench to read at the memorial service at Westminster Abbey. But she and Murdoch share an Anglo-Irish heritage, and each, in her own way, is a paradoxical amalgam of propriety and wildness.

With a leafy home in Surrey, a silver Rover, a taste for simple if expensive clothes, a commitment to charities (she is a patron of a hundred and eighty-three of them), and her obbligato of drollery—what Billy Connolly, who starred opposite her in "Mrs. Brown," calls "that light, posh, self-effacing humor"—Dench, who is sixty-seven, cuts a deceptively sedate, suburban figure. At work, however, she trolls her turbulent Celtic interior, a vast tragicomic landscape that ranges between despair and indomitability. "There's a sort of crimson place deep within her—a fiery dark-red place that stokes all the things she does," Connolly says. "You don't get to see it. But you occasionally get glimpses of how tiresome she finds the doily-and-serviette crowd. You know, those English twittering fucking women—they think she's one of them, and she isn't." This complexity is what Dench brings to her acting, which is nowhere more inspired than in her depiction of Murdoch. Her performance parses every nuance in the writer's trajectory of decline—from embarrassment to bewilderment, from terror to loss, from nonentity to a final connection with an enduring life force, where, in the shuffle of dementia, Murdoch somehow finds a dance.

Dench is not much of a reader, but she has read most of Murdoch's novels, and before filming she went so far as to sit outside Bayley's house while he was away to absorb the shambolic atmosphere of the place. (She found his car in the driveway; unlocked and with a window open.) "I didn't want to miss that snapshot in my mind," she says. But her uncanny portrait emerged out of her own process, a combination of technical rigor and imaginative free fall, in which, according to Eyre, "she doesn't put anything of herself between her and the character." He explains, "I was really staggered at the way she transformed herself. Toward the end of the film, when Iris's mind has gone, and you look at Judi's face and see that implacability, the sense of peace and the absence in her eyes, that is alchemy. She didn't go to old people's homes. She didn't sit and study. It's intuitive. She's quick I mean, *really* quick."

* * *

Except for time out to have a child and to nurse her husband of thirty years, the actor Michael Williams, who died last January of lung cancer, Dench has been performing almost constantly for four and a half decades. She appeared in the first season of the Royal Shakespeare Company, in 1961, and in the eighties was a founding member of Kenneth Branagh's Renaissance Theatre Company, for which she has also directed plays. Under the auspices of the Old Vic, the R.S.C., and the Royal National Theatre, she has turned in some of the greatest classical performances in recent memory. Her Juliet in Franco Zeffirelli's 1960 stage production of "Romeo and Juliet"; her Titania in "A Midsummer Night's Dream," directed by Sir Peter Hall in 1962; her Viola in "Twelfth Night" in 1969; her Lady Macbeth in Trevor Nunn's magnificent 1976 production; her Cleopatra in Hall's 1987 "Antony and Cleopatra"—all are exemplars of contemporary Shakespearean performance. Her work in the modern repertoire—as Anya in "The Cherry Orchard," as Juno Boyle in "Juno and the Paycock," as Lady Bracknell in "The Importance of Being Earnest," and as Christine Foskett in Rodney Ackland's rediscovered fifties classic "Absolute Hell"—has also had a huge impact on English theatregoers. And Dench has inspired allegiance as well through her television career, which includes thirty-four films and two popular long-running comedy series, "A Fine Romance" and "As Time Goes By."

"See you on the ice, darling," she has been known to call out from her dressing room to an actor headed toward the stage. For Dench, "the crack"—the Irish term for fun—is riding the exhilarating uncertainty of the moment. To that end, she is famous (some would say notorious) for not having read many of the parts she accepts. Instead, she has someone else paraphrase the script for her. (Williams usually had this duty before he died; now it has fallen to Dench's agent, Tor Belfrage.) "Michael said, 'Just read that one line;'" Dench recalls of "Pack of Lies," Hugh Whitemore's successful spy story, in which she and Williams starred. "It was just one line. I read it, and I knew then that it would be all right."

"It often seems absurd to me that a woman as intelligent as Judi could roll up at the beginning of the rehearsal not having read the play," says Branagh, who directed Dench in his films of "Hamlet" and "Henry V" and has, in turn, been directed by her onstage in "Much Ado About Nothing" and "Look Back in Anger." Although this method allows Dench to arrive at rehearsals with, as Branagh puts it, "the right kind of blank page to start writing on," from a professional point of view it is also sensationally reckless. "I don't know what it is in me, this kind of perversity," Dench told me when I visited her at home last July. "I don't understand it myself. I think some people think it's an affectation. It's thrilling, though, isn't it? You don't know what's coming."

The habit of not reading scripts has, over the years, landed Dench in a few sticky theatrical situations, such as Peter Shaffer's turgid "The Gift of the Gorgon," in 1992. And at first she wasn't keen to take on her current West End outing, in a revival of "The Royal Family," the slim 1927 Edna Ferber and George S. Kaufman satire of the theatrical Barrymores, but her mind was made up for her when she received a call from the director, Peter Hall. "It's entirely a roll of the dice, but it has to do with friends, with people I love and admire," she explained several weeks before rehearsals of "The Royal Family" began. "So if Peter rings me up and says, 'You ought to do this play,' I say, 'Sure.' I swear before God I have not read the play."

Dench's risk-taking onstage is in inverse proportion to her vulnerability off it. "When I go into a rehearsal room, my coat and bag have to be nearest the door," she said in a recent television interview. Performing, for Dench, is an antidote to chronic insecurity; it gives her, she says, what the Cockneys call "bottle": "It's courage. You know, like jumping into ice-cold water. If it's to be done—do it. Go!" Recently when Trevor Nunn offered her a role at the National, she replied, "I want to come back to the National, but not in that part. Would you ask me to do something more frightening?"

Dench's derring-do also seems necessary to keep her nearly perpetual routine of rehearsal and performance a fresh and vigorous challenge. "Her desire is to recreate each time, to reëxperience, and not simply reproduce," Branagh says. To that end, she refuses analysis. Without preconceived notions, she tries to let the character play *her*. "She absolutely hates to rationalize," Eyre says. "When you're working with her, she'll ask a question about a scene or a character, and when you go to talk about it, at some point she'll say, 'Yeah, O.K., I understand.' She doesn't want it spelled out. She has to find it herself." A long time ago, when Eyre was doing a play with

Dench at the National, where he was the artistic director for ten years, she left her script in the rehearsal room; the next day, Eyre handed it to her. "'Oh, you look terribly shocked,'" he recalls her saying. "'Is it because I didn't take my script home with me?' I said, 'Well, I guess so.' She talked to me about how she learned lines. The work that she does outside rehearsal is not sitting down with the script. She just sort of envisions the scene and colors it in her mind." Dench's method of bushwhacking through her unconscious to find the emotional core of a character is, she says, completely instinctive: "The subconscious is what works on the part. It's like coming back to a crossword at the end of the day and filling in seventeen answers straight off."

In one scene of "Iris," the senile Murdoch goes walkabout in the rain on a motorway and slips and falls down an embankment into the underbrush. This is the first and only scene in the film in which Dench's Murdoch, whose eyes are always turned inward, really sees and acknowledges Bayley. "I said to Judi, 'You have to find a way of doing it that reconciles a sort of rationality with the fact that her brain is more or less gone,'" Eyre says. "That's all she wanted to know." When the distressed Bayley (played by Jim Broadbent) finally finds her, Dench is covered with mud and laughing to herself. Out of her solitude, her eyes come to rest on Broadbent's face. "I love you," she says, and with a startling glimmer of clarity Dench manages to invoke the blessing and heartbreak of a lifetime of connection.

Dench describes herself as "an enormous console with hundreds of buttons, each of which I must press at exactly the right time." She adds, "If you're lucky enough to be asked to play many different parts, you have to have reserves of all sorts of emotions. When I was rehearsing a part I'd never, ever, ever discuss it with Michael, because I had that pressure-cooker syndrome. If I once open that little key—*pffft!*—the stuff goes."

In nature, as in art, the secret of conservation is not to disturb the wild things. Dench's brooding talent has its correlative in her five-acre Surrey domain, Wasp Green, and in the low-slung, wood-beamed 1680 yeoman's house where she lives with her twenty-nine-year-old daughter, the actress Finty Williams, her four-year-old grandson, Sammy, nine cats, and several ducks. The front of the house is bright, tidy, and picturesque in a *Country*

Life sort of way; the back acres, however, have been left alone, with only a small path cut through a thicket of brambles, nettles, and wild orchids. "You have to see the back garden to understand Judi," Franco Zeffirelli says. "She puts up a façade sometimes, but for herself she reserves a private garden. You discover there treasures that you don't see at the front of the house."

On the day I visited her there last summer, Dench, in Wellington boots, stepped lively on the overgrown path. "I've got to cut these back," she said, swiping at the nettles. She pointed out new plantings: a black poplar to commemorate a row that had blown down the previous year; "Sammy's oak," a tree planted in honor of her grandson's birth; and the place she'd chosen for "Mikey's oak," a sapling that was originally an opening night present from Williams to the director Anthony Page, whose production of "The Forest" was Williams's last acting job. "What's important to me is continuance—a line stretching on," Dench said. "I hate things that start and finish abruptly."

If the wild back garden is a kind of memory theatre for Dench, the theatre itself puts her in touch with her family, which she calls "a unit of tremendous encouragement." All the qualities that Judi has as a person, and, indeed, as an actress, come from the very close family background," Williams said on a 1995 "South Bank" TV biography of his wife. Dench's love of work, painting, swimming, jokes, and especially acting are passions she absorbed from her father, Dr. Reginald Dench, a physician who served as the official doctor for the Theatre Royal in York before he died, in 1964. "I remember going visiting with him," Dench says. "When we turned into a road, children would run and hold on to the car. That's the kind of doctor he was. He was a wonderful raconteur. He had the most incredible sense of humor—just spectacular." When Dench was about fifteen, on holiday in Spain, she admired a pair of expensive blue-and-white striped shoes. "Well, I think you could probably have those shoes," she recalls her father saying. "Let's go to lunch. We'll discuss it." At lunch, Dench—a fish lover— scanned the buffet of prawns and lobsters. "Daddy looked at me and said, 'Would you like that?' 'Yes, please.' So I had four big prawns and enjoyed every minute of it. Daddy said, 'You've just eaten your shoes.'"

The Dench children—Judi, Jeffrey, who is now an actor, and Peter, who became a doctor—grew up in York, in a sprawling Victorian house, where Judi, the youngest, had the attic room and was allowed to draw on the walls. "She got her own way," Jeffrey says. "Judi was Daddy's Beautiful Lady." According to her daughter, Finty, the only discrepancy between the public Dench and the private one is her temper. Her volatility is an inheritance from her flamboyant, sharp-tongued mother, Olave, who once threw a vacuum cleaner down the stairs at a representative who had called to inquire about it. "You didn't cross her, or *pow!*—not hitting, but a tongue-lashing, and you stayed lashed," Jeffrey says. Dench's contradictory nature—with its combination of mighty spirit and "nonconfidence," as she calls it—appears to have been forged as she tried to negotiate her mother's combustible personality. "She loved admonishing Judi," Trevor Nunn says of Olave. "I mean the kind of admonishment that comes from absolute worship. The privilege of being able to be the one who could put her in her place. 'Judi, you mustn't say that!' 'Judi, you're such an embarrassment!'" Dench says, "She was outrageous." In the late seventies, by which time she was having trouble with her sight, Olave had lunch with Nunn and Dench at a sophisticated, self-congratulatory Italian restaurant called the Lugger. "Olave ordered tomato soup, which came in a huge bowl," Nunn recalls. "A waiter arrived with a little sachet of cream, with which he spelled out the name of the restaurant on the soup and then left. 'Judi,' Olave said, 'a man has just come and written "bugger" in me soup!'"

Dench's parents took a keen interest in amateur dramatics and, when Dench became an actress, their support verged on the overprotective. They saw their daughter in "Romeo and Juliet" more than seventy times; once, Reginald got so involved in the play that when Judi, as Juliet, said, "Where is my father and my mother, nurse?" he was heard to say, "Here we are, darling. In Row H."

Whereas most stars seek a public to provide the attention they failed to get in childhood, Dench's commitment to the theatrical community is, she admits, an attempt to reproduce the endorsement and excitement of her first audience—her family. She claims not to be "good at my own company." Rather, to understand her own identity she needs to he in the attentive gaze of others—as the psychologist D. W. Winnicott puts it, "When I look I am seen, so I exist." Dench is clear on this point. "I need somebody to reflect me back, or to give me their reflection," she says. Ned Sherrin, who directed Dench and Williams in "Mr. and Mrs. Nobody" in 1986, says he was so aware of Dench's need "to create a family with each show" that he added a couple of walk-ons to what was otherwise a two-person play.

Dench, who keeps a collection of Teddy bears and hearts and a doll's house at Wasp Green, somehow contrives, as Branagh says, "to feel and be in the moment, as a child." In the collegial atmosphere of a theatre company; she is an adored and prankish catalyst, inevitably, as her brother Jeffrey points out, "at the center." "Eight going on sixty-seven" is how Geoffrey Palmer, her co-star in the nineties TV series "As Time Goes By," characterizes the innocence and spontaneity she brings to the daily routine of self-reinvention. Her process—her abdication of responsibility to intuition, her need to be told the story—is not so much about being lost as it is about being held. She casts the director as her father and exhibits an almost filial devotion. "When we did 'A Midsummer Night's Dream,' she did this extraordinary Titania," Hall says. "I said to her, 'One day, you'll play Cleopatra. I want you to make me a promise that when you do it you'll do it with me.' We shook hands on it." Hall goes on, "Twenty years later, she rang me up and said, 'I've just been asked to play Cleopatra by the R.S.C. I said I was promised to you. Now, do you want to do it?'"

From her first sighting onstage—as a seventeen-year-old Ariel in a production of "The Tempest," at the Mount School, in York, where she boarded from 1947 to 1953—Dench was transparently a natural. But neither Dench, who then aspired to be a set designer, nor her teachers took her ability very seriously. The novelist A. S. Byatt, a schoolmate, recalls, "I used to talk to Katharine MacDonald, the English mistress who taught her. 'You know, Judi will probably be content,' as she put it, 'to dabble her pretty feet in amateur dramatics.'"

Dench enrolled at London's Central School of Speech and Drama simply because her brother Jeffrey, who went there, had told her appealing stories about the place. Vanessa Redgrave, who was in Dench's class, and who was then self-conscious and gawky, remembers being both "admiring and jealous" of Dench's naturalness. "She skipped and hopped with pleasure and excitement up the stairs, down the corridors, and onto the stage," Redgrave wrote in her autobiography. "She wore jeans, the only girl who had them, a polo-neck sweater, and ballet slippers that flopped and flapped as she bounded around." The turning point in Dench's ambition came during a mime class in her second term, when she was required to perform an assignment—called "Recollection"—that she'd completely forgotten to prepare. "I don't remember thinking anything out," she says. "I walked into a garden. I bent down to smell something like rosemary or thyme. I walked and just looked at certain things. I picked up a pebble, and threw it into what I imagined was a pond and watched the ripples going out from it. I looked over and sat on a swing. And I swung, you know, like you do on a swing that isn't there. Then I walked out of the garden. That was my mime." Her teacher, Walter Mudd, gave her, she says, "the most glowing notice I think I've ever had. What is more, he said, 'You looked like a little Renoir doing it.' I thought, Well, I think that I will enjoy what I'm going to do, hopefully get work, go for it."

Dench graduated with a first-class degree and four acting prizes. According to her biography, the unfortunately titled "Judi Dench: With a Crack in Her Voice," by John Miller, a notice was posted on the school's bulletin board naming her the student most likely to become a star; and when the Old Vic offered her the role of Ophelia opposite John Neville's Hamlet it seemed a self-fulfilling prophecy. "ENTER JUDI—LONDON'S NEW OPHELIA—OLD VIC MAKE HER A FIRST-ROLE STAR," the Evening News announced. When Neville heard about his tyro Ophelia, "I blew my top," he says. He begged the theatre's publicity department not to hype her before the opening. "I thought, and still think, that it would have been best just to let the media discover her for themselves," he says. Dench was more or less annihilated by the press. "Hamlet's sweetheart is required to be something more than a piece of Danish patisserie," Richard Findlater wrote in the Sunday Dispatch; in the Observer, Kenneth Tynan swatted her away as "a pleasing but terribly sane little thing." At the end of the season, when the production toured America, the role was taken away from Dench. "That was a kind of dagger to the heart," she says. "I remember John Neville saying to me, 'You must decide what you're doing this for.' And I made my mind up, and I think that's what keeps me going." The answer remains Dench's secret. "The only part of her that is totally unreachable for me is that she's never told me why she's an actress," Finty says. "I would love to know what motivates her."

Dench came of age just as the definitions of femininity were being rewritten, and she was an incarnation of the freewheeling, bumptious independence of the eternally young New Woman. With a cap of close-cropped hair, a strong chin, high cheekbones, big alert eyes, and a wide smile, the five-foot-two Dench cut a gamine figure onstage. Zeffirelli still thinks of her as "a kind of irresistible bombshell." He says," She was funny and witty and biting. You had to be very careful what you said because she would answer back promptly. She was a dynamo, this girl. She just was an extraordinary surprise, because I was accustomed to Peggy Ashcroft and Dorothy Tutin, that style of acting."

David Jones, who directed one of the high-water marks of Dench's TV career, "Langrishe, Go Down" (1978), remembers her quicksilver quality in Zeffirelli's "Romeo and Juliet." He describes her "darting—like a bird coming onto the stage and going off again. You weren't quite aware of the feet touching the ground, this extraordinary agility of body and of mind." Dench's kinetic quality onstage finds different but no less startling expression in film. "She has a kind of sprung dynamic with her eyes," John Madden says. "They don't move gradually and settle or shift. They dart, then dart back, then settle again on the place that they just avoided looking at. It's almost like a double take, which suggests a kind of current flowing in an opposite direction from what she is saying."

When you meet Dench, it's hard not to feel the engine running inside her. She's nervy. Her fingers play across her lips; her feet tap under the table. Her lightness and quickness are very much a part of her metabolism as an actress and lend credibility to her performances. "She is the perfect Shakespearean, because the great characters in Shakespeare have fantastic speed of thought," Nunn says. "They have speed of wit, speed of response, speed of invention of the image. That only works if the actor convinces the audience that that language is being coined by that brain in that situation." He adds, "You live in the moment with her. There's never a sense that she's doing a recitation."

Dench's combination of insight and inspiration, charisma and cunning has made her one of Britain's two marquee players whose names guarantee

West End commercial success. (Her friend Dame Maggie Smith is the other.) Even with the drastic fall-off of tourism after September 11th, "The Royal Family" had half a million pounds in advance bookings, and, despite a tepid press, is still doing brisk business. Dench's drawing power, for which she is paid a five-figure salary every week, plus up to ten per cent of the gross, has been greatly enhanced since the mid-nineties by her emergence as an international film star. Before being touched by what she calls "the luck of John Madden," who directed her in both "Shakespeare in Love" and "Mrs. Brown," Dench had not shown much interest in films, though she'd appeared in twelve. When she was starting out, she was told by an industry swami that she didn't have "a movie face." "It put me completely off," says Dench, who nonetheless nearly got the starring role in Tony Richardson's 1961 film "A Taste of Honey." "But then I only ever really loved the stage. It's only recently that I've got to like film so much." For the last three James Bond films, Dench's severe side has been siphoned off into M, Bond's no-nonsense boss; and among the fifty-five awards she lists in her bio are three Oscar nominations in the past four years—for "Mrs. Brown," "Shakespeare in Love," and "Chocolat." (The command and wit of her seven-minute cameo as Elizabeth I in "Shakespeare in Love" earned her the 1999 Academy Award for Best Supporting Actress.)

Among theatre people, Dench's popularity is a source of some curmudgeonly grousing—"If she farted, they'd give her an award," one playwright said—and some good jokes. Eyre recounted a conversation he once had with the playwright Alan Bennett, who had seen a man wearing a heavy-metal-style T-shirt that read "Hitler: The European Tour." They tried to imagine a T-shirt in worse taste. Recalling the thirty-nine Turin soccer fans who had been killed at a match against Liverpool in 1995, Eyre suggested "Liverpool 39–Turin 0." "Yes, that's ghastly," Eyre recalls Bennett saying. "But the worst-taste T-shirt, the very, very worst, would be 'I Hate Judi Dench.'"

One clue to Dench's appeal is her husky voice, which has a natural catch in it; certain notes fail to operate. When Dench was at the Nottingham Playhouse in the mid-sixties, she had the box office display a notice that said, "Judi Dench is not ill, she just talks like this." Dench's sound is idiosyncratic but not mannered; it is full of intimations that, as Alan Bennett says, "open you up to whatever she's doing" and allow various interpretations. Sir Ian McKellen, who has performed with Dench in four plays, most memorably as Macbeth to her Lady Macbeth, calls it "a little girl's voice—the crack suggests she's not in control."

Another reason for Dench's popularity is her warmth. She communicates a palpable, deep-seated generosity. "You feel somehow, even as a member of the audience, that if you were in trouble she would help you and laugh you out of it," Hall says. Dench pays close attention to her audience. During the half hour before a show, she keeps the loudspeakers in her dressing room turned up, both to take the measure of the house and to pump up her adrenaline. "I have to hear the audience coming in," she says. "I need to be generated by it—for the jump-off. It's like a quickie ignition." Once, an American student asked Dench if the audience made a difference to her; Dench replied, "If it didn't make a difference, I'd be at home with me feet up the chimney. That's who I'm doing it for." "It's a little unnerving when you're working with her," McKellen says. "What's happening is that she's making love to the audience—not making love but providing the focus of attention to an audience that wants to love. You could be wrapped in Judi's arms onstage and acting as closely with her as possible, and she's capable of betraying you, because her main reason for being in your arms is for the audience's delectation. It isn't upstaging. That isn't taking away the focus. Her spirit is flowing, and it's a decision she's made that it will flow. And when I'm in the audience I want her to do that."

In performance, Dench is a minimalist: no gesture or movement is wasted. Richard Eyre refers to what he calls her "third eye." "It's the ability to walk on fire and yet he completely unburnt, to be red-hot with passion and at the same time there's this third eye that is looking down thinking, Am I doing this right?" Billy Connolly told me about filming one scene in "Mrs. Brown." In the first meeting between the widowed Queen Victoria and her Scottish manservant, John Brown, Brown's forthrightness catches the Queen offguard. "Honest to God, I never thought to see you in such a state," Brown says. "You must miss him dreadfully." In an astonishing closeup, the austere formality of Dench's visage suddenly transforms—a cloud of grief sweeps over her and she breaks up. "Judi did that twelve times," Con-

nolly says. "Every time, I thought I'd really wounded her. You see me looking all bewildered. Well, I actually was."

"Dench has a kind of glamour when she performs," says Hal Prince,
who directed her as Sally Bowles in "Cabaret" in 1968 and considers her
"the most effective of all the people who played the part." Glamour—the
word has its root in the Scottish word for "grammar"—is an artifice of elegant coherence; it requires distance. Dench, who is no Garbo or Dietrich,
manufactures this not through stage-managed aloofness but through a natural sense of containment. David Jones says, "Her gift is to step down the throt-
tle, so you don't get the full impact of her passion; you just know there's an
enormous amount in reserve. It's like a wave suspended." McKellen observes,
"She goes *out,* but she doesn't always invite you *in.*"

On a bright July morning, Dench picked me up outside Gatwick Airport
to ferry me hack to Wasp Green. She arrived with a story—one that she
retold three times during the day. She hadn't known what I looked like, she
said—though I later noticed on her desk a book I'd sent her with my jacket
photo prominently displayed—and she'd stopped two men before I loomed
up in her windshield. "I slowed down and this man says, 'I know you. Are
you with American Airlines?'" she said. At a stroke, she had levelled the
playing field, by making herself appear just an ordinary, unrecognized citizen. The story got us talking and laughing. Disarming others is one of
Dench's great social gifts, and one of her most skillful defenses. "She was
successful very young," Eyre says. "She developed some sort of tactic that
stopped people from disliking her."

As a diva Dench is something of a disappointment. Her dislike of public
display—what Branagh calls her "puritanical scrutiny of anything showy"—
can be attributed at least in part to the tenets of her faith. She was introduced to Quaker practice as a teenager at the Mount School, and she still
goes to Quaker meetings. "I have to have quietness inside me somewhere,
otherwise I'd burn myself up," she said in a recent television interview.
Quakerism requires its followers to look for the light in others, as well as in
themselves, and this, in a way, explains Dench's view of acting as a service
industry. "It's a very unselfish job," she says. "It's about being true to an
author, a director, a group of people, and stimulating a different audience

every night. If you're out for self-glorification, then you're in the wrong profession."

"There are a lot of people who are very willing to put my mother on a pedestal, which is a lonely existence," Finty says. "She wants to dispute that so much that she will literally do anything for anybody." For twelve years, Dench and Williams lived with all of their in-laws in one house, and Dench is a legendary sender of postcards and birthday cards; by Finty's reckoning, she gives about four hundred and fifty Christmas presents a year. She once gave Eyre a wooden heart carved from a tree trunk; and, for as long as Hall can remember, on his birthday Dench has managed to have delivered—as far afield as Australia—his favorite meal: oysters, French fries, and a bottle of Sancerre. "Comes my seventieth birthday, and there's no oysters, no Sancerre," Hall says. "I said to my wife, 'Well, I must be off the list.' We had my dinner"—a party for fifty, with Dench at his side—"and there's a Doulton china plate from Judi, specially made, with six oysters and chips painted on it."

This hubbub of good will and connection, however, skirts the issue of intimacy. "Judi has always found safety in numbers," says David Jones, who was involved with her briefly in his twenties. "When we were dating, I would arrange what I thought was a one-on-one meeting to go to a museum or the theatre. Quite often, I would turn up and find two other people invited. And Judi would say, 'Isn't it fun? They're free! They can come with us.'" Some of Dench's schoolmates, like the writer Margaret Drabble, found her buoyancy "a little Panglossian." Even Dench's husband, a man prone to the kind of melancholy that he called "black-dog days," and which could stretch into months, sent up her effervescence. "With Judi, it's bloody Christmas morning every day," he told Branagh.

"I'm a person who off-loads an enormous amount onto people," Dench told me. "Inside, there's a core that I won't off-load." According to Finty, Dench "doesn't like to talk about very emotional things," but throughout our day together at Wasp Green her gallant cheer was tested by small unsettling moments. Although her charm never faltered, I was left with mixed messages, as if I had wandered into some Chekhovian scenario full of distressing secrets. Our extended conversation at a garden table on the lawn was interrupted first by a series of visitors (the mailman, a next-door neighbor, and two secretaries, each of whom got Dench's full attention), then by phone calls from Anthony Page and Peter Hall, then by someone delivering a single pink rose (I learned later that it was from Finty—carrying on Williams's tradition of having a single red rose sent to Dench every Friday of their marriage), then by Dench's need to feed the herd of cats, and then by a panic over a credit card that might or might not have been stolen.

Finally, and most perplexingly, Finty, who moved back into her parents' house when Michael fell ill, walked over unbidden with a provocative and bewildering announcement. "Your granddaughter is being played by an eighteen-year-old," she said. Dench's bright face collapsed." Oh, Finty, I'm so sorry." "It's all right," Finty said, with a wave of her hand. "I'm all right." She turned back to the house, leaving her mother to struggle with her obvious disappointment. After a while, Dench said, "It'll be for a very good reason." Then, finally she explained: "'The Royal Family.' She saw Peter." Finty, who had recently finished filming in Robert Altman's "Gosford Park," had hoped for a part in the play.

A few minutes later, Finty came out again to say goodbye. "It doesn't matter about that, you know," Dench said. "It doesn't matter." Finty agreed. "She's only a little eighteen-year-old, and maybe it's her first job. Maybe she'll he celebrating with someone and getting very excited," she said. "Maybe you will have something else to do, you never know, "Dench said. "Never know," Finty said, nodding. "My audition's been cancelled on Tuesday." There was a long, fierce silence as she exited for the second time. "It's impossible being the child of an actor," Dench said. A certain gravity fell across her face as she seemed to push down feelings of remorse and guilt and got on with the professional task at hand.

Onstage, Dench has found her bliss; offstage, that bliss has cast a shadow on others—on her brother Jeffrey ("There is jealousy," he admits. "She's had the breaks. I'm a jobbing actor. You know that niggles"), on Michael ("In some way, his heart was broken by Judi's success," Eyre says), and now on Finty, who seemed, in a way that neither of them quite acknowledged or understood, both to adore her mother and to wish to subvert her. A few months later, Finty told me a story that reminded me of this. While she and Dench were watching television together one night,

Finty said, "Oh, I think Kylie Minogue"—the Australian pop singer and former soap-opera star—"is so talented." According to Finty, Dench got "massively uptight. 'Define "so talented,"' she said. 'She's a singer, isn't she? She looks good.' She got really cross with me. She was, like, 'If you think that's talented, what are you aspiring to?'"

In her time, Dench has been serenaded by Gerry Mulligan from beneath her New York hotel window. She has watched, in West Africa, as, at the finale of "Twelfth Night," people in the audience threw their programs into the air, then jumped to their feet to sing and dance for several minutes. She has clowned with the comedians Eric Morecambe and Ernie Wise. She has locked herself in a bathroom with Maggie Smith to escape the advances of the English comic character actor Miles Malleson. She has refused Billy Connolly's offer to show her his pierced nipples. As for her own nipples, she has stood in front of the camera, naked to the waist and unabashed, dabbing meringue on them. She has cooled herself on a summer day by jumping fully clothed into a swimming pool. At Buckingham Palace, she has scuttled away from the ballroom with Ian McKellen to sit on the royal thrones. In a Dublin restaurant, when Harold Pinter, a theatrical royal, barked about the tardiness of their dinner, Dench, according to David Jones, actually barked hack, "Mr. Pinter, you are not in London. Would you please adjust." She has made David Hare a needlepoint pillow as a Mother's Day present, with the words "Fuck Off" intricately stitched into the tapestry. On the day she became Dame Judi, Dench pinned her D.B.E. insignia on the jacket of the actor playing Don Pedro in a production of "Much Ado About Nothing" that she was directing. It is a barometer of her louche and lively life that, not long after that, the first ten rows of the National's Lyttelton Theatre heard Michael Bryant, who was playing Enobarbus to her Cleopatra, say to Dench under his breath, "I suppose a fuck is well out of the question now?"

Still, as Zeffirelli says, "She has known suffering." At the corner of her Surrey property is a rowan tree, planted on an exact axis with the backdoor of the house, which, according to folklore, is supposed to protect the house from witches; it has not been able to protect Dench from the caprices of life. Soon after Michael died, in January, an electrical fault in the garage—

an old barn—started a fire that gutted it to the frame. That charred skeleton is the first thing that rolls into view as you enter the property, and it stands in eerie contrast to the tranquillity behind it—wisteria by the front door, a sundial, a swimming pool, a flotilla of plastic slides and Winnie-the-Pooh toys tucked underneath the warped cantilevered timbers of the porch. Seven years earlier, Dench's house in Hampstead had burned down and a lifetime's memorabilia went up in flames. And in 1997, in a weird instance of life imitating art, Dench, like her character Esme in "Amy's View," which she was rehearsing at the time, learned that Finty, then twenty-five, was eight months pregnant and hadn't told her. She went immediately to Eyre's office at the National. "She stood in the doorway and just collapsed," he recalls. "She exploded. I'd never seen that. Unbelievably painful. She was massively wounded that the person she had thought of as her best friend in the world had not confided in her the not insignificant fact of her pregnancy." (Finty hadn't wanted Michael, a conservative Catholic, to know that she was having an illegitimate child.) Nevertheless, rehearsals of "Amy's View" went on. Eyre says of Dench, "Deep within her is the ethos that you don't let people down. If you're an actor, you go on. As Tennessee Williams says, you endure by enduring."

On July 9th of last year, a muggy Monday, at St. Paul's Church in Covent Garden, a standing-room-only crowd heard Trevor Nunn eulogize Michael Williams as a fine actor and partner. "I remember them courting," he said, standing opposite an enlarged photo of Williams, who was five feet four and puckishly handsome. "When they got married, Mike said to me, he was in the grip of feelings 'beyond any happiness he had ever dreamed of.' He told me more than once that his favorite line in Shakespeare was 'You have bereft me of all words, lady.' Because when he was with Jude, he knew the full extent of what Shakespeare was saying."

By the time Dench and Williams were married, in 1971, when she was thirty-six, Dench had done a lot of living. "When she likes something, she wants it like a wild animal," Zeffirelli says. Eyre adds, "She was prodigiously falling in love with the wrong man." One such man was the late comic actor Leonard Rossiter, who was in another relationship when they had an affair. "Some days, she'd come in and she'd had a wonderful day with him," recalls McKellen, who was then co-starring with her in "The Promise." "Other times, he'd have to leave early or hadn't turned up, and she was desperate. Tears, tears, tears. She was helpless and hopeless. What I was seeing was utterly vulnerable."

In 1969, on an R.S.C. tour of Australia, Charlie Thomas, a talented young actor with a drinking problem, who was playing the lovelorn Orsino to Dench's Viola, died under mysterious circumstances. Thomas had been very dependent on Dench, Nunn told me. "It was a shattering situation," he said. Williams, who was also a member of the R.S.C. and had become, in Nunn's words, "probably more than a friend," flew out to comfort her. "What was between them deepened enormously during that time," Nunn says. "Mike arriving made a fantastic difference." On that trip, Williams proposed, but Dench demurred. "No, it's too romantic here, with the sun and the sea and the sand," Williams remembered her saying. "Ask me on a rainy night in Battersea and I'll think about it." One rainy night in Battersea, in 1970, she said yes.

Williams, who came from Liverpool, had a more working-class pedigree than Dench, and he had the right combination of sturdiness and faith to both tether Dench and contain what her agent calls the "Dizzy Dora" side of her personality. "Michael was all-calming," Dench says. By every account, they were good companions. Dench recalls, "He used to say of himself, because he was Cancerian—the crab—and I'm a Sagittarian, 'I'm scuttling away toward the dark, and you're scuttling toward the light. What we do is we hold hands and keep ourselves in the middle.'"

But, as the decades wore on, and despite "A Fine Romance," the sitcom they starred in together in the early eighties, Williams was increasingly in Dench's shadow. "In a sense, every one of her successes was a diminution of him," Eyre says. Dench was acutely aware of the problem. "Judi was protective of Michael like a lioness," Geoffrey Palmer says. "I don't think Michael was an easy man. But the fact that all his married life he was Mr. Judi Dench—that's difficult for any man. He used to get very low. He sat at home feeding the bloody swans while she was doing three jobs a day." According to Dench, during these depressions Williams would become remote and "very, very silent." She says, "I had to give an incredible amount of confidence to Michael, who was very unconfident indeed."

On the inside of Dench's wedding ring is inscribed a modified line from "Troilus and Cressida," which Williams included in the first note he wrote to her: "I will weep you, as 'twere a man born in April." It proved to be somewhat prescient. On their twenty-fifth anniversary, Dench spoke of "just missing the rocks." The marriage, she says, was volatile. "I throw things," she adds. "I threw a hot cup of tea at him and his mother. And the saucer. I didn't hit either of them, unfortunately." Williams enjoyed spending time at the local pub. On several Sundays, when they had guests for lunch, Williams and the male guests rolled back from the pub late for the meal. "Mum's like 'Fine. Lock all the doors,'" Finty recalls. "'No, he's not coming in unless he can get through the top window.'" Williams and his crew climbed to their lunch on a thirty-foot ladder. And once, just before Christmas in 1983, an argument about the boiler sent Dench and Williams into such a blind fury that they refused to talk or look at each other on the long ride into London, where they were performing in "Pack of Lies." "The air was black, and we're bowling down Shaftesbury Avenue and not speaking and this person knocks on the window and begins to sing 'A Fine Romance,'" Dench says. "We howled with laughter. Howled. I realized it very much in the last year—he was a tremendous anchor to me. A real, proper anchor."

Just months before Williams died, the family took a trip to Aberdeen-shire, where Billy Connolly had gathered some friends at his castle. The week before, Williams had asked Dench whether he was going to die, and she'd told him he was. "When Judi told me about it, she started by looking me in the eye and ended up fiddling with the cutlery, then just went very quiet," Connolly recalls. "She went to a place in her head where she obviously feels much more comfortable and didn't say a thing." Connolly is a banjo player, and when Dench and Williams were in residence he and his other guests—Steve Martin (banjo), Eric Idle (guitar), the Incredible String Band's Robin Williamson (mandolin), and a local fisherman who played the fiddle—would go to a clearing in a nearby wood, build a fire, and sit on tree stumps to play, sing, and sometimes dance into the night. Connolly has a picture of the revels, with two green wicker chairs brought into the circle for Williams and Dench. Williams is laughing and holding a large glass of whiskey. He's looking beyond the fire at the fiddler; Dench is looking at him. "They were like young lovers," Connolly says. "They touched all the time. The wicker chairs are still there. We can't move them. Nobody wants to. 'Cause it's Judi and Michael."

"I have a huge amount of energy," Dench told me when we met at the Union Club in Soho for lunch in November. "Grief produces more energy, and all that needs burning up." In the ten months since Williams's death, Dench's herculean workload—"The Royal Family" and three films, "The Importance of Being Earnest," "The Shipping News," and "Iris"—had brought some of the shine back to her pale-blue, almond-shaped eyes. Her face was both animated and calm. "When my father died, it was almost like she was curiously liberated," Finty says. And although Dench still feels "lop-sided," she said, "I just want to learn new things all the time," and was full of news of her accomplishments in gardening, archery, and pool.

She had also learned to ride a Zappy scooter—a sort of skateboard with handlebars. Kevin Spacey, who before making "The Shipping News" told the director, Lasse Hallström, that he had two goals—"to give a good performance and to make Dench laugh"—had taught her in Central Park on his scooter, which has a turbo engine that goes up to about twenty miles per hour. "I was running along with her as she did it," Spacey says. "People were kind of recognizing us, particularly her. Someone said, 'Didn't you have something to do with James Bond?' And she said, 'Yes, I'm his boss,' and kept moving." From her gold-leafed diary, Dench produced a photo of Spacey on location; he was wearing a black baseball cap with "Actor" embroidered above the visor and a sweatshirt she'd had made for him with the legend "The Caramel Macchiato of Show Business," in honor of the cof-fee he'd brought her each day on the shoot. That evening, she told me, Spacey was coming to "The Royal Family."

On performing nights, Dench leaves Wasp Green by car at quarter to five and arrives at the Theatre Royal Haymarket in London at six-fifteen. Her dressing room—No. 10, on the third floor, John Gielgud's favorite—has a blue carpet, high ceilings, an antechamber, and a gold plaque on the front door with her name on it. First, Dench reads and responds to her let-ters. Her next order of business is to talk with the company. "We always will checkup with each other," she says. "Essential. It makes you laugh if you see them for the first time onstage. I don't know why. I'm on a knife edge in this play." Her ritual for getting dressed never varies. She puts on a body stocking, then black tights and a dressing gown. She bandages up her hair and does her face and, finally, her nails. Above her is an oval mirror festooned with greeting cards; to her right, a photo of Williams; and to her left a photo of her grandson, Sammy. Beside her on the dressing table are two lucky pigs, two trolls, and a snail (a memento of her very first role, at the age of four).

After our lunch, on the way out, I mentioned to Dench that I hadn't yet seen "The Royal Family." She paused at the front door of the club. "Will you tell me when you're coming in?" she said, holding out her cheek to be kissed. "And I'll overact for you." It was an exquisite exit. The line came so fast and was played so deftly and spoken with such warmth that, for a moment, I believed she'd never said it before.

BILL HICKS

GOAT BOY REDUX

I.

On October 1, 1993, the comedian Bill Hicks, after doing his twelfth gig on the David Letterman show, became the first comedy act to be censored at CBS's Ed Sullivan Theatre, where Letterman is now in residence, and where Elvis Presley was famously censored in 1956. Presley was not allowed to be shown from the waist down. Hicks was not allowed to be shown at all. It's not what's in Hicks's pants but what's in his head that scared the CBS panjandrums. Hicks, a tall, thirty-one-year-old Texan with a pudgy face aged beyond its years from hard living on the road, is no motormouth vulgarian but an exhilarating comic thinker in a renegade class all his own. Until the ban, which, according to Hicks, earned him "more attention than my other eleven appearances on Letterman times one hundred," Hicks's caustic observations and mischievous cultural connections had found a wide audience in England, where he is something of a cult figure. I caught up with Hicks backstage on a rainy Sunday last November at the Dominion Theatre, in London, where a record-breaking crowd of two thousand Brits was packed so tightly that they were standing three deep at the back of the dress circle to hear Hicks deliver some acid home truths about the U.S.A., which to him stands for United States of Advertising. Hicks thinks against society and insists on the importance of this intellectual freedom as a way to inspire others to think for themselves. "To me, the comic is the guy who says 'Wait a minute' as the consensus forms," Hicks told me as we climbed the stairs to his dressing room. "He's the antithesis of the mob mentality. The comic is a flame—like Shiva the Destroyer, toppling idols no matter what they are. He keeps cutting everything back to the moment."

Even then, the talk about courting comic danger had Hicks worrying about his prospects in America. "Comedy in the States has been totally gutted," he told me when we'd settled into the dressing room. "It's commercialized. They don't have people on TV who have points of view, because that defies the status quo, and we can't have that in the totalitarian mind-control government that runs the fuckin' airwaves. I can't get a shot there. I get David Letterman a lot. I love Letterman, but every time I go on, we have tiffs over material. They love me, but his people have this fictitious mainstream audience they think they play to. It's untrue. It doesn't exist. I like doing the show, but it's almost like working a puzzle: How can I be me in the context of doing this material? The best thing I do is make connections. I connect *everything*. It's hard to do it in six minutes."

Hicks certainly went for broke and pronounced his real comic self in the banned Letterman performance, which he wrote out for me in a thirty-nine-page letter that also recounts his version of events. Hicks had to write out his set because the tape of it, which the Letterman people said they'd send three weeks ago, had not yet reached him. He doubts it ever will. But the routine, which he had prepared for a Letterman appearance a week earlier (he was bumped because the show ran long), had been, he wrote, "approved and reapproved" by a segment producer of the show. Indicating stage directions and his recollection of significant audience response, Hicks set out some of the "hot points" to which the network took exception.

> You know who's really bugging me these days? These pro-lifers . . . (*Smattering of applause.*)
>
> You ever look at their faces? . . . "I'm pro-life!" (*Here Bill makes a pinched face of hate and fear; his lips are pursed as though he's just sucked on a lemon.*) "I'm pro-life!" Boy, they look it, don't they? They just exude *joie de vivre*. You just want to hang with them and play Trivial Pursuit all night long. (*Audience chuckles.*)
>
> You know what bugs me about them? If you're so pro-life, do me a favor—don't lock arms and block medical clinics. If you're

so pro-life, lock arms and block cemeteries. (*Audience laughs.*) . . .
I want to see pro-lifers at funerals opening caskets—"Get out!"
Then I'd really be impressed by their mission. (*Audience laughs
and applauds.*)

I've been travelling a lot lately. I was over in Australia during
Easter. It was interesting to note they celebrate Easter the same
way we do—commemorating the death and resurrection of
Jesus by telling our children a giant bunny rabbit . . . left
chocolate eggs in the night. (*Audience laughs.*)

Gee, I wonder why we're so messed up as a race. You know,
I've read the Bible. Can't find the words "bunny" or "chocolate"
in the whole book. (*Audience laughs.*)

I think it's interesting how people act on their beliefs. A lot
of Christians, for instance, wear crosses around their necks.
Nice sentiment, but do you think when Jesus comes back, he's
really going to want to look at a cross? (*Audience laughs. Bill
makes a face of pain and horror.*)

Ow! *Maybe* that's why he hasn't shown up yet. (*As Jesus looking
down from Heaven*) "I'm not going, Dad. No, they're still wearing
crosses—they totally missed the point. When they start wearing fishes, I might go back again . . . No, I'm not going . . .
O.K., I'll tell you what—I'll go back as a bunny."

Hicks, who delivered his monologue dressed not in his usual gunslinger
black but in "bright fall colors—an outfit bought just for the show and
reflective of my bright and cheerful mood," seemed to have a lot to smile
about. Letterman—who Hicks says greeted him as he sat down to talk with
"Good set, Bill! Always nice to have you drop by with an uplifting message!"
and signed off saying, "Bill, enjoy answering your mail for the next few
weeks"—had been seen to laugh. The word in the Green Room was also
good. A couple of hours later, Hicks was back in his hotel, wearing nothing
but a towel, when the call came from Robert Morton, the executive producer of the Letterman show, telling him he'd been deep-sixed. Hicks sat
down on the bed. "I don't understand, Robert. What's the problem? I

thought the show went great." The following is a condensed version of what Hicks remembers from the long conversation.

"You killed out there," Morton said, and went on to say, according to Hicks, that the CBS office of standards and practices felt that some of the material was unsuitable for broadcast.

"Ah, which material exactly did they find . . ."

"Well, almost all of it."

"Bob, they're so obviously jokes."

Hicks protested that he had run his routine by his sixty-three-year-old mother in Little Rock, Arkansas, and it passed the test. Morton insisted that the situation was out of his hands. He offered to set up another appearance and, according to Hicks, shouldered the blame for not having spent more time beforehand editing out the "hot points."

"Bob, they're just jokes. I don't want to be edited by you or anyone else. Why are people so afraid of jokes?"

"Bill, you've got to understand our audience."

"Your audience! Your audience is comprised of people, right? Well, I understand people, being one myself. People are who I play to every night, Bob. We get along just fine. We taped the show at five-thirty in the afternoon, and your audience had no problem with the material then. Does your audience become overly sensitive between the hours of 11.30 p.m. and 12.30 a.m.? And by the way, Bob, when I'm not performing on your show, I'm a member of the audience of your show. Are you saying my material is not suitable for me? This doesn't make any sense. Why do you underestimate the intelligence of your audience?"

"Bill, it's not our decision."

Morton apologized to Hicks, explaining that the show had to answer to the network, and said that he'd reschedule him soon. The conversation ended soon after that exchange, and in the intervening weeks Hicks had had no further word, he says, from Morton or Letterman. He has, however, heard indirectly from the CBS standards-and-practices office. A man who heard an interview with Hicks on the radio and was outraged over the censorship wrote to CBS to upbraid the network for not airing Hicks's set. He faxed the reply from CBS standards-and-practices to the radio station, which faxed it to Hicks's office. "It is true that Bill Hicks was taped that evening and that his performance did not air," the letter said. "What is inaccurate is that the deletion of his routine was required by CBS. In fact, although a CBS Program Practices editor works on that show, the decision was solely that of the producers of the program who decided to substitute his performance with that of another comedian. Therefore, your criticism that CBS censored the program is totally without foundation. Creative judgments must be made in the course of producing and airing any program and, while we regret that you disagreed with this one, the producers felt it necessary and that is not a decision we would override."

Hicks, who refers to the television set as Lucifer's Dream Box, is now in Lucifer's Limbo. He can't get the Letterman show to send him a tape of his performance. He can't get to the bottom of who censored him. And, as yet, he has no return date on Letterman. I called Robert Morton two weeks ago, and, when pressed, he finally grasped the nettle. He had begun by saying that the decision not to show Hicks's routine was made jointly by the Letterman show and CBS and ended up telling me that the producers of the show were solely responsible. "Ultimately, it was our decision," he said. "We're the packagers and owners of the program. It's our job to deliver a finished product to the network."

"It's been a strange little adventure for Willy," Hicks told me at the Dominion last year, referring to his American comedy career. And so it has proved—stranger, in fact, than Hicks's most maverick imaginings. The farce came full circle in the week following the Letterman debacle. A friend called Hicks to tell him about a commercial she'd seen during the Letterman show—a pro-life commercial. "The networks are delivering an audience to the advertisers," Hicks said later. "They showed their hand. They'll continue to pretend they're a hip talk show. And I'll continue to be me. As Bob Dylan said, the only way to live outside the law is to be totally honest. So I will remain lawless."

Outlaw is how Hicks was styling himself last year for the Dominion performance as he put on his black rifleman's coat and Stetson in the dressing room. When the curtain came up, Hicks was revealed in his hat, long coat, and cowboy boots, while behind him huge orange flames licked the air.

Images of heat and hunting are the perfect backdrop to Hicks's kind of comic attack. He was a hostile sharpshooter taking aim at the culture's received opinions and trying to shoot them down. The British, who have an appetite for this kind of intellectual anarchy, embraced Hicks with a rare and real enthusiasm from the moment he stumbled onto the vivacious English comedy scene in November 1990, as one of eighteen comedians in "Stand Up America!," a six-week limited engagement in the West End. The next year, Hicks was at the Edinburgh Festival, where he outclassed the native talent and won the Critics' Award. This led to his 1992 "Dangerous Tour" of Britain and Ireland, which culminated in appearances in the West End, at the Queen's Theatre, that May. The response was overwhelming, and now Hicks was doing one of the final performances of the "Relentless Tour," his second lap of honor around the British Isles in one year. Hicks was at home with the English, whose sense of irony made them more receptive to his combative humor than the credulous American public had been. "There's a greater respect for the performer," he said. "If you're onstage, people think you've earned it. In America—I'm not kidding—people bark their approval." I looked at him dubiously. "Ask around," Hicks said, and he simulated the sound. "They bark like animals. It's frightening. It's what American society has reduced people to. Ironically, in this show I call myself Goat Boy. They shouldn't be barking, they should be *baaing*."

My first encounter with Hicks was his Gulf War routine, which had been broadcast during the postwar euphoria at the beginning of 1992 on England's Channel 4. My sixteen-year-old son, Chris, was bellowing from the living room for me to come quickly. It was midnight, and he was sprawled, laughing, on the sofa, watching Hicks at the Montreal Comedy Festival calling a massacre a massacre. "So scary, watching the news. How they built it all out of proportion. Like Iraq was ever, or could ever, under any stretch of the imagination, be any threat to us *whatsoever*. But, watching the news, you never would have got that idea. Remember how it started? They kept talking about 'the élite Republican Guard' in these hushed tones, like these guys were the bogeyman or something. 'Yeah, we're doing well now, but we have yet to face . . . the élite Republican Guard.' Like these guys were twelve-feet-tall desert warriors—'NEVER LOST A BATTLE. WE SHIT BULLETS.' Well, after two months of continuous carpet bombing and not *one*

reaction at all from them, they became simply 'the Republican Guard'—
not nearly as élite as we may have led you to believe. And after another
month of bombing they went from 'the élite Republican Guard' to 'the
Republican Guard' to 'the Republicans made this shit up about there being
guards out there.'

"People said, 'Uh-uh, Bill, Iraq had the fourth-largest army in the
world.' Yeah, maybe, but you know what? After the first three largest
armies, there's a *real* big fuckin' drop-off. The Hare Krishnas are the fifth-
largest army in the world. And they've already got our airports."

Most TV comics trade in brand-name jokes or jokes that play off physical stereotypes. They don't question their culture so much as pander to its
insatiable hunger for distraction. But Hicks's mischievous flights of fantasy
bring the audience back to reality with a thump. Hicks is a kind of ventriloquist of his contradictory nature, letting voices and sound effects act out
both his angst and his appetites. Occasionally, the instinct for Goat Boy
comes over him, and Hicks, a man of instincts, goes with it. Goat Boy is
Pan, or Hicks's version of him—a randy goat "with a placid look in his eyes,
completely at peace with nature"—through which he celebrates his own
rampaging libido.

"I am Goat Boy," he would say in the act that night, in a grave baritone.
"Come here, my little fruit basket."

"What do you want, Goat Boy?" he answered, in a coy Southern
falsetto. "You big old shaggy thing."

"Ha, ha, ha, ha," Hicks growled into the microphone. "I am here to
please you."

"How?"

"Tie me to your headboard. Throw your legs over my shoulders, let me
roll you like a feed bag." Hicks brought the microphone close to his mouth.
He snorted, slurped, and finally screamed, "Hold on to my horns!" Then, as
suddenly as the impulse had come upon him, Hicks broke off the fantasy,
saying, "I need professional help at this point."

The secret of Hicks's psychic survival has always been comedy. He started
writing and performing his jokes as an alienated thirteen-year-old in Houston in 1975, and, by his own count, for the last five years he has been per-

forming about two hundred and sixty-five days a year, sometimes doing as many as three two-hour gigs a night. Few contemporary comics or actors have such an opportunity to get their education in public. Hicks uses the stage time to write his material in front of an audience. "I do it all onstage, *all* of it," he said, and then began to relate how he'd started on his eccentric journey. "When I was about eleven, it dawned on me that I didn't like where I was," he said, speaking of the subdivision where he lived, which was called Nottingham Forest; of Stratford High School, which looked like a prison and where he was bored out of his skull for four years; and of his father, who was a midrange executive with General Motors. The Hicks family lived in "strict Southern Baptist ozone." The memory still rankled. "One time a friend of mine—we were nine—runs over and goes, 'Bill, I just saw some hippies down at the store.' I go, 'No way.' He goes, 'I swear.' My dad goes, 'Get off his property! We don't swear on this property!'"

"We were living the American dream. This was the best life had to offer. But there was no life, and no creativity. My dad, for instance, plays the piano. The same song for thirty years—I think it's 'Kitten on the Keys.' I don't play the piano, but all my friends are musicians. My dad goes, 'Do they read music?' I go, 'No.' 'Well, how do they play it?' I go to the piano and I write a song. What's the difference? He can't improvise. That, to me, is the suburbs. You get to a point, and that's it—it's over."

Once he'd seized on the idea of writing jokes, Hicks closeted himself in his bedroom and went to school on comedians. He started watching Johnny Carson. "I thought he was the only comic in the world, because I never stayed up later," he said. Soon Hicks began burning the midnight oil, taping other comic acts on television. "I'd take their jokes and also write my own. I performed them around school, and what I loved was when both got equal laughs. I knew which one was me and which one I'd seen on TV the night before. I learned how to mesh these things. How to get into character. I was very, very popular and known as a comedian at school. I'd always have to have material, constantly, all day. It got to the point where my English teacher gave me five minutes to do before class. My older brother Steve encouraged me. I typed up about two pages of jokes—whimsical stuff in the Woody Allen vein, which really appealed to me—and slipped them under his door. He came in later that night and said, 'What's this?' I said, 'I dunno. I'm writing these things. They're jokes.' He couldn't believe it. 'These are funny, man. Keep doing this.'"

Hicks's first partner in comedy was Dwight Slade, with whom he formed the act Bill and Dwight in the eighth grade. A tape exists of Hicks and Slade giggling through some of their early routines, which involved pretending to be brothers with "many, many problems." "Ladies and gentlemen, the comedy sensation Dwight Slade and Bill Hicks. And here they are!" it begins, and then the two of them collapse into roars of amusement at their own vain attempts to strike adult postures while reading gags about God, sex, abortion, and parents.

The jokes illustrated Hicks's precocity, and suggested how comedy both masked and admitted the hostility that kept him sullen and virtually silent around his family. "I can remember being at dinner when Bill would come down to eat," Steve Hicks told me. "He'd sit there with his face buried in a book. Absolutely no conversation from him or to him. Nothing. Then he would go up to his room and close and lock the door. We had no idea what he was doing." Hicks's room, which had nothing on the walls but a guitar, was a cell of rebellious solitude. He kept a typewriter under his bed and hid his pages of jokes inside its case.

In 1976, there were no comedy clubs in Houston. Except for school, the only outlets for Bill and Dwight's routines were talent shows and nightclubs. They scoured the paper for auditions, and often rode their bikes the seventeen miles into town and back for a tryout. That summer, when they were both fourteen, a talent agent to whom they'd sent a tape liked it enough to get them airtime on Jerry Lewis's Telethon from 2 to 2:45 A.M. Their big break posed three immediate problems: (1) they didn't have forty-five minutes of material, (2) they'd never performed as Bill and Dwight in front of a live audience, and (3) they had to tell their parents. The first two problems were surmountable, but the third proved the sticking point. Hicks's parents said no. Hicks and Slade had to cancel, explaining that they were too young to drive themselves to the job. But in 1978, when the Comedy Workshop opened on San Felipe, in Houston, they talked their way into the lineup. This time, they made the gig. To get to it, Hicks had to climb out his window, shin down the drainpipe to the garage roof, jump from the roof to the ground, and hightail it to the Catholic church behind his house, where Kevin Booth, a friend who had a car, picked him up and then drove both performers to the club. Bill and Dwight did fifteen minutes—a kind of double solo performance, each doing Woody Allen shtick without the actual give-and-take of a comedy team. "What was really funny was when my friends would come and I'd go, 'I . . . uh . . . I have trouble . . . trouble with women,'" Hicks said. "And my friends would go, 'No, you don't!' I'd go, 'My parents are very poor.' 'No, they're not!' They were amazed we were in this adult world. They were seventeen and could drive us there, but when they got us there we were in this adult world."

The comedy team performed five times before Slade moved to Portland, Oregon, where he still lives, working as a standup comic. Hicks put his anarchic energy into a hapless punk-rock group called Stress, in which he sang a song called "I'm Glad I'm Not a Hubcap (Hubcaps Don't Get Laid)." At some point in his seventeenth year, Hicks's parents took him to a psychotherapist. "There was no connection between me and my parents—none," he said. "They had no idea of who I was. They still don't get what I do. How could they have understood it fifteen years ago?" The therapist met with the family, then with Hicks. At the end of the session, the therapist took Hicks aside. "Listen, you can continue to come if you feel like it," Hicks recalled him saying. "But it's them, not you." Soon afterward, at the beginning of Hicks's senior year, his father was transferred to Little Rock, Arkansas. He and his wife left Hicks behind in the house and gave him the keys to the car. Hicks began doing comedy every night. His parents thought he was studying. The comedy club put him on first, because he had to get home early. Sometimes the phone would be ringing just as he walked in the door. "The conversations were like this," Hicks said. He fell easily into his father's Southern accent: "'Where were you?' 'Library.' 'Again?'" Even after his parents left, his material was almost entirely about them.

To this day, Hicks continues to mythologize his parents and his relationship with them, in comic routines that spoof their Southern propriety. But this is only professional acrimony, and doesn't stop Hicks from thanking his parents on his record albums or turning up regularly for ritual family

occasions. Hicks, like all comedians, picks at ancient wounds to keep open
the soreness that feeds his laughter and to demonstrate his mastery over the
past.

In 1982, Hicks's parents finally saw him perform. They had been visiting Steve in Dallas, where the family had assembled for Thanksgiving, and
his parents decided to surprise him. The plan was to drive the three hours
to Austin, see the show, and drive back to Dallas the same night before setting out the next day for the six-hour ride to Little Rock. Steve and his wife
waited up for them but finally fell asleep around 3 A.M. At nine, their
phone rang. The Hickses had been so appalled by their son's act that they'd
got in their car and driven nonstop to Little Rock. "They were in a state of
shock," Steve says. "They didn't say a word to each other for nine hours.
They didn't even realize they'd driven through Dallas!"

At one end of Hick's long, corridorlike dressing room at the Dominion was a
window overlooking the stage. Hicks walked over and looked out at the paying
customers. "It's about that time," he said. Isolation suddenly fell over him like
some fog blown in by his unconscious. Showtime was approaching, and he
wanted to be alone. Fifteen minutes later, he brought his aggression roaring
onstage. The narrative swung into attack as Hicks, like a man driven to distraction by the media, fought his way free of its overload by momentarily becoming its exaggerated voice: "Go back to bed! America is in control again . . .
Here . . . here is 'American Gladiators.' Watch this! Shut up. Go back to
bed. Here's fifty-six channels of it. Watch these pituitary retards bang their
fuckin' skulls together and congratulate yourself on living in the land of freedom. Here you go, America! You are free to do as we tell you! You are free!"

Hicks worked at a tremendous rate, pounding away at the absurdities of
American culture with short jabs of wit and following up with a flurry of
counterpunches. "Ever notice how people who believe in creationism look
really unevolved?" he said. "Their eyes real close together. Eyebrow ridges.
Big, furry hands and feet. 'I believe God created me in one day.' Looks like
he rushed it." Later, near the end of the evening, Hicks drew one final lesson. "The world is like a ride at an amusement park," he said. "And when
you choose to go on it, you think that it's real. Because that's how powerful
our minds are." A young Englishman three seats away from me shouted

"Bollocks!" And, without missing a beat, completely caught up in the dialogue he was having with his audience, Hicks said, "There is a lot of denial in this ride. The ride, in fact, is made up of denial. All things work in Goat Boy's favor!" Thrilled by the improvised insight, the audience burst into applause, and then Hicks guided the rest of the show smoothly to its conclusion, which, for all its combativeness, ended on the word "peace."

Hicks came to my house the next day for tea. He was tired and a little distracted, and was wondering out loud which way to take his quirky talent. "Once this stuff is done, it's over with—I'm not married to any of it," he said. "Goat Boy is the only thing that really intrigues me right now. He's not Satan. He's not Evil. He's Nature." Hicks paused and added, "I'm trying to come up with this thing about 'Conversations with Goat Boy.'" Then, suddenly, the interrogator and Goat Boy started a conversation at my tea table:

"You don't like America?"

"I don't *see* America. To me, there is just a rapidly decreasing wilderness."

Hicks stopped and smiled. "That is Goat Boy. There is no America. It's just a big pavement now to him. That's the whole point. What is America anyway—a landmass including the Philippines? There are so many different Americas. To him, to Nature, it's just land, the earth. Indian spirit—Indians would understand randy Pan, the Goat Boy. They'd probably have a mask and a celebration."

My son wandered into the kitchen and lingered to eavesdrop on the conversation. At one point, he broke in. "I don't know how you have the courage to say those things," he said. "I could never talk like that in front of people."

Hicks smiled but had no response. Saying the unsayable was just his job. He analyzed the previous night's performance, which had been filmed for an HBO special. (It was broadcast in September to good reviews.) "People watch TV *not* to think," he said. "I'd like the opportunity to stir things up once, and see what happens. But I've got options. Do I even want to be a part of it anymore? Show business or art—these are choices. It's hard to get a grip on me. It's also hard for me to have a career, because there's no archetype for what I do. I have to create it, or uncover it." To that end, he said, he and Fallon Woodland, a standup from Kansas City, were writing "The Counts of the Netherworld," a TV comedy commissioned for England's Channel 4 and set in the collective unconscious of mankind. Hicks was doing a column for the English satire magazine *Scallywag*. He was planning a comedy album, called "Arizona Bay," a narrative rant against California with his own guitar accompaniment. Should he stay in England, where he was already a cult figure, or return to America? He recounted a joke on the subject by his friend Barry Crimmins, another American political comedian. "'Hey, buddy,' this guy says to him after a show. 'America— love it or leave it!' And Crimmins goes, 'What? And be a victim of our foreign policy?'"

As Hicks was about to go, he said, "We are facilitators of our creative evolution. We can ignite our brains with light." The line brought back something his high-school friend Kevin Booth had told me: "Bill was the first person I ever met whose goal was to become enlightened." At various times in his life, Hicks has meditated, studied Hindu texts, gobbled hallucinogens, searched for U.F.O.s—anything to make some larger spiritual and intellectual connection. His comedy takes an audience on a journey to places in the heart where it can't or won't go without him. Through laughter, Hicks makes unacceptable ideas irresistible. He is particularly lethal because he persuades not with reason but with joy. "I believe everyone has this fuckin' poem in his heart," he said on his way out.

‖

My *New Yorker* profile about Bill Hicks sat unpublished at the magazine for nearly four months. Hicks's ban from the David Letterman Show and his subsequent thirty-nine-page hand-written screed to me provided the impetus to get the profile into print by November 1st. "The phones are ringing off the hook, the offers are pouring in, and all because of you," Hicks wrote to me the following week, signing himself "Willy Hicks." "I've read the article three times, and each time I'm stunned. Being the comedy fan that I am, I've ended the article every time thinking, 'This guy sounds interesting.'" Hicks continued, "It's almost as though I've been lifted out of a ten-year rut and placed in a position where the offers finally match my long held and deeply cherished creative aspirations . . . Somehow, people are listening in a new light. Somehow the possibilities (creatively) seem limitless."

Rereading Hicks's letter now, ten years later, the parentheses in the last sentence hit me like a punch to the heart. Hicks was suddenly, to his amazement, no longer perceived as "a joke blower," his word for the kind of pandering stand-up he hated. In the two months following the publication of the New Yorker profile, seven publishers approached him about writing a book; "The Nation" asked him to write a column; Robert De Niro met with him to discuss the possibility of recording his comedy on his Tribeca label; and Britain's Channel 4 with Tiger Aspect green-lighted Hicks's "Counts of the Netherworld" ("Channel 4 wants our first show to somehow tie in with their celebration of the birth of Democracy two thousand year ago," Hicks wrote to me. "Democracy may have been born then, I just can't wait till it starts speaking and walking.") The creative possibilities may have seemed limitless to Hicks, but, even as he was writing me letters about "the hoopla" and his newfound calm ("I'm very grateful for it"), he knew that he was dying.

In June, touring Australia with the comedian Steven Wright, Hicks had begun to complain to his manager and girlfriend Colleen McGarr about horrible indigestion. He hadn't had a proper physical exam in ten years; so when they returned, later in the month, to West Palm Beach for a week's engagement at the Comedy Corner, McGarr booked a check-up for Hicks. On June 15th, his first night at the Comedy Corner, Hicks came offstage clutching his side. "The physical had been set up for the following Thursday," McGarr recalls. "But when I took a look at him, I said 'We gotta get you in tomorrow.'" Hicks was thirty-one. Because of his relative youth, the doctor, William Donovan, seemed convinced that the swelling on Hicks's side was a gall-bladder problem. He sent Hicks for an ultrasound. "The ultrasound guy said, 'We have to get him over to the hospital. We have to do a biopsy because this isn't gall bladder,'" McGarr says. "They looked very grim at the time."

On the night of his liver biopsy, Hicks slept at the Good Samaritan Hospital. "He was really digging it," McGarr says. "I was going out to get him his favourite treats—grilled-cheese sandwiches and soup. It was like an enforced rest after all the touring. He was kind of chipper." At five the next morning, William Donovan phoned her. "Colleen, it's the worst news possible," he said. "You've got to get down here now. We have to talk to him." In person, Donovan explained to McGarr that Hicks had pancreatic cancer; he had only about three months to live. At 7:30, they went into see Hicks, and Donovan told him that he had stage-four pancreatic cancer and that there was very little that could be done about it. At first poleaxed by the news— "He looked like he'd been shot," Donovan is reported as saying, in Cynthia True's *"American Scream: The Bill Hicks Story"*—Hicks finally said, "What's the battle plan?" What had to be decided, Donovan explained, was how Hicks wanted to live the time he had left. Aggressive treatment would leave him mostly incapacitated. Since Hicks felt "at the peak of his powers," according to McGarr, a compromise treatment was arranged, so that he could continue to write and to perform. "There was no crying. There was no going nuts," McGarr says. "It was really, really calm." She adds, "He'd known for awhile, I'm sure, that something was wrong. I mean people don't have indigestion for six months."

The following Monday, Hicks started chemotherapy. A network of doctors around the country was set up so that Hicks could get treatment wherever he happened to be touring. Hicks responded well to the therapy. "No one knew about his illness," McGarr says. "The only people who knew were my business partner, Duncan Strauss, and Bill's immediate family. Nobody else. We didn't tell anyone. That was also Bill's decision. He had a lot to do—he was finishing the record 'Arizona Bay' and he had a ton of gigs." She adds, "He wanted the work to get out without the taint of any sentimentality."

In the months that remained to him, by all accounts, Hicks seemed to inhabit the world in a different way. Instead of scourging it, he beheld it. "Things became a lot more meaningful than he'd ever given them credit for," says McGarr, who saw him "growing on a spiritual level." "Flowers. The beach. He started swimming in the ocean for the first time, splashing around like a dolphin which is not really Hicks-like—at the beach, when he was dragged there, he was always the guy dressed head-to-toe in black." Hicks referred to his cancer as a "wake-up call." Where, in the past, Hicks had styled himself as an outlaw onstage and a loner off it; now he sought out people and engaged them. His spirit and his wardrobe started to lighten. "He was astounded by how much love came around him as a result of this," McGarr says. "He realized that people really did care about him and that he didn't have to be alone." For a time, he moved into McGarr's West Palm Beach apartment, and he "began to take some actual joy" in domestic life. "This is a guy who had been on the road for about fifteen years," McGarr says. "He's used to eating crap spaghetti sauce out of a jar. 'I need you to get me some Ragu,' he'd say. I'm like, 'We don't have jarred spaghetti sauce in this house, we have homemade.' Fun stuff like that. It was a revelation to him."

Before returning to Little Rock, Arkansas, for his birthday—December 16th—and for Christmas with his family, Hicks celebrated his own unofficial Yuletime with McGarr in Florida. They brought a Christmas tree and decorated it with homemade ornaments. Hicks drew a reindeer on a card and tied it to the front bough of the tree. He told McGarr to open it. "Will you marry me?" it said. The question was academic. By late December, according to McGarr, Hicks was "really, really bad."

"On a work level, everything was done," she says. "He'd recorded 'Arizona Bay,' performed his last complete sold-out set at Igby's in Los Angeles on November 17th, pitched the TV show at Channel 4.' In just four months, Hicks had acquired what had eluded him for fifteen years—a receptive American audience. But on a physical level he was now fading. Nonetheless, after Christmas, he insisted on meeting McGarr in Las Vegas to watch Frank Sinatra and Don Rickles in concert. "I almost passed out, he looked so bad," McGarr recalls. The day after the Sinatra show, they flew back to West Palm Beach. The doctors wanted to admit Hicks to the hospital; he refused to go. "Things got very tense," says McGarr, who had to enlist the help of hospice nurses and of Hicks's mother, Mary.

On January 5, 1994—against McGarr's wishes—Hicks did the eight o'clock how at Caroline's Comedy Club, in New York. In her attempt to prevent Hicks from doing the gig, McGarr rang Dr. Donovan. "Colleen, Bill is ready to die. He just won't lie down," Donovan told her. She hung up on him. Hicks was about thirty minutes into his set when he looked up over the microphone and scanned the crowd. "Colleen, are you out there?" he said. From the back of the room, McGarr called out, "Bill, I'm right here." "I can't do this anymore," he said. McGarr rushed to the side of the stage. Hicks glanced over at her, paused, then put the mic back in its stand, and stepped into the wings. It was his last performance.

On January 26th, McGarr put Hicks on a plane to Little Rock. "Bill always wanted to die with his parents at their house in Little Rock," she says. "He wanted the circle complete—that was very important to him." On Valentine's Day, after making a few calls to old friends, Hicks announced that he was finished with speaking. Although he hardly uttered another word, except to ask for water, he wandered around the house, according to his mother, almost every night. On February 26th, at 11:20 p.m., Hicks died with his parents at his bedside. His radiant comic light had burned for thirty-two years, two months, and ten days.

When a great comedian dies, the culture loses a little of its flavor. The world rolls on, of course, but without the comedian to both witness and illuminate the deliria of his moment. In Hicks's case, the loss is even more piquant, given that the American public discovered him largely after he'd departed it. "This is the material by the way, that's kept me virtually anonymous in America," Hicks joked in his last complete set, after a detour into philosophy. "You know, no one fucking knows me. No one gives a fuck. Meanwhile, they're draining the Pacific and putting up bench seats for Carrot Top's next Showtime special. Carrot Top: for people who didn't get Gallagher." He continued, "*Gallagher!* Only America could produce a comic who ends his show by *destroying* food with a sledgehammer. Gee, I wonder why we're *hated* the world over." At the end of the set—in an inspired moment that was captured on film—Hicks came back on stage for his encore with a large paper bag, from which he extracted a watermelon. He put it on a stool, grabbed the microphone, raised it high above his head and brought it down on the side of the stool. He'd missed the melon but hit the target. The audience howled. As Rage Against the Machine's "Killing in the Name" blared over the loudspeakers—"*Fuck you, I won't do what you tell me*"— Hicks shouted in unison with the lead singer: "*Motherfucker!!!!!!*" Hicks made his exit, flipping the finger wildly with both hands to the room, to the world, to the cosmic order that his jokes frequently invoked.

The revenge that Hicks took with laughter—his almost infantile glee at getting even for the credulity of the republic ("You're a moron!" "You suck Satan's cock!" he frequently yelled to the idiots in his mind and in the audience)—marked him as the genuine comic article. "Listen to my message, not the words," Hicks told his mother. Composed in equal parts of skepticism, scatology, and spirituality, Hicks's humour gave off a very special acrid perfume. "Pro-lifers murdering people," Hicks heehawed. "It's irony on a base level, but I like it. It's a hoot. It's a fuckin' hoot. That's what fundamentalism breeds, though—no irony." To the spellbound and the spellbinders, Hicks bequeathed a heritage of roaring disgust. If he wanted to force the public to descry a corrupt society, he also wanted it to descry the low standard of commercial American comedy, which raised laughs but not thoughts and, in his eyes, hawked "fucking beer commercials," while leaving the public "without any kind, of social fucking awareness."

The white heat of Hick's fulminations was meant, in part, to purify comedy itself—a notion explicitly stated in a film script he developed in the last year of his life, which told the story of a serial killer who murders hack comics. "I loved those who gave their lives to find the perfect laugh, the real laugh, the gut laugh, the healing laugh. For love, I killed those comedians," the murderer explains when he's finally caught. Hicks wanted to play the serial killer; his act was part of the same search-and-destroy mission.

Hicks came of age when the sitcom showcase was king. At a time when the romance of the road was over for American comedians, and the goal was to get a development deal—your own show and a big payday—Hicks returned comedy to its essential atmosphere of challenge and unpredictability. In a riff about "Tonight Show" host Jay Leno doing Dorito commercials ("What a fucking whore!"), Hicks said, "Here's the deal folks. You do a commercial, you're off the artistic roll-call. Forever. End of story. You're another fuckin' corporate shill . . . Everything you say is suspect, everything that comes out of your mouth is like a turd falling into my drink."

As the Letterman incident and his reaction to it dramatized, Hicks was as hungry as the next comedian for mainstream success, but only on his own terms. He was not prepared to sacrifice the emotional integrity of his material for popularity. "There's dick jokes on the way," he'd say to his listeners when he raised ideas that flummoxed them, then he'd put on his cracker accent: "'This guy better have a big-veined purple dick joke to pull himself out of this comedy hole.'" As a comedian, Hicks was never soft and cuddly. For the first-class members of the next generation of American comedians, such as Jon Stewart of "The Daily Show," the purity of Hicks's comic quest was inspirational. "Hicks was one of the guys fighting the good fight," says Stewart, who considered Hicks "a legendary figure" and who worked with him a couple of times on the road. "He was the guy you looked to. He wasn't trying to be mediocre; he wasn't trying to satisfy some need for fame; he wasn't trying to get a sitcom; he was trying to be expert." Stewart adds, "Hicks was an adult among children." Among the daring lessons that Hicks's comedy taught Stewart and other comedians of the next generation was "to walk the room"—if Hicks didn't think that the room was worthy of him, he would "walk it," that is, drive his comedy further than even he might normally think of doing. "The audience's apathy spurred him on," Stewart says. For instance, at one gig, as Hicks was launching into a bit about the Zapruder film, a drunken blonde called up to him, "You suck!" Hicks rolled the words around in his mouth, stepped downstage, and pointed to the woman. "Get out! Get out, you fucking drunk bitch! Take her out! Take her fucking *out!* Take her somewhere that's good. Go see fuckin' Madonna, you fucking idiot piece of shit!" Hicks began to imitate her voice—"'You suck, buddy! You suck!'"—and ended up skipping around the stage in her persona. "'I got a cunt and I'm drunk. I can do anything I wa-aant! I don't have a cock! I can yell at performers! I'm a fucking idiot 'cause I got a cunt!'" He knelt down. "*I want you to find a fucking SOUL!!!!*"

As a performer, Hicks was not short on soul or on charisma. In front of the paying customers, he was powerful, unpredictable, and thrilling. "He was bigger than the room," Stewart says. A great comedian is by definition inimitable. Nonetheless, since his death, and even before it, American comedians like Dennis Leary have made a good living reworking his lines and faking his bad-ass attitude. The indicators of posthumous longevity for

Hicks are good. A biography has been published ("the most outspoken, uncompromising and famous unknown comic of all time," the jacket says); Hicks's record sales are bullish; in a recent TV documentary about censorship for which Hicks's expletives were deleted, his name was added to the short list of comic martyrs.

Since his death, history has caught up with his comedy. In the early nineties, he was already talking about Iraq and the first President Bush. "If Bush had died there," he said, in a bit about why we should kill Bush ourselves instead of launching twenty-two Cruise missiles at Baghdad in response to his alleged attempted assassination, "there would have been no loss of innocent life." In a culture made increasingly woozy by spin-doctors, Hicks's straight-talking about political chicanery was a few years ahead of its time. If Hicks didn't pave the way for comic civic disobedience in such popular TV shows as "Politically Incorrect" and "The Daily Show," he was an immanence of subterranean rumblings. "When they were putting together 'Politically Incorrect,'" Colleen McGarr says, of the controversial American TV show, "they were actually considering Bill as the original host instead of Bill Maher."

A dream is something you wake up from. It is compelling and significant that the final words on Hicks's last record, "Rant in E-Minor," are a prayer: "Lift me up out of this illusion, Lord. Heal my perception, so that I may know only reality." Hicks mocked society's enchanters—advertisers, TV networks, rock-and-roll icons, religious fanatics, politicians—with the sure knowledge that as in all fairytales only the disenchanted are free. He made that show of freedom by turns terrifying, exhilarating, and hilarious. He was what only a great comedian can be for any age: an enemy of boundaries, a disturber of the peace, a bringer of insight and of joy, a comic distillation of his own rampaging spirit.

RICHARD RODGERS

WALKING ALONE

Wᴴᴇɴ ᴛʜᴇ ᴄᴏᴍᴘᴏsᴇʀ Rɪᴄʜᴀʀᴅ
Rodgers died, in 1979, after sixty-two years in show business, forty musicals, and more than nine hundred songs, Lionel Trilling—an éminence grise not given to hyperbole—announced, "Few men have given so much pleasure to so many." Leonard Bernstein said, "He has established new levels of taste, distinction, simplicity in the best sense, and inventiveness." Rodgers's music, alternately mischievous and elegant, playful and brooding, stately and surprising—what Ethan Mordden called his sunbeam of melody—sometimes struck a sentimental note but never a vulgar one. To speak the titles of some of his most famous songs—"Isn't It Romantic?," "Some Enchanted Evening," "The Lady Is a Tramp," "Oh, What a Beautiful Mornin'," "Getting to Know You," "My Funny Valentine," "Hello, Young Lovers," "Manhattan"—is to hear sound, a blithe sound that lifted the nation out of its Depression doldrums and, in the postwar boom, fired it with a sense of idealism. "People have a need for melody, just as they need food or personal contact," said Rodgers, for whom music, which manufactured happiness even as it inspired a longing for it, was dream made manifest.

Jonathan Schwartz, the swami of the American songbook and the keeper of its flame in a weekly four-hour public-radio show, recently called Richard Rodgers the most performed composer in history, and, although the assertion is unprovable, certain statistical indicators show just how deeply his music has penetrated into the American interior. According to ASCAP, three hundred and seventy-six of Rodgers's works are still in active circulation (the Beatles, by comparison, have a mere hundred and fifty-four). Thirty movies have been made from his scores, including "The Sound of Music" (1965), which is by every standard the most successful movie musical of all time, and, if you adjust for inflation, the third-largest-grossing film, after "Gone with the Wind" and "Star Wars." Rodgers's music has been heard in two hundred and eighty-five other feature films, and in more than twenty-seven hundred television shows. In 2001 alone, the Rodgers & Hammerstein Organization, which oversees all of Rodgers's musical and theatrical interests, licensed three thousand and eighty-five productions of his shows. If you were to calculate the number of performances that Rodgers's shows have had on Broadway, the total would be twenty thousand four hundred and fifty-seven, or, figuring eight a week, the equivalent of fifty years of a Broadway run.

No wonder, then, that the centennial of Rodgers's birth, on June 28th, is being celebrated with more hoopla than a monarch's. In addition to three Broadway productions (revivals of "Oklahoma," "Flower Drum Song," and "The Boys from Syracuse"), there will be twelve musicals in concert; ten museum exhibitions; four new records; five books, including the excellent "Richard Rodgers Reader," the lacklustre Meryle Secrest biography "Somewhere for Me," and a reissue of Rodgers's own emotionally opaque memoir, "Musical Stages"; plus scores of musical tributes from the Hollywood Bowl to the Boston Pops. Still, Rodgers's legacy, like his life, is replete with tantalizing contradictions, the first of which is the issue of just what happened to his body. Although his music is still with us, the remains of the great man himself have disappeared. There is no hallowed plot, no venerated gravestone, no funerary urn, and his own daughters have been unable to locate one. Rodgers has vanished as definitively as the Lone Ranger, leaving us only the silver bullet of his sound—an absence that serves as a piquant metaphor for his sometimes slippery negotiations with the world.

"My recollection is that I've been scared all my life," Rodgers said in 1960. The series of Manhattan town houses in which he grew up with his parents and maternal grandparents resounded with acrimony. "Bickering, yelling, or unnatural silence were the norm," he wrote in his memoir, recalling the "sheer hell" of the household atmosphere, which left him with "a deep feeling of tension and insecurity." Rodgers's mother, for whom, he wrote, the "display of affection did not come easily," was so morbidly fearful that she had to be accompanied to the corner store by his grandmother. His father, a doctor, worked long hours. Rodgers's older brother, Mortimer, bullied him so much in his early years that he ran away from home.

Music was the only thing that calmed the fractious family. Rodgers's parents were avid theatregoers who bought the sheet music to the show tunes of the day and sang together around the piano, which his mother played expertly. As a toddler, Rodgers could "reproduce the melodies with accuracy"; at nine he was composing his own, a talent that brought the members of his family closer to him and to one another. "These were the happy moments in not very happy days," Rodgers wrote. "There were no loud-voiced arguments then; voices were raised only in song. And in the middle of the fun stood little Richard, who received nothing but praise and love because his ear was so quick and he sang so well." Rodgers added, "I quickly discovered, too, that my parents' response to my love of music was their love of me." (For years, Rodgers's father laboriously maintained his son's scrapbooks.) In a household where, he said, "almost everything contradicted everything else," Rodgers's music literally and figuratively made harmony.

From childhood on, Rodgers learned to let the bright surface of his music stand in for him. At school assemblies, he amused his teachers by improvising marches to play the students in and out of the hall. "Occasionally, I made a musical joke," he said. "Whenever the principal said, 'Students, sit,' I would play the familiar musical doggerel 'Shave and Haircut.' Then as the students sat, I'd play 'Two bits.'" At summer camp, he found that "my piano-playing made me the pet of visiting parents and sisters." On his first day as a Columbia University freshman (he went there for the sole purpose of composing the Varsity Shows, and switched after two years to the Institute of Musical Art), Rodgers saw an announcement for a singing contest between the four Columbia classes and promptly wrote music and lyrics for a number that he taught to the Class of '23. The song won, and Rodgers became "the class hero." On August 26, 1919, his stock went up even further when a song of his—"Any Old Place with You"—was performed on the Broadway stage for the first time, in the musical comedy "A Lonely Romeo." Rodgers was only seventeen years old, younger even than George Gershwin had been when his first song made it to Broadway, but he

had already found just the right person to put words to his music: an imp-
ish, well-educated twenty-three-year-old Columbia dropout who was a
descendant of the German poet Heinrich Heine—Lorenz Hart.

When the dapper sixteen-year-old Rodgers went to meet Hart for the first
time, referred by a mutual friend, Hart appeared at his front door unshaven
and dishevelled, wearing frayed carpet slippers, a pair of tuxedo trousers,
and a checked jacket. He was five feet tall. "All he needed was a tin cup and
some pencils," wrote Rodgers, who liked to portray himself as the responsible square to Hart's feckless hipster. He added, "I left Hart's house having
acquired in one afternoon a career, a partner, a best friend, and a source of
permanent irritation." Hart's bohemian mufti—his combination of finesse
and undress—foreshadowed the stylistic verve of his lyrics: the happy coex-
istence of the sophisticated and the demotic. Hart had a deep knowledge of
verse forms, a prodigiously light touch, and a mission to liberate the musical from what he called the "brutally cretin aspect of light entertainment."
"You can't sing 'Kiss Me Again' to the sound of a slapping chain-tire," he
said, of the need for popular song to reflect America's changing momentum.

Hart's manic lyric playfulness—his use of internal, male-female, and
double and triple rhymes—coaxed Rodgers down comparably daring
musical paths. "There was an almost feverish demand in Hart's writing,
which reflected itself in Rodgers's melodies," Alec Wilder writes in "American Popular Song." In their first hit, "Manhattan," from "Garrick Gaieties"
(1925), for instance, Rodgers's abrupt turns, sharp rests, and wide intervals
bent the song structure to match the jazzy fragmentation of Hart's lyric:

> We'll go to Greenwich
> Where modern men itch
> To be Free . . .

Hart's special gift was to distill the complex into the colloquial—
"Vexed again / Perplexed again / Thank God I can be oversexed again."
Likewise, Rodgers's musical language was deceptively simple. By saunter-
ing up and down the major scale—as he did in "Manhattan" and "Mountain

Greenery," for example—he could create wonders. (Rodgers later played the same game with his second long-term musical partner, Oscar Hammerstein II, running up the scale in "Oklahoma!" and even hymning it in his last big hit, "Do Re Mi," from "The Sound of Music.") Rodgers's wistful lyricism was a fetching counterpoint to Hart's cynical urbanity, and the combination, Rodgers felt, was the secret of their success—"sentimental melody and unsentimental lyrics." Their songs were the era's high-water mark of verbal and emotional sophistication. As Cole Porter—who once joked that every Rodgers melody had a certain "holiness" about it—sang, "It's smooth! / It's smart! / It's Rodgers! / It's Hart!"

The contrast between music and lyrics was mirrored in Rodgers and Hart's seemingly opposite natures. Rodgers was a detached, disciplined workaholic with an eye to his own legend; Hart was a warm-hearted, undisciplined wastrel, who was more interested in seizing the day than the brass ring. "That boy will never see twenty-five," Rodgers's mother told him in the early days of their collaboration. (Her instincts weren't wrong, and Hart did die young, of pneumonia, in 1943, at the age of forty-eight.) Rodgers had social ambitions and moved easily in high society; Hart's view of the rich was that they were "a lot of crumbs held together by their own dough." Rodgers was empty without work; Hart was empty with it. ("What have I lived for?" were his last words.) Rodgers was emotionally contained; the idiosyncratic Hart seemed to spill out over everything. "When he liked something apparently his whole body itched," Rodgers said of his partner. Rodgers was a womanizer who longed for a happiness that always seemed to elude him; Hart was a closeted gay man—a romantic who couldn't get a date—the poignancy of which is broadcast in so many of the team's memorable songs ("A Ship Without a Sail," "Spring Is Here," It Never Entered My Mind," "Where's That Rainbow?," and—note the pun—"Nobody's Heart"). "Let me buy you a stimulant" was the diminutive Hart's mantra. Cigarchomping and night-loving, he was, as he once described Falstaff in a prizewinning high-school essay, a "blustering, boisterous boy of Bacchus."

No one made more of a myth of the duo's contradictions than Rodgers himself. Just as Hart's size made Rodgers look bigger than he was—five feet seven—his wild ways made Rodgers look better than he was. Hart's bad behavior allowed Rodgers to camouflage, from the world and from himself, his anxieties about his own fragility; next to Hart, he was a model of normality and rectitude. "I was pretty much a thorn in Larry's side, because I lived a much more conventional life," Rodgers said in an oral history stored at Columbia University. (The section of the oral history relating to Hart remained sealed until Rodgers's death.) "His mother used to badger him. She used to say, 'Why can't you get married like Dick and have children?' Well, this was the last thing that Larry wanted to do. . . . I know that it bothered him. There it was in front of him, every day, the conventional good citizen."

In fact, Rodgers was an alcoholic, too, excessive in his philandering appetites (all his life he kept an apartment for *cinq à septs*), and phobic about, among other things, germs, airplanes, fire, elevators, tunnels, bridges, and homosexuals. "Had dinner with the shrimp last night and hit the hay at a very early hour while he went on about his nefarious (get it?) business," Rodgers wrote to his wife, Dorothy, the sister of a childhood friend, whom he had married in 1930. Decades later, Diahann Carroll, who starred in "No Strings," for which Rodgers wrote the words as well as the music, recounted the shock of his saying to her, "You just can't imagine how wonderful it feels to have written this score, and not have to search all over the globe for that drunken little fag."

Many of the songs that Rodgers subsequently composed with Oscar Hammerstein—"Climb Ev'ry Mountain," "You'll Never Walk Alone," "A Hundred Million Miracles," "You've Got to Be Carefully Taught"—express a particular sense of American charity, blessing, decency, and justice. Rodgers could preach it, but he didn't practice it. After Hart died, the team of Rodgers and Hammerstein became a multinational corporation. "We had written 'Oklahoma!' and every time one of us blew his nose it was a symphony," Rodgers said. But their success had serious implications for the Rodgers-and-Hart legacy, which was controlled by the Rodgers & Hammerstein Organization. "He preferred to keep Rodgers and Hart dormant," Hart's sister-in-law, Dorothy Hart, wrote of Rodgers, in a memorandum. "Actually to keep the trade name down. . . . He did not want over-exposure and as Rodgers and Hammerstein shows and songs were going great guns, it was Rodgers and Hart that had to be buried." (After Rodgers's death, the president of the Rodgers & Hammerstein Organization, Ted Chapin, and Rodgers's elder daughter, the composer and author Mary Rodgers Guettel, put an end to this favoritism.)

In his oral history, Rodgers tells about how he and his father had helped the profligate Hart save money. "We arranged to steal Larry's money from him," he explained. "I put an accountant to work with Larry. He was doing my accounting. This was a man named William Kron. . . . He took Larry's money and distributed it in savings accounts all over the city, in Larry's name. There was no way for Larry to get at it and no way for anybody else to get at it." After Hart's death, however, the deposited money was never found. His brother, the actor Teddy Hart, with whom he lived until 1938, had been left a hundred-thousand-dollar insurance policy, but a clerical error resulted in the money being paid to the estate, and not to him. Teddy even had to buy back his brother's personal effects from the estate, and he got no help from Rodgers, who was one of the executors.

Hart's will turned out to have been rewritten five months before his death, under the supervision of Kron, who became a sort of keeper to Hart in his later years. Whereas the original will had left the bulk of Hart's wealth and the control of his intellectual property to his mother, in the revision Kron and his "lawful issue" got thirty per cent of Hart's royalties. The phrase "lawful issue" was omitted when it came to the Hart family: Teddy was to receive a percentage of Hart's royalties while he was alive, but after he and his wife, Dorothy, died the corpus of the estate would pass not to their heirs but to the Federation for the Support of Jewish Philanthropic Societies of New York, a charity in which Dorothy Rodgers was active. As evidence of Lorenz Hart's wish in this regard, Rodgers's lawyers produced a check for twenty-five dollars which Hart had donated to the charity in 1933.

Teddy contested the will, arguing that Hart had not been of sound mind at the time that it was drafted, and probably hadn't even read the eight pages of small print. The wrangling went on for more than four years. Finally, exhausted, demoralized, and poor, Teddy and Dorothy Hart—who had to fight the best lawyers that Rodgers, the Guaranty Trust Company Bank, and the Federation could buy—dropped their case. But their petition, which has not previously been made public, contains significant evidence that Hart truly was unstable. According to medical records, Hart saw his doctor a hundred and twenty-two times in the last nine months of his life. In one sworn deposition, Milton Bender, a friend of thirty years, said, "In the last three years I would say that the decedent was under the influence of liquor for at least eighty per cent of the time. He drank morning, noon, and night, rarely ate, and was difficult to manage." Dorothy Hart, in her deposition, recounted that in the last year of Hart's life Rodgers himself had suggested that Hart be sent to a psychiatrist or, if he refused, "committed by the State and . . . declared mentally incompetent." Rodgers, however, cited the success of "Pal Joey" (1941), "By Jupiter" (1942), and a rewrite of "A Connecticut Yankee," on which he and Hart had begun work in May, 1943, six months before Hart died. He unhesitatingly testified that Hart had been "in complete possession of all his mental faculties and aware of his every act and competent to understand the nature of same." (This despite the fact that Hart had spent a large part of the time that he was working on "A Connecticut Yankee" drying out—according to Teddy Hart, "frequently against his will"—at Doctors Hospital, in New York.) Dorothy Hart died in 2000. Until the end of her days, her son Larry, a Washington consultant, says, she felt that Rodgers had "helped commit a terrible fraud." By the terms of the will that Rodgers helped to engineer, Hart family members now receive no royalties; nor can they claim any newly discovered manuscripts, which officially belong to the United Jewish Appeal-Federation of New York, the successor to the Federation for the Support of Jewish Philanthropic Societies.

On the subject, Rodgers showed the world a tough and unrepentant face. "There's a statute of limitations on gratitude," he said in later years when asked about his partnership with Hart. In the mid-fifties, at Sardi's, Dorothy Hart and her son ran into Rodgers, who was recovering from surgery for cancer of the jaw. "He suddenly burst into tears and hugged my mother," Larry Hart recalls. "'I'm sorry,' he said. My mother didn't say anything. It's just something I'll never forget. She said, 'He must feel this terrible guilt.'"

In "Something Good," a song from the film version of "The Sound of Music," for which Rodgers wrote both music and lyrics, after Hammerstein's death, in 1964, he obliquely addressed his lifelong guilt and bewilderment over the fact that although his work had done good in the world, he had not:

> For here you are, standing there, loving me,
> Whether or not you should . . .
> Nothing comes from nothing,
> Nothing ever could.
> So, somewhere in my youth or childhood
> I must have done something good.

Rodgers's extraordinary musical prowess was an equally extraordinary defense against his imperfections as a friend, father, and husband. He and his wife—an inventor, interior designer, and hostess, whose eye for detail got her nicknamed La Perfecta—inhabited a Superbia of their own making, whose pressure for excellence weighed on their two daughters. "We weren't perfect people," Mary Rodgers Guettel told me. "That meant that we didn't love them—because, if we really had, we would have been perfect." In fact, Guettel claims, her parents "were quite crazy, disturbed, unhappy, miserable people." Dorothy Rodgers was addicted to Demerol, and, according to Guettel, frigid. "She was genuinely an awful person," Stephen Sondheim, who collaborated with Rodgers on "Do I Hear a Waltz?," says, in the Secrest biography. Rodgers's alcoholism made him prey to fierce mood swings; he was a man with secrets, wedded only to his music. "I was, I think, the most important person in his life," Dorothy Rodgers wrote in "Letters to Dorothy," her judiciously edited attempt to turn their marriage into a legend. "But his work was quite simply his life." Guettel adds, "He wanted people to think he was good, but he was a very suspicious, angry guy, easily hurt. He was sour and terrifying as a father. He cared so much about what people looked like." "You're so fat when you walk down the hall, your arms swing out by your sides like an ape," he told Mary, who was a pudgy youngster; she was also nearsighted, and this imperfection so displeased Rodgers that he made her remove her eyeglasses at the dinner table. "I saw a home movie of him playing with me when I was about ten months old," Guettel says. "My whole stomach turned over. Here was this wonderful, handsome, sweet, affectionate man playing with this baby. And I thought, I've never seen that person!" She adds, "We were just living this gigantic lie."

In 1979, during the Philadelphia run of "I Remember Mama," Rodgers asked Guettel, who was by then a theatre professional herself, to sit in on an important production meeting. Later, she went by her mother's room at their hotel: "There was Daddy in the doorway. My mother was . . . screaming at him at the top of her lungs. You've never heard such venom coming out of a woman in your life—everything she'd done for him, everything she'd put up with. It turns out she was in a rage because he had asked me to sit in on this meeting instead of her. . . . It was terrifying—everything I had feared and hoped for at the same time. She really didn't want to share him with me." In Roger Sherman's recent "American Masters" documentary on Rodgers, Guettel expanded on the theme of her parents' bad faith: "I think my mother resented every second of her life that was not spent with Daddy. I think Daddy resented every second of her life that she spent with him when he was working, because he had to feel guilty about her."

Rodgers, who saw five psychoanalysts during his lifetime, was more or less permanently depressed. "I suspect he feels in some way cut off," the choreographer Agnes de Mille wrote of Rodgers, with whom she had worked on "Oklahoma!" and "Carousel," in her memoir "And Promenade Home." "The banter is too constant, the quips too quick and sharp to betoken anything but vulnerability." She continued, "In his eyes (when he is off guard), there is a brooding quiet, a kind of unappeased hunger, a woe." Guettel says, "He was committed entirely to himself his worries, his pains, his phobias, and primarily his music."

Hunting a melody at the piano was his most effective antidepressant. "When I finish a tune, I'm high," Rodgers said. "I feel fulfilled, full of energy." The charm of musical theatre, he argued, was its remove from reality, and he took up more or less permanent residence in its world of make-believe. As his output indicates, he contrived to be "in production" almost all of his waking life. When Rodgers was at the piano, composing each morning in his gray cashmere cardigan, Guettel says, "there would be enthusiasm and excitement. He was Jolly Johnny—showing off." She adds, recalling her father's dramatically split personality, "The experience of writing music is like nothing else. You are completely protected from everything that hurts you. You own the world. You own yourself. You're the boy in the bubble."

Rodgers was only forty when he teamed up with Hammerstein, whom he had known since his Columbia days. Unlike Hart, who often needed to be in the room with Rodgers to write, Hammerstein preferred to give him completed lyrics. This, Rodgers said, provided him with "an almost inevitable musical pathway." The first lyric that Hammerstein gave Rodgers was for "Oh, What a Beautiful Mornin'." "From there on the stuff just flowed," Rodgers said in his oral history. "Very easy for both of us. . . . The whole thing was a kind of picnic." A tall, soft-spoken, disciplined man of moderation, Hammerstein was, in fact, the "cockeyed optimist" he would invoke in song. Whereas Hart had charmed the world with his wordplay, Hammerstein believed that "if a listener is made rhyme-conscious, his interest may be diverted from the story of the song." His compact, vivid folk lyricism and his working method changed Rodgers's musical palette—the phrases became longer, the sound richer and more grand.

Together, in nine musicals over nearly twenty years, the pair revolutionized the nature of musical storytelling. "One could no more think of their failing than the war effort failing," de Mille wrote. The range of their success and the depth of their influence gave Rodgers an almost imperial stature among his cohorts. De Mille went on, "He kids and jokes companionably at all rehearsals but he is a figure of some terror through sheer nervous tension, high voltage, and the unforgettable overtones of his world power. . . . He does not converse, he pronounces with judgments frequently unexpected and sharp, like summer lightning. Most of his comments are coups de grâce."

Inevitably, Rodgers's power made him a source of paranoia in others. Teddy Hart, who had worked consistently on Broadway before contesting his brother's will, never did again. The costume designer Lucinda Ballard, who worked with Rodgers on "Higher and Higher," was convinced that his "enmity" was responsible for her subsequent difficulty in getting jobs. "You are one of the most important people in the theatre and also have a very strong personality. I wonder if you realize the harm you have done me," she wrote him in 1949. In four terse and regal paragraphs, Rodgers swatted Ballard and her claims away: "You will have to accept this letter as factual and truthful and with it goes one word of advice. . . . I would like to take the liberty of suggesting you had better get hold of yourself."

Rodgers's co-workers, however, found it hard to get hold of him. The director Joshua Logan, who was responsible for the Broadway productions of four of Rodgers's musicals, admitted in his biography that after "Oklahoma!" Rodgers became, "almost in front of your eyes, a monument." He went on, "To me, his fun seemed to be gone—the fun he and I used to have. And I tried to decide for myself—what is a Richard Rodgers?" Logan's pronominal shift and his references to Rodgers as "it"—"It's a brilliant, talented, highly intelligent superbrain. . . . It's not given to smiling too much"—suggest a performing machine rather than a human being. When Hammerstein's son confessed to his father that he wasn't comfortable around Rodgers, Hammerstein replied, "Nobody is. It's not you. It's Dick."

Sondheim, characterizing the two giants whose work he subsequently deconstructed in his own musicals, told Newsweek, "Oscar Hammerstein was a man of limited talent and infinite soul. Richard Rodgers was a man of infinite talent and limited soul." In his music, especially in the gorgeous waltzes—"Falling in Love with Love," "Lover," "The Most Beautiful Girl in the World," "Wait till You See Her"—Rodgers made palpable the thrilling promise of connection. The heartbreak that he never showed to others was revealed in the haunting beauty of his songs, which became a kind of virtual representation of him, a simulacrum that allowed him to be present in the world without actually being a part of it. Although his music was familiar to the public, he remained a stranger to himself. The critic Brooks Atkinson, in an unfavorable review of "Pal Joey" in the Times, asked, "Can you draw sweet water from a foul well?" Richard Rodgers's life seems to suggest that the answer is yes.

TONY KUSHNER

On MAY 2, 2004, THE HUMID Sunday that his musical "Caroline, or Change" was to transfer from the Public Theatre, downtown, to the Eugene O'Neill Theatre, on Broadway, Tony Kushner left his apartment on the Upper West Side and ambled east through Central Park. He was seeking out Bethesda Fountain and the statue of an angel that graces it to ask for blessing. For luck, on opening nights, Kushner usually performs two rituals: before the curtain goes up he sings Cole Porter's "Begin the Beguine"—a song that, according to his will, must be played, along with Brahms's Fourth and Mahler's Resurrection Symphony, at his funeral ("I envision a lengthy service," he has written. "Bring lunch"); then, while the show is on, he slips away for a Chinese meal. On this occasion, however, Kushner found himself doubly in need of luck. Not only would the opening of "Caroline" mark his return to Broadway after more than a decade but a revised, nearly four-hour version of his play "Homebody/Kabul" was beginning a limited engagement at the Brooklyn Academy of Music.

Kushner had last been represented on Broadway in 1993, with "Perestroika," the second part of his seven-hour epic, "Angels in America." The first major play to put homosexual life at the center of its moral debate, "Angels" covered territory that ranged from Heaven to earth, from the AIDS epidemic to conservative politics, encapsulating, in its visionary sweep, the sense of confusion and longing that defined late-twentieth-century American life. "It gave a language to that generation," the director George C. Wolfe, who staged both "Angels in America" and "Caroline, or Change" on Broadway, says. "It gave playwrights permission to think about theatre in a whole new way. A play could be poetic, ridiculous, fragile, overtly political, sentimental, and brave all at the same time." "Angels" won Kushner two

Tonys and a Pulitzer Prize. Last December, HBO aired Mike Nichols's sixty-million-dollar film version, for which Kushner adapted the play and which starred Al Pacino and Meryl Streep. (The film was nominated for twenty-one Emmys and won a record eleven.)

In Kushner's view, however, "Caroline, or Change"—a semi-autobiographical account of the relationship between a Southern Jewish boy, who has lost his mother, and his family's saturnine maid, Caroline—is his best-told story. Based on the "unexpected hidden life" of the Kushner family's maid, Maudie Lee Davis, the script is a radical departure from the standard forms of Broadway musical distraction. With its focus on race, class, and even economics, "Caroline" celebrates the ambivalent, instead of the upbeat. When it opened last year at the Public, it earned a strong critical response, not all of it positive. For some critics, the show's psychological subtlety was hidden beneath the folkloric, seemingly simplistic style of the production. ("'Caroline' might be regarded as the brooding person's 'Hairspray,'" Ben Brantley wrote in the *Times*.) Kushner felt, he says, "hugely disappointed" and only "cautiously, but definitely, endorsed."

Nevertheless, throughout the winter and into the spring, bolstered by the growing demand of the Public's audiences and by the success of the Nichols film, Kushner worked the phones and called in favors until a consortium of twenty Broadway producers put up five million dollars to move the musical to Broadway. No one was going to get rich, their mantra went, but Broadway would be the richer for it. The Broadway opening meant another round of reviews. "It would be lovely if suddenly there was sort of this Pauline conversion and people were coming and saying, 'I was wrong the first time; it's great now,'" Kushner said. "But that isn't going to happen. Tomorrow there'll be some wonderful things and also maybe some not-so-wonderful things. Then we have to take a deep breath and figure out how we're going to give this a respectable run on Broadway." Kushner admits that he is "preternaturally, even *prenatally,* thin-skinned." He says, "I would like to care less about the things other people say about me, but I can't imagine caring less. I think people pay heavy prices for armor and callousness." Still, he adds, "it's very hard to take criticism when it's inept, when it kills the chances of that show being seen."

For a while, he sat on the low perimeter wall of the Bethesda plaza, enjoying the scene. His gaze finally came to rest on the blousy bronze angel in the center of the fountain, which plays an important role in the finale of "Angels in America." In the Biblical tale of Bethesda, an angel appears on the surface of a pool and gives the water healing powers. The statue, Kushner explained, "commemorates the naval dead of the Civil War. It's the first commissioned sculpture by a woman in New York—Emma Stebbins, the sister of the parks board president and a lesbian." He went on, "The other thing I love about it is that it got terrible reviews when it was unveiled."

Kushner is a purveyor of what he calls "brave art"—"the best sense we can make of our times." Several weeks before "Caroline" opened on Broadway, in a debate sponsored by the Classic Stage Company, one of Kushner's great champions, the critic Harold Bloom, spent the better part of two hours trying in vain to get Kushner to admit that he was a theological writer. "I'm somebody who believes in . . . a kind of relationship of complaint and struggle and pursuit between the human and the divine," Kushner said finally. "And part of that struggle involves politics. For me, drama without politics is inconceivable."

He is fond of quoting Melville's heroic prayer from "Mardi and a Voyage Thither" ("Better to sink in boundless deeps, than float on vulgar shoals"), and takes an almost carnal glee in tackling the most difficult subjects in contemporary history—among them, AIDS and the conservative counter-revolution ("Angels in America"), Afghanistan and the West ("Homebody/Kabul"), German Fascism and Reaganism ("A Bright Room Called Day"), the rise of capitalism ("Hydriotaphia, or the Death of Dr. Brown"), and racism and the civil-rights movement in the South ("Caroline, or Change"). But his plays, which are invariably political, are rarely polemical. Instead, Kushner rejects ideology in favor of what he calls "a dialectically shaped truth," which must be "outrageously funny" and "absolutely agonizing," and must "move us forward." He gives voice to characters who have been rendered powerless by the forces of circumstance—a drag queen dying of AIDS, an uneducated Southern maid, contemporary Afghans—and his attempt to see all sides of their predicament has a sly subversiveness. He forces the audience to identify with the marginalized—a humanizing act of imagination.

Kushner also has what he calls "a boundless appetite" for exploring the dramatic form. An early dance-theatre piece, "La Fin de la Baleine: An Opera for the Apocalypse"—about bad love, the blues, the bomb, and bulimia—included a woman dancing on point with a tuba and spouting water from her mouth. "Homebody/Kabul," which began with a first-person monologue, morphed into a third-person drama, moving unexpectedly from closeup to long shot. With its visions and poetic fulminations, "Angels in America" expanded the expressive limits of naturalistic theatre. Likewise, "Caroline, or Change" used its visual, sonic, and linguistic vernacular to create a kind of American folk opera, in which the worlds of white privilege and African-American impoverishment were woven together in a dreamlike fable that bore the influence of Kushner's friend Maurice Sendak, with whom he has written a children's book and an opera libretto.

Underneath Kushner's prodigious flow of language is a sense of incantation, which draws the spectator in and compels him to listen. His writing is defined by fluency and excess. He wrote the first draft of the opening monologue for "Homebody/Kabul" in forty-eight hours, "Caroline" in four and a half months, and he had just finished a two-hundred-and-eighty-three-page draft of a screenplay for Steven Spielberg about the aftermath of the 1972 terrorist attack during the Olympic Games in Munich, which he wrote in three weeks. "I like big, splashy, juicy plays," Kushner says. "I like the audience to feel space to roam around in." (He refers to Samuel Beckett as "that matzoh of a playwright.") In his 1995 collection of essays, "Thinking About the Longstanding Problems of Virtue and Happiness," Kushner writes, "A good play, like good lasagna, should be overstuffed. It has a pomposity, and an overreach. Its ambitions extend in the direction of not-missing-a-trick, it has a bursting omnipotence up its sleeve."

The swashbuckling quality of Kushner's intellectual aspirations is not borne out by his demeanor. At forty-eight, he is tall, courtly, unassuming, and flat-footed, with a tangle of wiry black curls—his "wackadoo hair," as his friend the director Michael Mayer calls it. He is by nature a "fummfler"—what Sendak calls "the jewish fumbler who is in perfect control, who uses his comic character to somehow make everyone feel comfortable and loose." He talks extraordinarily fast, with a machine-gun-style delivery that reflects both his swiftness of mind and his nervousness. At the same time, his pace gives him a distinct comic advantage. When delivering the Class Day speech at Columbia University earlier this year, he reminded the students that he had been their fourth choice—after Warren Buffett, Supreme Court Justice Ruth Bader Ginsburg, and Jon Stewart. "I think I should begin by acknowledging your disappointment that I am not Jon Stewart," he said. "Your disappointment that I am not Jon Stewart will last one morning. I am disappointed at not being Jon Stewart every morning of my life." To graduates at Bard, where he was awarded an honorary degree, he observed, "I cherish my bile duct as much as any other organ. I take good care of it. I make sure it gets its daily vitamins and antioxidants and invigorating exposure to news of Antonin Scalia and everyone else working for the Bush family." At Cooper Union, receiving another degree, he began his speech by pronouncing President Bush's words of the previous day: "Thank you and good evening. I'm honored to visit the Army War College. Generations of officers have come here to study the strategies and history of warfare. I've come here tonight to report to all Americans, and to the Iraqi people, on the strategy our nation is pursuing in Iraq and the specific steps we're taking to achieve our goals." He paused, then added, "I just wanted to feel what it felt like to say that."

When Kushner speaks in public, his gambit is often to share with his audience a little secret, some complaint that downplays his own prestige: he's tired; he's nervous; he's unprepared; he's overworked; he doesn't know what to say. "He keeps dismantling himself, reminding himself of how weak he is and how many frailties he has," Nichols says. "He lets you see the vulnerability. It's part of a genius's self-protection."

"I don't look like Keanu Reeves," Kushner said in a 1994 interview. "So when people express an interest, which happens rarely but does . . . I sort of go, 'Well, why?'" Mayer says, "He's very disparaging about his chin, his nose, his weight. You don't imagine him lying on the beach in a bathing suit." Kushner is constantly at war with his body, alternately indulging and starving it. Between 1988 and 1993, when he was writing "Angels in America," he gained about a hundred pounds. "I used to say, I'm pregnant. I'm eating for eight," he says. Then, just as dramatically, he shrank himself down.

* * *

In 1969, when Kushner was twelve, his mother, Sylvia, learned that she had breast cancer. (After a long remission, she died of inoperable lung cancer, on August 27, 1990.) At one point, when she was in a hospital in New York, he badgered his father, William, to buy him a pocket watch, then had it engraved with the words "Cogito, Ergo Sum" (a motto he'd acquired from Marvel comic books, not Descartes). "A thinker or nothing," he explains. "Because the body, clearly, betrays."

William Kushner, a Southern Jew from Lake Charles, Louisiana, who had studied at Juilliard, had been playing first clarinet with the New Orleans Symphony when he met Sylvia Deutscher, who, as first bassoonist, was one of the first American women to hold a chair in a major orchestra. She had been a professional musician since she was twenty-three. In addition to touring with Sadler's Wells and playing with the New York City Opera, she had recorded with Stravinsky and played at the first Pablo Casals Festival. Kushner says of his mother's music, "That nasal but open-throated, deep wooden vibrato sound echoed through my childhood. I think the idea of fluency made itself felt in me as something musical before it became something lingual. She had huge lung power. She could breathe into a candle flame and control the flicker of it with her breath." He also says, "She saved a good deal of her truthfulness, the things she couldn't say in the quotidian, for her music."

The youngest of four children from a first-generation socialist Jewish family in New York, Sylvia was noisy and emotional. Her father, an early member of the glazier's union, had been fierce and abusive. As a result, according to her sister, Martha Deutscher, Sylvia "was a needy person who was massively insecure about herself." Kushner's older sister, the artist Lesley Kushner, was born, in 1954, with severe hearing loss; she couldn't speak and couldn't easily comprehend what was said to her. Her frustration kept her in a more or less permanent tantrum. To spend more time with her and Tony, William and Sylvia, then in their early thirties and playing for the New York City Opera, decided to move back to Lake Charles, where William could earn a living in his father's lumber business. But Sylvia felt isolated in the South. "Leaving music professionally was very difficult for her,"

William says. "She hadn't succeeded as an artist," Kushner explains. "There was a sense of the world having not gotten her, and not appreciated her. She was furious about it."

When Kushner was born, in 1956, he entered a family dominated by an atmosphere of regret, disappointment, and, in the case of his older sister, murderous rage. "There was just no way to tell her, no way to make her understand," William recalls of Lesley's rancor over the sudden appearance of her brother. She had to be physically removed from Kushner's third birthday party; when her father drove her away from the house, she tried to throw herself out of the car. The brutality of her behavior was, William says, "pretty devastating" to Tony—"it gave him a great sympathy with other people who were mistreated." Until Kushner reached high school, he and Lesley were at war. Adding to the tension, according to Kushner, was the fact that Sylvia had different notions of femininity than Lesley, who was a tomboy. "She took you and kind of rejected me," Lesley wrote in a recent e-mail to Tony. "Or as she put it, 'My father was an angry man and you were angry so I gave you to Daddy.'" A third child, Eric, who was born in 1961, absorbed his parents' professional ambitions. "They pushed Eric into music," Lesley says. "Every single week, they would drive him to New Orleans for horn lessons, four hours each way." (Eric is now first horn for the Vienna Symphony Orchestra.)

In 1969, Sylvia underwent a mastectomy, and nine years later William became the maestro of the Lake Charles Symphony—events that changed the family dynamic. While Lesley and Eric gravitated toward their father, Tony maintained the closest bond to Sylvia. From an early age, he'd been a fervent reader of comics—"I wanted to write books, to be an illustrator," he says. He made up his own stories for the comic characters and wrote their dialogue. "Momma read them and would delight in them," Lesley recalls. "She thought they were funny. Everything he said she just found delightful." Tony was equally enchanted by his mother, who had theatrical aspirations. At six, he watched her perform in Arthur Miller's "Death of a Salesman" at the local theatre-in-the-round. "As Linda Loman, she changed from my beautiful young mother . . . to an old woman in the course of the evening," he wrote in 1997. "It was terrifying and wonderful. . . . I don't think I ever saw her the same way again." Over the years, he watched Sylvia play Anne Frank's mother, and Beatrice in "The Effect of Gamma Rays on Man-in-the-Moon Marigolds." "I really think that it was seeing those plays and the special sort of power that her being in them gave to them that started me on a lifelong fascination with the theatre," he has said.

Kushner has come to realize that William's love of writing—he and his family were great reciters of poetry and doggerel—was also an important influence on him. But, in his youth, what he got from his father was a sense of worry—the idea "that there was something wrong that he was trying to fix." As a boy, Kushner was not assertive or athletic. "I would become angry with Tony, frustrated with his helplessness," William says. "He wanted something from me that I wasn't giving him," Kushner recalls. William tried unsuccessfully to interest him in chess, ball games, bird-watching, sailing, and an Outward Bound course (they got as far as the orientation meeting). Around puberty, he began to give his son pep talks about sex. Kushner says, "As I got older, he figured it out. He finally said, 'I think you're a homosexual, and I want you not to be a homosexual. I want you to go to a therapist and fix it.' I was about sixteen."

Kushner had known that he was gay for almost a decade. He remembers rubbing the shoulders of his handsome Sunday-school teacher and thinking, Oh, this is fun, and also I shouldn't be doing this. Those impulses sent him through childhood with a sense of fraudulence. "You feel you are unacceptable to everyone, even to your parents, who love you but wouldn't if they knew," Kushner says. His persistent nightmare was of his classmates finding out "and killing me or burning the house down." His high-school friend Tom Tolin, an economist, says, "I remember him sitting in the bleachers and these guys around him giving him a hard time, calling him 'Kush-Kush.' He just sat there with his head buried in a book. It was painful." Kushner recalls, "I hated the kids that I was going to school with, the boys especially—aggressive, nasty, physically intimidating. I didn't know how to get protection, because I was too embarrassed."

For years, Kushner was, by his own admission, a terrible student. Then, to his astonishment, in high school he became a verbal athlete: a champion debater. "I may have been a sissy, but I was not without aggression," he says. "I became this incredibly mean arguer. I would not be defeated." He was also opinionated: in high school, he refused to stand for the Pledge of Allegiance;

he leafletted Ku Klux Klan members for George McGovern; as early as junior high school, he alone on his debate team argued in favor of feminism. But his talent gave him, for the first time, a sense of his own power and a society to which he belonged. "I found the smart kids," he says.

As Kushner was finding his lung power, his mother was losing hers. In 1969, following her mastectomy, she was overradiated and developed osteomyelitis in her ribs, some of which had to be removed. "She was in a lot of pain, couldn't laugh, couldn't be hugged, and, of course, she couldn't play the bassoon," Kushner says. Her ambition settled instead on Tony, whose Promethean itch had its origins in her aspirations for him. "It was this huge thing to her if I succeeded," he says. "I don't recall her ever lavishing a huge amount of praise on me, but I remember the thrill in her voice when I told her I had won some debate tournament, or when I got an agent, or when I got a grant or a good review or any indication that what she expected—which was that I would be a successful artist—was going to come to pass. She would simply say, 'Go! Go! Go!' in a crescendo of pitch and volume, when I brought her good news." Speaking of the special connection between Sylvia and her children, Lesley says, "She kind of moved into your skin with you. You couldn't tell if it was what you wanted for yourself or what she wanted for you. It was a sort of ventriloquist sensation." When Kushner was accepted to the graduate program at New York University's Tisch School of the Arts, Sylvia came to see him a couple of times a year. "She visited with him and nobody else," Martha Deutscher says. "It was always the two of them." Once, when Sylvia, Kushner, and Deutscher were having coffee in the Village, Kushner and his aunt began to tease his mother about some of her attitudes. "She turned to me and said, 'Don't you turn my son against me!'" Deutscher recalls. "She was not joking. She didn't want to share him."

When Kushner's play "A Bright Room Called Day" was staged in London in 1988, Sylvia flew over for the opening. It was panned. "She collapsed," Deutscher says. "When my mother died, I realized that a certain degree of my ability to take pleasure in my own accomplishments was gone," Kushner says. "Without her to show it to, to do it for—a circuit had been broken." Above his writing desk at his country house, in Manitou,

New York, is a huge framed copy—signed by the poet—of Robert Duncan's "My Mother Would Be a Falconress," which reads, in part:

> My mother would be a falconress,
> and I her gerfalcon, raised at her will,
> from her wrist sent flying, as if I were her own
> pride, as if her pride
> knew no limits, as if her mind
> sought in me flight beyond the horizon.

Sexuality was one of the ways in which Kushner broke away from his mother and, like the poem's falcon, flew "far, far beyond the curb of her will." Kushner's parents had hoped that with therapy his latent heterosexuality could be reinforced. When he was twenty-five, he called home to tell Sylvia that he was gay. "She cried for a month," he says. "She was just heartbroken by it. I finally said, I'm not going to call you anymore until you stop, because it's getting creepy. I feel like I've died."

Although he now refers to his "desire-based identity" and an "endlessly raging libido," he had difficulty, at first, accepting his orientation. In his second week as an undergraduate at Columbia, in 1974, Kushner presented himself at the health center and asked to see a therapist. "I'm gay and I want to be straight," he said. He is, he says, "sexually flusterable." "The first time I ever saw two men kiss was when I was a freshman at Columbia and it completely freaked me out," he said in an interview last year. "It still took another three years before I began to come out of the closet." When Kushner did come out, according to the actor Stephen Spinella—who met Kushner in graduate school at New York University, and later starred in "Angels in America"—"he exploded. It was like a train. He was out, out, out."

A decade later, in 1995, Kushner and Michael Mayer, who had also met as students at N.Y.U., found themselves, in the company of such celebrities as Roy Lichtenstein and Bob Hope, at the White House, during the first term of the Clinton Administration. Kushner was seated at Al Gore's table. "I wore a triangle made out of pink rhinestones. Gore asked me what it was and I got to explain it to him," Kushner recalls. After dinner, there was a dance. "We were slow-dancing together next to Senator Alan Simpson and his wife, the Gores, everyone," Mayer recalls. "We may be the first men ever to dance together in the White House."

Kushner, in his senior year at Columbia, took Edward Tayler's famous course on Shakespeare. "Tayler taught Shakespeare in a profoundly dialectical way," Kushner says. To understand Shakespeare, Tayler told his students, "you only need to count to two." From him, Kushner learned that everything in Shakespeare was paradoxical and contradictory—and that this collision of opposites was the first principle of drama. He left Tayler's lecture on "Henry IV, Part 1" "shaking and in a fog." He recalls, "I was having trouble breathing. I felt like, Oh, I'm beginning to understand something about life, the idea that a thing can be both one thing and its opposite, that two opposites can exist simultaneously and not cancel each other out. Or they can transform one another through conflict into something new." Kushner had already gravitated toward the stage. He had attended theatre and opera in New York, designed sets and props for university productions of "The Fantasticks" and "Marat/Sade," served for a year and a half as the drama critic of the Columbia *Spectator*, and written his first dialogue in a playwriting class. By the time he graduated, he had also fallen under the spell of Brecht's "A Short Organum for the Theatre," which set out the playwright's aesthetic for epic theatre—his attempt to engage the audience in a play of contradiction that encouraged active critical thought and departed from the passive emotional catharsis encouraged by the Aristotelian principles of drama. "I wanted to *be* Bertolt Brecht," Kushner says. He applied to N.Y.U., and, once there, studied under the German-born director Carl Weber, a Brecht specialist.

In his senior year at Columbia, while directing a university production of Ben Jonson's sprawling epic "Bartholomew Fair," Kushner had become friends with Kimberly Flynn, a Barnard psychology major from New Orleans, who was working on the stage crew. "We fit together intellectually and, in some ways, emotionally, on a kind of molecular level," he says. Kushner and Flynn went everywhere together; they had no secrets. Flynn had, Kushner says, a "vast appetite for pedagogy—she loves explaining things to people" and was "a great synthesizer." Kushner, in turn, had a vast curiosity. "She led and I followed," he says. "She read Walter Benjamin and told me I should. And Marcuse, Adorno, Horkheimer. I had read some Freud and some Marx, but not nearly as widely." He continues, "As soon as I started writing, or constructing plays, she would read, comment, make suggestions. I would call her my dramaturge, but Kim was that to the power of twenty." Inevitably, though, there were struggles over ownership of ideas. In 1982, Kushner formed a theatre company with several people, including Flynn and his first boyfriend, Mark Bronnenberg, to produce "La Fin de la Baleine," among other plays. Flynn contributed the ideas; Kushner created the stage images, and got most of the credit for the show, which caused some bad feeling between the friends.

In 1984, Flynn was riding in a cab as it sped up the West Side Highway when the car went out of control and off the road, ramming into a tree in Riverside Park. During the next few days at the hospital, Flynn's garbled sentences, her repetitions, and her inability to distinguish left from right indicated to her, even before the doctors confirmed it, that she had suffered brain damage. Just as Kushner's theatrical career was taking off—he was appointed the assistant director of the St. Louis Repertory Theatre in 1985, and became the associate artistic director of the New York Theatre Workshop in 1987— Flynn was stymied, and she directed some of her enormous fury at Kushner. She told The New Yorker, "It was hard to deal with how angry I was, and with the idea that I was jealous and that I was in no position to be jealous—I was out of the game." Kushner agonized over moving to St. Louis. "I've had to make the hardest decisions of my life around Kim's illness," he has said. His guilt about her disaster and the difficulty of taking care of her is evident in "Millennium Approaches," the first part of "Angels in America." "She was everywhere in it," he says. (He gave Flynn ten per cent of the profits.)

Flynn eventually recovered sufficiently to become a full-time political activist, focussing on environmental issues. But in 1996, right before Kushner began work on "Homebody" and "Caroline," he and Flynn decided to alter the nature of their friendship. "We tried very hard to figure out a way of staying close," he says. "We were just making each other, by the end, terribly, terribly unhappy." He continues, "It was an important turning point for me." In his cramped one-room office in Union Square, Kushner keeps a photograph of himself with Flynn at Bethesda Fountain.

Kushner's "A Bright Room Called Day," which is dedicated, in part, to Flynn, crosscut the effect of the rise of Hitler on a group of friends in Berlin in the early thirties with a rant on American politics that linked Fascism with the Reagan revolution. It was meant, Kushner says, as "a warning signal, not a prediction." The play, which was workshopped in New York in 1985, drew little press attention, but the director Oskar Eustis saw one of the performances. "Tony's gift for language was completely apparent," he says. "He was deeply, specifically interested in politics, in political theory and how it related to political practice." He goes on, "'Bright Room' was about what all Tony's plays are about—people who feel themselves inadequate for the demands that history has put on them."

Eustis produced and directed "Bright Room" in 1987 at San Francisco's Eureka Theatre, where it had a succès d'estime. But East Coast critics were less enthusiastic when they saw a reworked version in 1991 at the Public Theatre in New York. "A fatuous new drama," Frank Rich called it in the *Times*. "An early front-runner for the most infuriating play of 1991." For all its intelligence and ambition, the play was dramatically inert. "I made an outline of twenty-four scenes," Kushner says. "I wrote twenty-four scenes. Each scene was exactly what I put down in the outline." Eustis says, "Tony understood everything else about theatre, but he didn't understand about reversals, how that worked. The theatre is about change, so change has to happen in the course of the play. In 'Bright Room,' you'd have scene after scene of characters coming out, beautifully expressing how they feel, then leaving the stage without changing at all."

After the San Francisco run ended, Kushner began work on what he envisioned as a taut, one-set musical about AIDS. As he started to write for the first time about his own time and place—about homosexuality, AIDS, and right-wing American politics—the play quickly began to exceed his ambitions for it. "For the first-rate artist, there is a moment when he's really getting revved up, and the time just flows into him," Mike Nichols says. "It only happens once. It happens without his awareness at all. He planned nothing. He was just going ahead doing this next thing."

As Kushner was writing "Angels in America," he gave himself to the characters, not to the outline; instead of imposing an ideology on them, he followed their lead. "I was two acts into 'Millennium' and I didn't know what the fuck I was doing," he says. "So I thought, I'm gonna ask a character. Who's most like me? Louis. So I sat down, and I said, 'What is this play about?' I waited a few minutes and then 'Why has democracy succeeded in America?' popped into my head. Then Louis began to qualify himself as he always did—the first of my big logorrheics. I wrote the line 'There are no angels in America.' Then I wrote on the side to myself, 'Louis is wrong.'" The story seemed to suggest itself from there. Still, the writing wasn't easy for Kushner. "I can't get these people to change fast enough," he complained to Eustis. "At first, I thought he was being self-indulgent," Eustis says. "What became clear is that the difficulty in these people changing *was* the subject of the play."

What eventually emerged was an epic discourse on American life that mixed social reality with theatrical fantasy, naturalism with Judaism and magical realism. It told its story in numerous dialects—camp, black, Jewish, Wasp, even Biblical tones. At the same time, it provided a detailed map of the nation's sense of loss. "Millennium Approaches" charts the heyday of the Reagan Presidency through a series of characters who ruthlessly pursue their own sexual and public destinies: Prior Walter, an AIDS patient, is abandoned by his lover, Louis, at the time of his most profound need; Joe, an ambitious bisexual Mormon Republican chief clerk, leaves his lost, pill-popping wife, Harper, for a man; and Roy Cohn, the notorious right-wing lawyer and fixer, a closeted homosexual who is also dying of AIDS, rationalizes his own sensational rapacity. (Cohn, whom Kushner portrayed with Jacobean relish, personifies the barbarity of individualism.) In "Perestroika," which ends four years after "Millennium," in 1990, Kushner explores the possibility of progress and community, of redemption. Harper finally accepts the failure of her marriage and sets out on her own. Louis reconciles with Prior—in a scene that took Kushner years to write. "Failing in love isn't the same as not loving," Louis says. "It doesn't let you off the hook, it doesn't mean . . . you're free to not love."

Twenty-four characters, eight acts, fifty-nine scenes, and an epilogue: "Angels in America" turned the struggle of a minority into a metaphor for

America's search for self-definition. "I hate this country," a gay black nurse called Belize says to Louis. "It's just big ideas, and stories, and people dying, and people like you. The white cracker who wrote the national anthem knew what he was doing. He set the word 'free' to a note so high nobody can reach it." Although "Angels" was not the first play to explore the AIDS pandemic—Larry Kramer's polemical "The Normal Heart" (1985) pre-ceded it—it was the first to explore the particular claim of the disenfran-chised to a romantic vision of America. "We will be citizens," Prior announces to the audience at the finale. "The time has come."

By the fall of 1988, it had become clear that the play would need two evenings to run its course, which meant that Eustis couldn't afford to pro-duce it at the Eureka Theatre. "A two-evening show about AIDS by a play-wright nobody had heard of. I mean, it was just disastrous," Eustis says. In the end, he chose the play over his theatre company. He left the Eureka for the Mark Taper Forum, in Los Angeles, where the artistic director, Gordon Davidson, had agreed to workshop "Millennium" and, eventually, to mount both halves of the play together under Eustis's directorship. The plan took a few years to complete. It wasn't until the spring of 1991, almost a year after Kushner's mother had died, that he was able to wrench the three-hundred-page draft of "Perestroika" out of himself—in an eight-day writing spree in a cabin on the Russian River, in Northern California, where he holed up with a box full of junk food and cold cuts. "I would sleep two hours at a stretch, get up, write the next scene, and it just went on and on," he says. He finished the play on April 11th. "It was maybe one of the happiest days of my entire life," he says.

"Millennium" had its first major production in Declan Donnellan's ver-sion at London's Royal National Theatre, in January, 1992. After a work-shop of "Perestroika" at the Taper in May of that year, both parts of the play were performed together for the first time, over two nights, in November. By then, "Millennium" had won the London *Evening Standard*'s award for best play. When the Mark Taper box office opened for the complete pro-duction of "Angels," the receipts broke the theatre's record. At the Taper première, most of New York's theatrical establishment and its major critics were in the audience. Backstage, Kushner wrote a letter to the cast and pinned it on the bulletin board. "And how else should an angel land on earth but with the utmost difficulty?" it said. "If we are to be visited by angels we will have to call them down with sweat and strain, we will have to drag them out of the skies."

The plays, if not the Taper production, were triumphant. "Angels" was hailed as a turning point for theatre, for gay life, and for American culture. Frank Rich, in the *Times,* spoke of "Angels" as "this vast, miraculous play," and Jeremy Gerard of *Variety* went even further: "'Angels in America' is a monumental achievement, the work of a defiantly theatrical imagination." In Charlotte, North Carolina—and in university towns in rural parts of Indiana and Texas—fundamentalists staged protests to stop subsequent local productions, a move that Kushner referred to in *The Nation* as "unconstitutional, undemocratic and deeply unwise." (A decade later, when the Nichols film aired on television, the climate of tolerance that "Angels" helped to create was used as a criticism of the play. When Kushner begins writing, he jokes about needing to banish his "inner John Simon," the voice of the acerbic theatre critic of *New York*, whom he imagines saying, "You're completely terrible and everything you write is shit." But Simon's attacks— real or imagined—are nothing compared with the grapeshot vitriol of Lee Seigel in *The New Republic*. "'Angels in America' is a second-rate play written by a second-rate playwright who happens to be gay, and because he has written a play about being gay, and about AIDS, no one—and I mean no one— is going to call 'Angels in America' the overwrought, coarse, posturing, formulaic mess that it is," Seigel wrote.)

After "Angels in America," Kushner found it hard to start another play. Nonetheless, he wanted to be useful. He thought about training to be a teacher, a lawyer, a nurse. Instead, according to Eustis, "he reinvented himself as a public intellectual," becoming, among other things, one of America's most prominent gay-rights activists. His essays—some of which began as speeches delivered at gay-rights events—addressed sex, homosexual liberation, and socialism. He argued in defense of the activist and playwright Larry Kramer; of the controversial choreographer Bill T. Jones; and of Matthew Shepard, the Wyoming student who was murdered because of his sexuality. "Campaign for homosexual and all civil rights—campaign, not just passively support," Kushner exhorted the readers of his article on

Shepard, which appeared in *The Nation* in 1998. "Matthew Shepard shouldn't have died. We should all burn with shame."

In 1995, Kushner was asked by President Clinton to submit some ideas for the forthcoming State of the Union address. In a letter, Kushner set out the tenets of his version of American democracy: "You need to be the full-blooded liberal Democrat I believe you want to be. You need to tell the American people that you stand for a strong Federal government, fully empowered to regulate industry; protect the jobs and lives of American workers, and protect our *extremely* endangered environment (and our health along with it). You have to declare war on the anti-tax, anti-government movement, calling it what it is: a scam perpetrated against the middle class, the working class and the poor in the interests of maximizing profits for multinational corporations and the very rich. . . . You have to have the courage you had in 1992 to declare that grown-up responsible citizens of a democracy *pay taxes*." He ended his eight-page letter with a plea for social justice: "You must support affirmative action, poverty, education, child care and jobs creation programs, and anti-discrimination legislation which *includes sexual orientation*."(Clinton read the letter, but nothing from it made it into the speech.)

These days, when Kushner visits college campuses, where he can command more than twelve thousand dollars a talk, he is the equivalent of a rock star. (Once when he spoke at Brown, loudspeakers had to be placed outside the hall for the overflow audience; last April, at Middlebury; in the school's auditorium, he spoke to a standing-room-only crowd.) Still, Kushner is a playwright who is an activist, not an activist who happens to write plays. One of the few serious playwrights who know how to write a joke, he is also one of the few political speakers who know how to deliver one. "When Republicans are upset, they fall over. Have you noticed this?" he asked Cooper Union's graduating class last June, before pointing out that Nixon had tripped at a New Orleans trade show, Gerald Ford often fell down stairs, Bush senior had fallen and then vomited on the Japanese Prime Minister ("And he was the Bush who was *good* at foreign relations!"), and Bush junior had collapsed while eating a pretzel. "What are they expressing, these falling people?" he asked. "A spiritual vertigo? The insupportable weight of all the power and ponderous wealth they have arrogated unto themselves, beneath which their legs eventually buckle? . . . Is it an unseemly yet uncontrollable desire to slither?"

The apotheosis of Kushner's kvetching persona was his appearance, in robe and slippers, at a fund-raising event for Friends in Deed, a charity that provides support for people with life-threatening diseases. Declaiming at a panic-stricken Gilbert-and-Sullivan clip, he read from his "diary":

Wednesday, August 28, 2002. Mike Nichols called today. He wants a favor: Could I write a funny ten-minute play for a bene-fit for some group he's on the board of, Friends of something-or-other. I love Mike. I would do anything for him. There's no one I admire or adore more in the whole industry, maybe in the whole world. He's really a great man, so busy and yet has the time to organize something like this. Wow! Me sharing the stage with six other incredibly intimidating playwrights of whom I am insanely jealous. Sounds like fun! I'm sure Mike doesn't love Robbie Baitz more than me.

"Two people alone on an empty stage for ten minutes." They can't mean a literally empty stage. Props and costumes, surely. And sets. Maybe five people. Would anyone complain if mine was fifteen minutes long? And does it have to be funny? Funny is hard. I wonder if we get paid for this. . . .

Friday, October 25, 2002. I have a cold. I think I'm gaining weight again. I wish Mike had never asked me. I can't write. . . . Why did Mike ask me? Maybe he was mad at me. Maybe he's resentful that he's been stuck filming my play since before the first Bush administration and he's doing this to humiliate me. I bet he wishes he could call Nora Ephron in for rewrites. . . . My God, my God, why have you abandoned me? STEVE MARTIN is writing one! I'm doomed! It's not a competition. It's not a competition . . . .

Tuesday, November 5, 2002. I couldn't write today, I had to go vote. I am optimistic, no matter what the polls say. Tomorrow, WITHOUT FAIL, I will write this play. . . . I will be in a good mood after the election. It'll be easier to write then.

Wednesday, November 6, 2002. I wish I was dead....

Wednesday, November 13, 2002. . . . Something will come. ANYTHING. Who cares? It's a benefit, for God's sake! They took my name off the goddam ad! . . .

Thursday, November 14, 2002. Mike just nixed my idea: a Nichols and May reunion. "Two people alone on an empty stage," that's what he said. And then he refuses to cooperate! He's ruined everything. Thanks a LOT, Mike. Schmuck! See if I ever do you a favor again!

If Kushner's laughter is combustible, so, in certain theatrical circumstances, is his temper. Eustis recalls, "One time, after seeing a run-through of 'The Illusion'"—Kushner's 1989 adaptation of Corneille's comedy and his first commercial success—"he called me from his apartment after he'd destroyed every piece of furniture." He adds, "There was one particular moment where Tony told me that it was a mistake for me to ever have directed and I should give up the field. That was devastating. I can't tell you how many directors he's tried to get fired at crucial moments in the process." Although Eustis didn't finish the job on "Angels," Kushner has worked hard to make sure that their relationship didn't end there and he now pays Eustis to dramaturge his plays. "I still consider Oskar one of my most important collaborators," Kushner says. "I spend hours with him weekly when I'm writing, talking about what I'm doing. I send him everything I write."

For Broadway, George Wolfe was brought in to energize the production of "Angels." "Tony is nothing if not intrusive," Wolfe says. "He completely trusts me, but I think, ultimately, he'd prefer to do it himself." Wolfe admits to occasionally burning Kushner's extensive and fevered production notes, "because I get so hostile about some of the things he writes." As a play gets closer to previews, according to Wolfe, "his mind, not having a lot to do, starts to obsess about everybody else's work. He starts to spin his wheels. Now, the first time you encounter the spinning of the wheels you try to go inside and figure out every single spoke of the wheel. Then, over time, you go, 'Madness, madness, madness, madness, oh, really strong truth. Let me hold on to that.' You have to reach inside the hurricane and pull out that beautiful little baby." Kushner is quite aware that Wolfe thinks he's a few sandwiches short of a picnic. "He doesn't think I'm insane, just a very neurotic person," Kushner says. "We were at dinner somewhere, and he looked at a bouquet of beautiful flowers. 'This is what you're like,' he said, and snapped off one of the smallest flowers. 'Oh, now the whole thing is completely ruined.'"

Kushner's intrusiveness was so pervasive that, while "Caroline, or Change" was in rehearsals, Wolfe and the company made a legend of it. They were working in the large, high-ceilinged Martinson auditorium at the Public Theatre—where a roof window looks down on the stage—when a pebble fell down onto the floor. Wolfe joked, "Tony's hiding up there. Jeanine"—Jeanine Tesori, who wrote the music for "Caroline"—"takes food up there so he can eat while watching us 'destroying' his piece."

Taking issue with Kushner is not easy. "It's like standing in front of a Mack truck," Tesori says. A few days before the show was to open on Broadway, she and Kushner still hadn't fine-tuned the epilogue. Wolfe insisted that he needed the scene the following night. Sitting at a table in her studio, Tesori said to Kushner, "It's too long."

"No, it's not," he replied. "Sometimes you need length. 'Angels' is full of places that shouldn't work but do, and they're long."

"I don't care what worked in that," Tesori said. "That's not this. It's too long."

"Well, we're just gonna have to agree to disagree."

"Well, we're just gonna have to stare at each other till one of us does something," Tesori said.

For ten minutes or so, Kushner and Tesori stared at each other in silence.

"Finally, he conceded, 'Well, maybe we can move the first line?'" Tesori recalls. "I said, 'Maybe we could.' Then he started shifting."

*   *   *

In May, Kushner broke his usual pattern and agreed to attend the Broadway opening of "Caroline," along with Mark Harris, his partner of six years, whom he married in a ceremony on April 27, 2003. (They were the first same-sex couple to have their wedding announced in the "Vows" column of the Sunday *Times*.) By the time the couple took their seats at the Eugene O'Neill—they were in Row T of the orchestra, the seats farthest from the stage—they had already consumed their lucky sesame noodles and dumplings and Kushner had successfully sung "Begin the Beguine." The lights went down, and Kushner leaned forward, with his chin in his hands, to watch as the reimagined drab basement of his childhood home came into view and Caroline, played by Tonya Pinkins, entered with an armful of laundry to broadcast the mood of the brooding household:

> Nothing ever happen underground
> In Louisiana
> 'Cause they ain't no underground
> In Louisiana
> There is only
> Underwater.

When the show was over, the audience, including Kushner, stood and cheered. Then he slipped into the aisle, where he, Tesori, and Wolfe, with their arms around each other and their heads touching, jumped up and down in a huddle. A few minutes later, for the first time on an opening night, Kushner took a bow from the stage. He made a dismissive flourish to the crowd with his left hand, then disappeared into the back row of the cast. Afterward, when the rehearsal light was up and only a few people lingered in the orchestra, Kushner looked at the ropes and winches and out at the empty auditorium. "Western civilization can't have been so terrible if it made a machine like this," he said. "It really is a great gadget."

The joy of the opening dissipated in the following weeks under the pressure of the awards season, which was likely to decide the commercial future of the show. The prospect of competing in the musicals category rattled Kushner, who saw "Caroline" as "more like a play." In an e-mail, he wrote, "'Caroline' has as much in common with the shows it's up against, some of which I really like, as marquetry has to do with Olympic tobogganing. It makes me nuts." In the end, "Caroline" won only one Tony, losing the awards for best musical and for best book to "Avenue Q," a jaunty show with puppets. But by the time "Caroline" got its closing notice, in mid-July—its final Broadway performance was on August 29th—Kushner had fought his way through the gloom. "I'm devastated but fine," he said. "I can't join in with the general lamentation over the wretched state of Broadway, which has never really been in any other kind of state." ("Caroline," at least, has had a successful second life at the Ahmanson Theatre, in Los Angeles.

On a hazy afternoon in late June, Kushner and I drove to his country place in Manitou, in the Hudson Valley, a two-story house, with forest-green shingles and a red door, shaded on all sides by towering maples and oaks. Through the sloping trees, the river was visible. Amtrak's Hudson Line hugged the shore, and every twenty minutes or so a train hurtled by, blaring its presence. Kushner barely registered the sound. "I always write best here," he said. "It reminds me of Louisiana, in that it's so verdant." He went on, "Inside me, it's like a fist unclenching."

For Kushner, the house has other happy associations. When he found it, six years ago, he had been ready to renounce New York altogether. "I thought, Fuck this," he says. "I'm just giving up on men. It hasn't happened. It's not going to happen. I'll give up and move out of the city." Kushner closed on the house in March of 1998; on April 16th of that year, at a party given by Michael Mayer, he met Harris, a droll and intelligent man, seven years his junior, and an editor at large at *Entertainment Weekly*. "Tony had this lovely combination of brazen confidence, enthusiasm, and huge insecurity that I found appealing," Harris recalls. A few days later, Kushner invited Harris to dinner at his place and prepared about five pounds of pasta. "This was so Tony," Harris says. "It was like a cauldron the size of a chemical-waste container on his stove. He bought a focaccia the size of a tire. He'd made a salad that could comfortably feed ten. I was completely terrified. 'This guy is gonna think I hate his food because he's given me a week's worth.'"

Kushner stayed in the city, but Manitou is still his favorite retreat. In his house, he has gathered pictures of Sylvia and her bassoon and of William and his clarinet, as well as the last photograph taken of his maternal great-grandparents in Vilnius before the Holocaust. Even the light fixtures outside his front door carry a memory of the past—they are from Temple Sinai, his childhood synagogue, in Lake Charles. Above his desk, in a cabin at the bottom of the garden, where he goes to write, hangs a photograph of Tennessee Williams, smiling over a bottle of wine. Harold Bloom told Kushner recently that Williams "is your most distinguished ancestor in the American drama and one who I think you'll wind up rivalling." The two playwrights share, at least, a belief that struggle is the natural order of things. "I'm deeply aware of what developmental psychologists call 'optimal frustration,'" Kushner says. "The way children learn is that the task they have in front of them is always a little too difficult and forces a degree of concentrated angry attention. It should be a struggle. Its fun to struggle. We're born to it."

Just as he was leaving Manitou, Kushner got a call from a distraught Larry Kramer, whose play "The Normal Heart," recently revived at the Public, had failed to find Broadway backing. Kramer was calling to say that the producers were closing the show that night. Kushner paced the driveway, commiserating, and they agreed to lament together over dinner. "We'll meet up and set ourselves on fire," he said.

A couple of weeks later, Kushner was back at work, mixing his activism with his art. For a MoveOn.org fund-raiser last summer, he went back to "Only We Who Guard the Mystery Shall Be Unhappy," a play-in-progress that depicts Laura Bush attending an after-school reading program for dead Iraqi children. For the event, he added a second scene, in which the First Lady, an admirer of Dostoyevsky's writing, comes onstage to debate the play's literary merits with the playwright himself. Since the first scene was published in *The Nation*—the first play that the magazine has printed in its hundred-and-thirty-nine-year history—Patricia Clarkson, Marcia Gay Harden, and Vanessa Redgrave have all played the role of Laura Bush, who was invited to read the part herself. (Her office did not respond.)

Kushner likes to collect amusing tidbits about political figures. According to his research, Supreme Court Justice William Rehnquist has led judges and lawyers in sing-alongs of "Dixie"; Judge Jay S. Bybee, who wrote a controversial memo justifying torture, plays in an all-kazoo orchestra; and President Bush refers to the First Lady as "my lump in the bed." In the new scene of "Only We Who Guard," Kushner, in full "fummfle," brings this up. "So I guess my point is that we're all like you," his character says to Laura Bush. "That we're all being fucked by your husband." The First Lady takes umbrage and gets up to leave. As a parting shot, she scolds Kushner. "Using the stage, the theatre, ART! For, for tawdry propagandizing? You oughta be ashamed of yourself," she says.

"I always am," Kushner replies.

The articles in this volume first appeared in *The New Yorker*

August Wilson (April 16, 2001), Cole Porter (July 12, 2004),
Billy Connolly (November 17, 2003), Mira Nair (December 9, 2002),
Laurence Fishburne (April 5, 2004), Ang Lee (June 30, 2003),
Dame Edna Everage (July 1, 1991), Yip Harburg (September 30, 1996),
Baz Luhrmann (December 2, 2002), Kenneth Tynan (August 7, 2000),
Dame Judi Dench (January 21, 2002), Bill Hicks (November 1, 1993),
Richard Rodgers (July 1, 2002), Tony Kushner (January 3, 2005)

INDEX